PRODUCING CULTURE
AND CAPITAL

PRODUCING CULTURE AND CAPITAL

FAMILY FIRMS IN ITALY

Sylvia Junko Yanagisako

PRINCETON UNIVERSITY PRESS   Princeton and Oxford

Copyright © 2002 by Princeton University Press
Published by Princeton University Press, 41 William Street, Princeton,
New Jersey 08540

In the United Kingdom: Princeton University Press, 3 Market Place,
Woodstock, Oxfordshire OX20 1SY

All Rights Reserved

Library of Congress Cataloging-in-Publication Data

Yanagisako, Sylvia Junko, 1945–
Producing culture and capital : family firms in Italy / Sylvia Junko
Yanagisako.
p. cm.
Includes bibliographical references (p.   ) and index.
ISBN 0-691-09509-4 (cloth : alk. paper) — ISBN 0-691-09510-8
(pbk. : alk. paper)
1. Silk industry — Italy — Como.   2. Family-owned business
enterprises — Italy — Como.   I. Title.
HD9915.I83 Y36 2002
338.4'767739'094523 — dc21   2002069294

British Library Cataloging-in-Publication Data is available

This book has been composed in Sabon

Printed on acid-free paper. ∞

www.pupress.princeton.edu

Printed in the United States of America

10 9 8 7 6 5 4 3 2 1

For John Merwin Sullivan

Contents

❧❦

Figures and Tables

✌

Preface and Acknowledgments

೪๙

This study is the attempt by an anthropologist to face up to capitalism in a new way. Rather than trace the effects of "Western capitalism" on the cultural lives of the discipline's usual subjects — peasants, migrants, workers, racial and ethnic minorities, and, above all, those outside the West — I investigate the cultural processes through which a group of people produce a form of "Western capitalism." I have chosen a technologically advanced European manufacturing industry as my object of study to counter the widespread notion that only "non-Western" capitalism is shaped by culture. Instead of assuming that capitalists in the silk industry of Como, Italy, pursue rational strategies motivated by a universal bourgeois interest in capital accumulation, I ask what cultural sentiments, meanings, and subjectivities motivate and shape their entrepreneurial actions.

Anthropology has always had a troubled relation with capitalism. The roots of this disciplinary legacy can be traced to the division of labor that emerged along with the social sciences in the nineteenth century and that defined their disciplinary boundaries. Like the other social sciences, anthropology came into being as an intellectual project of Western capitalist modernity aimed at coming to grips with the economic, political, and cultural transformations that both constituted and troubled that modernity. Unlike the other social sciences, however, the scholarly mandate of anthropology was the study of that which was *not-capitalist*. While sociology focused on the forms and functions of the emerging social institutions of industrial-capitalist society, anthropology focused on the precapitalist, preindustrial societies that were perceived to have been left in the dust by European modernity. In the "othering" of these societies, perhaps nothing was more iconic of their purported "marginality" to the "modern world" than their lack of involvement in capitalist production and consumption, which relegated them to the domain of "primitive economies."

More than a hundred years later, as those peoples and societies who were considered the appropriate subjects of ethnographic inquiry have been drawn willy-nilly, but not always unwillingly, into capitalist relations, anthropology has found it impossible to ignore the far-reaching social and cultural consequences of capitalism. Numerous ethnographic studies have documented in rich detail the transformative effects of capitalism on the lives of people in all areas of the globe. Several have demonstrated that "peripheral" peoples have not become the passive objects of Western capitalist expansion, but rather have resisted and employed "Western capitalism" in ways that have strengthened and developed their own cultural systems. Yet in these studies, "Western capitalism" itself has been left unexamined as a cultural practice.[1] Either it is assumed to be an undifferentiated European and North American economic system or it takes the shadowy form of an omnipotent structure of domination. The view of "Western capitalism" as a homogenizing, penetrating, acultural economic force is by no means new,[2] although recent discussions of globalization and global capitalism have breathed new life into it. Rather, as I argue in chapter 1, it has deep roots in the models of capitalism's two major theorists: Marx and Weber.

Anthropology's contribution to understanding capitalism and culture will continue to be severely hampered unless we break out of the discipline's predominant focus on working-class, "subaltern," and "non-Western" peoples. The moment when some social theorists seriously entertained the idea that those at the bottom of social hierarchies have a more accurate view of its workings (the idea being that they must in order to survive) has passed, opening the way to a more rigorous and comprehensive examination of capitalist cultural formations. If we limit our ethnographic studies to workers—or expand them only to include the middle class—we will be no closer to understanding capitalism than we will be to understanding racism if we study only the racially oppressed, or sexism if we study only women. If we are to understand capitalist societies, we need to understand how capitalist motives, capitalist selves, and capitalist strategies are produced through the everyday practices and experiences of the bourgeoisie as well as of workers.[3]

This study is based on eighteen months of ethnographic and archival research on the silk industry of Como, Italy. After an initial year of research from September 1984 to August 1985, I returned for shorter periods in 1989, 1995, and 2000. Although I collected information on a larger number of firms, this book focuses on the thirty-eight firms for which I collected the most complete information and that constitute a rough stratified sample of the approximately four hundred firms that operated in the industry in 1985 (see chapter 3 for a description of the firms and the families that own and manage them). In each case, I began by interviewing one of the owner-managers of the firm, usually several times. In a third of the cases, I went on to interview additional family members and relatives — both those who worked in the firm and those who did not. I also interviewed industry officials, business consultants, financial advisers, notary publics, lawyers, and union leaders. The archival component of my research included government records of firm histories, government censuses, industry surveys, industry reports, and notarial records of property transfers.

In the aftermath of the reflexive turn in ethnography, it would be disingenuous not to admit to the guilty pleasures of fieldwork in exotic places. In this case, these pleasures — which have drawn many an anthropologist to the field even while they have troubled the discipline — were complicated by the mutual exoticism in which my subjects and I participated. It was common for firm owners to think that I was from Japan or China rather than from the United States. A particularly humorous incident occurred when the elderly uncle of a firm owner-manager leaned over and whispered to me, sotto voce: "You say that you are American, but I can see with my own eyes that you are Chinese." Given my appearance, this misrecognition was hardly surprising, especially in initial encounters. But it persisted among some people even after I explained that I was a third-generation American of Japanese descent, and a few may even have harbored suspicions that I was an undercover agent for the Chinese silk industry. Others, however, were intrigued by the novelty of being the object of study of an American professor who looked Chinese. Indeed, I think this is one of the reasons many firm owners initially agreed to meet with me. More rare among my informants were those who were sufficiently familiar with anthropology to appreciate the ethnographic irony of my research. One firm owner, in particular, did. He found it very amusing that an Asian woman who had been born and raised on a Polynesian island — the quintessential object of the Western ethnographic gaze — would have come to Italy to study industrialists like himself. So did I.

A brief note is in order here on the use of pseudonyms in this book. In order to honor my promise of confidentiality to the people I studied, I have used pseudonyms for all the firms, families, and individuals in the Como silk industry. The only names that I have not changed are those of industry associations and individuals who were cited or quoted in newspapers or magazines.

My commitment to not revealing the identities of the people in this study has one unfortunate consequence; it means that I am unable to identify those to whom I owe the most for making this study possible. I am immensely grateful to the firm owners and their family members who took time out of their busy schedules to meet with me, suffer my prying questions, supply detailed histories of their families and firms, and invite me into their offices, factories, and homes. Although they will remain unnamed, their generosity will not be forgotten.

Other friends and colleagues in Italy who supported this research can, fortunately, be named. Simona Segre, Paola Schellenbaum, and Martino Marazzi were invaluable research assistants in Italy. Without their perceptive and thoughtful guidance and research, the range and depth of this study would have been much more limited. I thank them for their energetic contributions and continuing friendship. I am indebted to Antonio Marazzi for steering me to them and for providing me with invaluable contacts and a "home base" in Milan. In Como, the warm welcome and generosity of friends in Moltrasio, Argegno, and Molina Faggetto Lario nurtured and sustained my family and me during periods of fieldwork. Among them are Renato and Eliana Patriarca, Tamara Patriarca, Gianmario and Elide Brenna, Alessandro Donegana, Paolo and Daniella Peroni, Zaira Cazzulani, and the late Sergio and late Susanna Bello-Gallina.

At Stanford I have been aided by the able library research of Carole Blackburn, Karen Morris, Orin Starn, and Mei Zhan. Phil Ansell conducted both library research at Stanford and field research in Como during the initial phase of this study. Donald Donham, Donald Moore, Lisa Rofel, Anna Tsing, and Mei Zhan have been invaluable interlocutors throughout the writing of this book, which has benefited immensely from their insights and critical commentary. I am grateful to colleagues who have commented on drafts of the manuscript and its chapters: Marc Abélès, Pam Ballinger, Carol Delaney, Michael Herzfeld, Charles Hirschkind, Lyn Jeffery, Saba Mahmood, Joanne Martin, Martino Marazzi, Sherry Ortner, Paola Schellenbaum, Jane Schneider, and Simona Segre.

A seed money grant from United Parcel Service in 1982 enabled me to survey several potential field sites for this study. Fieldwork in 1984–85 was supported by the National Science Foundation and the Wenner-Gren Foundation for Anthropological Research. A grant from the Rockefeller Foundation enabled me to conduct further research in 1989. The writing of this manuscript was begun in 1991–92, while I was a Fellow at the Center for Advanced Study in the Behavioral Sciences at Stanford. An Associates' Fellowship from the Institute for Research on Women and Gender at Stanford also supported my writing that year.

I thank my children, Nathan and Emi Sullivan, for their good humor and patience throughout the writing of this book and for bravely going off to preschool and elementary school in Italy knowing, at first, hardly a word of Italian. This book is dedicated to John Merwin Sullivan, who has sustained me throughout this project, from beginning to end. As he shopped and cooked, learned local recipes, dealt with the intricacies of state bureaucracies, researched inheritance laws, and nurtured friendships, he made this study a possibility and a pleasure.

PRODUCING CULTURE
AND CAPITAL

☙

CHAPTER ONE

PRODUCING CULTURE AND CAPITAL

Three stories have been told about the silk industry of Como, Italy. The first is encapsulated in an adage that I first heard from an industry official soon after I had begun my research in Como. "Il nonno fondò, i figli sviluppano, i nipoti distruggono"—The grandfather founded (the firm), the sons develop it, and the grandsons destroy it. This adage, which distilled local knowledge about the rise and fall of firms in Como, was subsequently repeated to me by several firm owners. A less frequently cited, but notable, variation of the adage ends "i nipoti mangiano." In other words, the grandsons eat the firm. My translation of this adage is intentionally gendered. It could, after all, be translated "the grandfather founded [the firm], the children develop it, and the grandchildren destroy it," because the plural nouns *figli* and *nipoti* can include both males and females. It was clear from those who elaborated the adage, however, that this was a story about grandfathers, fathers, and sons.

In this tale of patrifilial succession, one generation of men succeeds in carrying forward their father's project, while the next fails. The grandfather is characterized as a "self-made man," much like the founder of a silk dyeing and printing firm whose son described him in precisely these terms. This was a man who began working in arduous, laboring jobs at the age of nine, who acquired his vocation through practical experience and education in evening classes, who worked long hours and lived a frugal life while he built a firm that flourished because of his technical expertise and dedication. The founder's sons, in turn, acquire their father's technical know-how and discipline by working at his side in the firm. Having inherited the business reputation and contacts accumulated by their father, these sons have the social as well as financial capital to expand the firm. By the third generation, so the story goes, the drive and self-discipline that enabled the grandfather to build the firm no longer exist among the grandsons, who squander the firm's assets in ill-considered schemes and frivolous expenditures. The picture painted is more or less one of dilettante bourgeois youths who prefer to sail the Bahamas rather than put in the long hours needed to advance the firm.

Like all adages, this three-generational tale of firm succession has a moral to it. And like all compelling moral tales, it leaves several things out. First, it leaves out history. Fathers, sons, and grandsons play out their generational destinies in a timeless tale of succession detached from any historical context. Second, and perhaps most obviously, it leaves out women. The exclusive concern with male productive force and its dissipation over time reflects a monogenetic theory of procreation (Delaney 1986), in which males alone supply the creative force that produces succeeding generations and, in this case, capitalist firms. It replicates in the profane world of business the cosmological model of male reproduction embodied in the sacred origin myths of Christianity. Finally, the adage leaves out gender. Not only are there no women in this tale, but the goals of the three generations of men are ungendered. Indeed, the self-evident character of men's ambitions forecloses the possibility of asking why fathers would want their sons to develop the firm in the first place.

The second story told about the Como silk industry is a prophetic account of the coming of a second era of industrial capitalism. In a book widely read in the 1980s, *The Second Industrial Divide*, the economist Michael J. Piore and the sociologist Charles F. Sabel herald the coming of a new epoch of industrialism based on innovative small firms. According to the authors, the limitations of an industrial system based on mass production in vertically integrated firms, which emerged in the nineteenth century, have become apparent in the wake of political and economic events that transformed the international market in the early 1970s. The most promising alternative to mass production lies in the networks of technologically sophisticated, innovative small firms that rely on craft forms of production. The flexible specialization of these firms has enabled certain industrial districts, including those of northern and central Italy, to ride the rough economic waters of the 1970s and 1980s and to usher in a new era of industrialism.

In contrast to the adage, Piore and Sabel's account situates this shift in a specific historical period of industrial capitalism. Moreover, it pays heed to the crucial role that politics plays in this transformation, recognizing that neither firms nor industries are autonomous from broad social and political movements. In their model of flexible specialization, "it is hard to tell where society . . . ends and where economic organization begins" (1984, 275). Thus, they highlight the political ideas and developments that created the preconditions for the emergence of such networks of flexible firms.

Like the adage, however, Piore and Sabel's account leaves out gender. There are no women, wives, daughters, mothers, or sisters, or for that matter men, husbands, sons, fathers, or brothers, in their industrial history—only artisans, subcontractors, skilled craftsmen, and other occupationally defined social actors. The political ideas and commitments that Piore and Sabel identify as having made possible the emergence and survival of flexible manufacturing include the struggle by nations for a place in the international order, by states to establish their power, and by Italian migrants to define a place for themselves in the large factories of the north. The politics of gender go unmentioned. Kinship, on the other hand, is attended to, as Piore and Sabel are aware that the innovative small firms in these industrial districts are predominantly family owned. They treat the "tradition of familialism" on which the firm owners draw, however, as a stable cultural resource rather than a historically situated, negotiated process that is itself continually being produced.

The third story is one in which Como's silk industry plays only a cameo role. The geographer David Harvey (1989) has fashioned an encompassing narrative linking an array of recent shifts in cultural life around the globe to structural adjustments in capitalism. Harvey attributes the rise of postmodern sensibilities and tastes in domains of cultural consumption as wide-ranging as art and architecture, cinema and coffee drinking, to the emergence of a new regime of capital accumulation—that of flexible accumulation. Like Piore and Sabel, Harvey identifies the early 1970s as the moment when new political and economic conditions necessitated the shift in capitalist strategies of accumulation from a Fordist regime of mass production and mass consumption to a late-capitalist regime of decentralized production and differentiated (lifestyle) consumption. In Harvey's thesis, however, the primary impetus for this shift comes from above—driven by capitalists' need to develop technological and organizational innovations to enhance profits and to control workers by undercutting their bargaining power (103). A key shift in industrial organization entailed in this new regime of accumulation has been increased subcontracting, which has both opened up opportunities for small business formation and "in some instances permits older systems of domestic, artisanal, familial (patriarchal), and paternalistic ("godfather," "guv'nor" or even mafia-like) labour systems to revive and flourish as centrepieces rather than as appendages of the production system" (152).

Harvey's thesis of the postmodern consequences of late capitalism brings in kinship only marginally, treating it, like culture, as a dependent variable. Flexible accumulation has broad and pervasive cultural effects on people's political identities and commitments and on their perception of time and space, but is itself not shaped by culture. "Cultural life" is pervaded with the logic of capital circulation and held within the embrace of the capitalist logic of our times, but capitalist production is itself outside the embrace of culture. As in most models of the global economy, late capitalism and the new institutional structures it has spawned are portrayed as acultural forces relentlessly bent on penetrating local communities and absorbing them into homogeneous regimes of accumulation. Local communities with culturally specific ways of life may mediate the effects of capitalism, but capitalism itself is not envisioned as shaped by cultural meanings and processes.[1]

Each of these three stories offers useful perspectives on the economic, political, and social forces shaping the silk industry of Como. Each contributes to the analytic narrative of this ethnography. Each, however, overlooks the cultural forces that incite and shape capitalist production and capital accumulation in the industry. In placing the local adage of generational succession alongside the two scholarly theses of the post-1960s transformation in capitalism, my aim is to expand and enrich the theoretical narrative to include what they leave out: an analysis of the sentiments, desires, and meanings of kinship, gender, and capital that are crucial to the production of the industry at a particular historical conjuncture. Like the local adage, my primary concern is with the character and motives of the people who own and manage the industry's firms. Like the adage, I situate them in families. In contrast to the adage, however, I am interested in understanding how these individuals have arrived at the sentiments and desires that lead them to pursue the particular entrepreneurial projects that, in turn, have shaped both their families and the silk industry of Como.

Toward a Cultural Analysis of Capitalist Action

This ethnography of Italian family firms eschews a model of capitalism as an economic system governed by universal laws. If we define capitalism, as did Marx, as a mode of production that is constituted by the class relation between capital and wage-labor,[2] then a universal model of capitalism entails two assumptions. First, we would have to assume that those who own and control the means of production and purchase labor power everywhere engage in the same "economic action" in pursuit of the same goals. Second, we would also have to assume that workers who sell their labor power are everywhere endowed with identical motives and subjectivities. In other words, a universal theory of capitalism is predicated on a universally homogeneous bourgeoisie and a universally homogeneous proletariat, As several recent historical and ethnographic monographs (Chakrabarty 1989; Rofel 1999; Donham 1999) have persuasively demonstrated, labor is never abstract, but is always provided by people with particular social identities and histories. Workers are always constituted through historically situated cultural processes as particular kinds of persons whose labor is employed, extracted, valued, and commodified in particular ways. This ethnography demonstrates that, like labor, capital also is never abstract, save in economic theory. Like workers, capitalists are always constituted as particular kinds of persons through historically specific cultural processes. As a consequence, capital is accumulated, invested, dispersed, and reproduced through historically specific cultural processes.

Among the refinements in cultural theory that the turn away from structuralism has enabled is a recognition that people's sentiments, identities, and social agency are not dictated by culture but are formed through everyday practices that are themselves culturally produced. It follows from this that bourgeois selves and orientations are constituted through these everyday practices, including what are conventionally construed as "business" practices.[3] For the most part, these "business" practices have been treated by social scientists as forms of "economic action"; in other words, as utilitarian actions aimed at singularly material ends. But this assumes that people organize their thoughts and actions according to the analytic abstractions (institutions and domains) of social theorists.

Building on Weber, whose theory of economic action I discuss at length later in this chapter, Parsons's (1955) division of modern society into the logico-meaningful and functional domains of economy, family, religion, education, and politics has led to an institutionally based theory of social action in which analytic abstractions (institutions, domains) have been mistaken for the actual processes through which people formulate action. The Parsonian model of institutional domains too readily grants cultural significance to the observer's analytic categories without adequate ethnographic evidence as to how people actually organize their thoughts and actions. While this institutional model can be a useful analytic device, it also has profound limitations, because people do not necessarily organize their everyday actions according to institutional domains. Instead, people think and act in ways that crosscut institutional boundaries.

All social action is constituted by a multiplicity of discourses and meanings. Consequently, cataloging and explicating these discourses and meanings will not, by itself, enable us to understand their articulation in the formation of social action. Such an understanding requires knowledge of the ways in which people in specific circumstances connect these discourses and negotiate their complex meanings. Rather than succumb to the temptations of a utilitarian-reductionist logic, I ask instead how capitalist strategies and actions are negotiated and forged by the members of entrepreneurial families who have heterogeneous desires, sentiments, and goals; how these change over time; and how they produce capitalist firms that are complex relations of love and profit, accumulation and distribution, communal solidarity and individual achievement.

This study draws on a second refinement in cultural theory that has been strengthened by the poststructuralist turn: the concept of culture as a process rather than a stable structure or system. If we think of culture in these terms, it makes little sense to speak of culture as something outside of "capitalism" or of capitalism as something outside of culture. A nondichotomous processual model of culture and capitalism treats capitalist action as culturally produced and, therefore, always infused with cultural meaning and value. It enables us to transcend the limitations of a passive concept of culture as either a resource to be used in the advancement of capitalist goals or a constraining system that must be broken through if capitalist logic is to be actualized. Treating capitalism as a culturally enabled process through which people continually rethink and reformulate goals, meanings, and practices allows us to better comprehend the creative, unfolding dynamic of capitalist action.

In proposing a model of culture and capitalism as mutually constituted processes rather than as distinct structures or institutions, I argue against Harvey's conception of capital as a logic that lies outside culture. According to Harvey, "because capitalism is expansionary and imperialistic, cultural life in more and more areas gets brought within the grasp of the cash nexus and the logic of capital circulation" (1989, 344). For Harvey, capital is process and cultural life is that which has been pervaded by the logic of capital. Yet the logic of capital lies outside the embrace of culture. As an alternative to Harvey's concept of the logic of capital, I argue that all capitalist practices are the product of historically situated cultural processes. The historical phenomenon that Harvey identifies as capitalism has certainly been expansionary and imperialistic, but it does not follow that it has been structured by a single "capitalist logic" or even that it is a single historical process.

I view capitalism as a complex and uneven historical process that entails heterogeneous capitalist practices shaped by diverse meanings, sentiments, and representations. I argue for a model of culture and capitalism that posits neither the existence of a single homogeneous capitalist mode of production nor culturally specific capitalist modes of production that are enacted by culturally distinct groups located in different national or regional spaces. I am not interested in salvaging the concept of culture as a distinctive system of symbols and meanings in the hope of discovering the distinctive characteristics of "Asian capitalism" and "European capitalism" or "Italian capitalism" and "Japanese capitalism." Instead, I leave open the possibility of the coexistence in any geopolitical space — whether local or translocal, national or global — of heterogeneous capitalist practices, all of which are culturally mediated. In other words, the model I propose is not one of distinctive "cultures of capitalism" or "capitalist cultures" but one in which diverse capitalist practices coexist in the same geopolitical spaces and flow across their boundaries. The forms that these diverse capitalist practices take and their articulation with each other must be empirically investigated rather than assumed.

Beyond Capitalist Interest: Sentiments as Forces of Production

A key issue in the study of capitalism has been how and under what historical conditions the working class comes to realize its collective class interests. Indeed, a century and a half of Marxist theory and historiography has been devoted to the question of the relation between proletarian class interests, subjective consciousness, and collective political action. The class interests of the bourgeoisie have received considerably less attention. It has been more or less assumed that we know where bourgeois interests lie — namely, in accumulating capital, maintaining control of the means of production, and establishing and reproducing bourgeois political hegemony. While the proletariat must struggle to break through the mystifications of capitalist hegemony to realize their collective interests, the bourgeoisie apparently do not. Their class interests are transparent enough to be obvious to anyone, even themselves. While the French bourgeoisie may have engaged in self-deception "to conceal from themselves the bourgeois limitations of the content of their struggles and to keep their enthusiasm on a high plane" (Marx [1852] 1963; 17), they appear to have been well aware of their political interest in the French state.

The problem does not lie in the Marxist theory of the inherent structural conflict between the bourgeoisie and the proletariat, but in the slippage between a theory of class interests and a theory of capitalist subjectivity and motivation. An abstract model of collective class interests may be useful in understanding why and how the bourgeoisie or any of its fractions takes political action to protect its interests, but it does not help us understand how and why people come to be interested in accumulating capital and reproducing capitalist firms. An abstract theory of bourgeois class interests has only limited usefulness for understanding the subjectivity and practices of a historically specific group of capitalists. Marx himself was well aware of this.[4] We can appreciate the insight offered by Marx's general theory of class interest without universalizing and naturalizing the dispositions, desires, and subjectivity of the bourgeoisie. The latter cannot be deduced from an abstract model of capitalism.

If we acknowledge—and as this study will show—that the bourgeoisie is not a homogeneous, undifferentiated group, then we cannot assume that they naturally share a set of common interests. Instead, we need to investigate whether and how particular interests come to be viewed as the common interests of the bourgeoisie as a whole. How, for instance, do particular ideas and practices concerning inheritance, the division of labor, forms of management, gender, hierarchy, and authority come to be seen as in the interests of the bourgeois family? How do particular ideas about family and business come to be accepted as the core values and goals of the bourgeoisie in an industrial network in northern Italy, especially when significant differences exist among them as regards capital resources, symbolic capital, past class trajectories, and opportunities for future mobility?

The concept of "interest" has been crucial in the slippage between a Marxist theory of class conflict and a theory of bourgeois subjectivity and social action. Critical scrutiny of this concept, however, calls into question its usefulness in social analysis. Hirschman's history of the ideological formation and transformation of "interest" in the sixteenth to eighteenth centuries offers valuable insight into the process by which the idea of economic advantage emerged as its core meaning.[5] The overwhelming acceptance of the concept of "interest" in the late-sixteenth and early-seventeenth centuries derived from the promise it offered as a hybrid form of human motivation and action that could mediate between "the destructiveness of passion and the ineffectuality of reason" (Hirschman 1977, 44). In other words, interest offered a way to resolve the long-standing tension between passion and reason in Western thought. It was perceived, moreover, to have the assets of predictability and constancy. Money making, in particular, as a "calm desire" that acts with calculation and rationality would enable its triumph over a variety of turbulent and destructive passions.[6] By the eighteenth century, "interests" and "passions" appear as synonyms in Adam Smith's argument that the material welfare of "the whole society" is advanced when everyone is allowed to follow his own private interests. Smith held that the lust for power and the desire for respect could all be satisfied by economic improvement, virtually equating the passions with the interests in a key passage of *The Wealth of Nations*. By substituting the blander terms "advantage" and "interests" for the terms "passion" and "vice," moreover, Smith purified the concept sufficiently for it to prosper as a central construct of economic theory (Hirschman 1977, 19).

My concern here is not with the historical twists and turns that led from the Renaissance philosophers to the bourgeois political theorists of the nineteenth century, but with the deconstruction of the concept of interest that Hirschman's history makes possible. Whether one agrees with his thesis that these philosophical arguments paved the way for the acceptance of capitalism, Hirschman's excavation enables us to understand how interest became so self-evident a concept that no one bothered to define it precisely. In short, a compelling bourgeois theory of human motivation was fashioned.

Hirschman's history ends at the close of the eighteenth century, setting the stage for the theories of economic action that have dominated contemporary analyses of capitalism. Sometime between *The Wealth of Nations* and Talcott Parsons's twentieth-century theory of social action (Parsons and Bales 1955), "interest" was cleansed of the "passion" that Smith had incorporated into it, and the older antimony between the two concepts reemerged. Parsons's concept of "instrumentality" entails a passionless interest, fashioned by reason and pursued through calculated rational action. "Affect," on the other hand, like passion, incites uncalculated, irrational action. The instrumental/affective dichotomy is central to the Parsonian theory of social action that has facilitated the acceptance of the concept of *interest* as a motivating force for economic action and the failure to recognize its emotional component. Once instrumentality was defined as rooted purely in objective interest, the unpredictability and unmanageability associated with emotion were relegated to other institutional domains in the Parsonian model of modern society. Family and religion might be governed by affect, but the economy is governed by instrumental action.

As we shall soon see, Weber's concept of economic action is the paradigm for Parsonian instrumentality, in spite of the former's recognition that any activity, including making love, can be rationally pursued with calculation.[7] Parsons's instrumental/affective dichotomy closely parallels Weber's distinction between economic action and other social action. For Weber, economic action is the quintessential pursuit of interest by means of rational technique — that is, technique consciously and systematically oriented to the experience and reflection of the actor (1978, 65).

The distrust of emotion as a force shaping economic action in all but the most affective ("female") spheres of social life evidences a model of human subjectivity and social action that has deep roots in Western European cosmology. In the 1980s, Michelle Rosaldo characterized these oppositions of thought/feeling, cognition/affect, outer "mask"/inner "essence," and "custom"/personality as products of a "bifurcating and Western cast of mind" (1984, 137), wedded to a Western cosmology of self and society. Rosaldo argued that the interpretive turn in anthropology (Geertz 1973) provided potent conceptual resources for challenging these dichotomies and rethinking our notions of selves, affects, and personalities (137). She pointed to developments in psychology (Ricoer 1970) and philosophy (Foucault 1972, 1978) that enable us to comprehend that human self-understanding does not emerge from an inner, presocial world, but "from experience in a world of meanings, images and social bonds, in which all persons are inevitably involved" (Rosaldo 1984, 139).

> instead of seeing feeling as a private (often animal, presocial) realm that is — ironically enough — most universal and at the same time most particular to the self, it will make sense to see emotions not as things opposed to thought but as cognitions implicating the immediate, carnal "me" — as thought embodied. (Rosaldo 1984, 138)

> Recognition of the fact that thought is always culturally patterned and infused with feelings, which themselves reflect a culturally ordered past, suggests that just as thought does not exist in isolation from affective life, so affect is culturally ordered and does not exist apart from thought. (137)

The idea that emotions are no less cultural and no more private than beliefs would seem obvious after a couple of decades in which cultural constructivist approaches have been in ascendance. Yet Rosaldo's argument that selves and feelings are more productively understood as the creation of particular sorts of polities and social relations seems yet to have significantly affected studies of "economic action." Such a change would open the door to a cultural analysis of emotion and economic action, reclaiming emotion as a product of social practices as well as a force shaping the production, reproduction, and transformation of economic action.[8]

In this study, I use the term *sentiment* to bridge the dichotomy between emotion and thought. As affective ideas and ideas with affect, sentiments are both emotional orientations and embodied dispositions. I include among them what are often described as concepts of selfhood and identity. Under particular conditions, sentiments generate particular desires and incite particular social actions. The patriarchal desire for succession by a son or children, which I discuss in chapter 3, is an example of such an incitement. My use of the terms *desire* and *sentiment* rather than *value, ideal, goal,* or objective is intentionally provocative. I hope to blur the boundaries that have come to be taken for granted in much of cultural and social theory between desire, which is conceptualized as an embodied yearning—sometimes even viewed as originating in the body (as in the case of sexual desire)—and ideals or goals, which are characterized as mental constructs originating outside the body and internalized by means of ideological enculturation, thus lacking the physicality and energy associated with the body.

Bourgeois "economic" actions, like all culturally meaningful actions, are incited, enabled, and constrained by sentiments that are themselves the products of historically contingent cultural processes. The Como silk industry is the result of the continuous generation and regeneration of family capitalism by people whose desires for capital accumulation have been incited by sentiments of family unity and communalism, but also by sentiments of individualism, independence, and competition. The latter are as integral to the generation and regeneration of firms as the former. In chapter 4, for example, I trace the ways in which trust and betrayal, as conjoined sentiments, incite and are incited by processes of firm production and reproduction in the Como silk industry. As sentiments in play at different moments in the developmental histories of family firms, trust and betrayal shape the character of technological diffusion, firm competition, and the creation of new firms. They are, on the one hand, products of the workings of Italian family capitalism. On the other hand, they operate as *forces of production* of Italian family capitalism.

My conception of sentiments as forces of production follows Donham's (1990) usage of Marx's concept of *produktivkräfte,* which is usually translated into English as "forces of production." Donham (1990, 59), following Cohen (1978), uses the alternate translation "productive powers" in order to highlight the fact that human capacities, rather than things outside human beings, were among the central referents of *produktivkrafte* for Marx. Like Donham, I am concerned with the ways in which human capacities, including skills, sentiments, and knowledge, influence and shape material production. In contrast to Donham, however, I construe these human capacities as both resources that are used in production and as cultural forces that incite, enable, constrain, and shape production. All human capacities that can be used in production, after all, also constrain and shape processes of production. As human capacities, they are not mere passive resources to be used in a neutral way for the sake of an acultural process of production. These human capacities, moreover, are constitutive of social actors themselves. In other words, I am interested in the ways in which sentiments, knowledge, and skills operate simultaneously as material and cultural forces of production to incite, enable, constrain, and shape processes of production, in this case, specifically, Italian family capitalism.

Kinship and Gender: Bringing It All Back Home

In the 1970s and 1980s, feminist scholars engaged in rethinking the links between work, family, and economy identified a major limitation of Marxist analyses of capitalism—namely, their failure to address processes of reproduction. By "reproduction" feminist scholars meant more than the biological processes through which new generations of humans are produced; they also meant the social production of humans with labor capacity. They challenged androcentric Marxist formulations that omitted "domestic relations" from the analysis of capitalism because they do not produce exchange value, arguing that such exclusion overlooks the social reproduction upon which capitalist production depends. Crucial to social reproduction is the domestic work of women in nurturing and socializing children who will be future workers and in caring for husbands whose labor capacity is reproduced on a daily basis. Feminist scholars argued that women's work in families includes not just the housework of cooking, cleaning, and shopping, but their emotional labor in creating a home and family that give meaning to wage-labor. The family as a refuge from the demands of work, the commodification of labor, and the market depends on women's unremunerated labor. This feminist critique led to the recognition that a domain of relations, sentiments, and values that had been construed as "noncapitalist" in both popular discourse and academic theory is crucial to capitalist production and to the reproduction of capitalist relations of production.

The socialist feminist critique of Marxist theory in the 1970s and 1980s focused almost exclusively on the reproduction of the labor capacity of workers—in other words, on the uncompensated work of women as wives and mothers. The reproduction of the bourgeoisie was largely ignored. The reasons for this lie in Marx's conception of the bourgeoisie as a class that is defined by the ownership of capital rather than by its labor. As we shall see in the discussion to follow, in Marx's view capital reproduces itself through the estrangement of labor and commodity fetishism. Thus, the reproduction of capital is a systemic process of capitalism as a mode of production, rather than a human process. Even if we grant that capital reproduces itself through these processes, however, it remains that the bourgeoisie does not. The capital/labor distinction—while extremely productive for Marx's analysis of relations of production—has the drawback of blinding us to the human productive capacities of the bourgeoisie and to the processes by which they are reproduced. Defining the working class in terms of its labor power and the bourgeoisie in terms of its ownership of capital can lead us to overlook the fact that the productive capacities of the bourgeoisie are also produced and reproduced through cultural and material processes. In short, capitalists, like workers, are made, not born.

I do not mean by this that capitalists, both as individuals and as a class, must be biologically reproduced or even socially reproduced by bourgeois women through child rearing and socialization in bourgeois families. Obviously, the bourgeoisie as a class can be reproduced through the recruitment of individuals from nonbourgeois families. Regardless of whether those who make up the bourgeoisie are raised in capitalist families or are recruited from other classes, however, they must be sustained, nurtured, and endowed with the sentiments and motives to pursue capitalist goals. In other words, just as the labor power of workers—their productive capacities, which include knowledge, skill, and physical prowess—is socially and culturally produced, so are capitalists productive capacities. Like workers, capitalists must have not only knowledge and skills, but sentiments and desires that enable and incite them to engage in particular kinds of productive activities. As capitalism entails more than mere commodity production and the pursuit of profit—it has at its core the relation between wage-labor and capital—it follows that capitalists must have both the capacity and the desire to own and control the means of production.

Family and kinship processes, relations, and sentiments are crucial for the production and reproduction of all forms of capitalism, whether family capitalism or nonfamily capitalism. Family capitalism, however, brings more clearly into view these processes, relations, and sentiments. Indeed, one of the benefits of studying family firms is that it brings to the fore the "other" supposedly "noncapitalist" processes crucial to capitalism. The study of family capitalism—a form of capitalism that has been marginalized in both Marxist and Weberian theories—enables us to see that its marginalization is itself part of the hegemonic process through which capitalism is made to appear as an economic system that is autonomous from family and kinship processes. One of the analytic projects of this ethnography, on which I focus in the concluding chapter, is to understand the discursive and material processes through which some relations, sentiments, and activities of the Como bourgeoisie come to be viewed as falling outside the realm of the "firm" and "business" and within the realm of the "family." These processes parallel wider processes in capitalist society through which certain kinds of relations, sentiments, actions, and entire institutions come to be defined as outside the realm of the economy. The opposition between "family" and "business" and the irrelevance of "family" to the "economy" in popular discourse mirrors this process. In social theory it is evidenced in the division of society into "capitalist" and "noncapitalist" relations and domains.[9]

That social theory would relegate family and kinship to a marginal role in capitalist society is ironic in light of the fact that the intergenerational transmission of property through family inheritance is a primary determinant of an individual's relation to the means of production and, thus, to his or her location in the class structure. Inheritance is also crucial in shaping the dynamics of firm development, expansion, diversification, reproduction, and decline. As we shall see, inheritance in Italian family firms is shaped by a dense cluster of sentiments about kinship and gender.

Gender pervades not only ideas and practices of inheritance and succession but all aspects of Italian family capitalism. Anthropological studies (Kondo 1993; Ong 1999; Greenhalgh 1994; Marcus 1992, 1998) suggest this is true of family capitalism everywhere. These studies provide useful comparative material on gender hierarchy and the marginalization of women in bourgeois families. Little attention, however, has been paid to the formation of bourgeois male identities. Yet, asking how particular capitalist masculinities motivate particular kinds of capitalist action would seem a powerful analytic strategy for challenging assumptions about the existence of a universal capitalist motive. In the absence of such analyses of bourgeois male subjectivity, it is tempting to naturalize and universalize particular forms of bourgeois masculinity and particular modes of accumulation.

Having learned from feminist theory the crucial role that discourse plays in producing women's subjectivities, we need to consider how men are discursively constituted as persons with certain kinds of desires, characters, orientations, and limitations. We need to broaden our gender analysis to investigate how men's subjectivities are produced in relation to women's subjectivities through everyday discourses and practices. In the chapters to follow, I scrutinize the discourses and practices through which both husbands and wives, fathers and mothers, daughters and sons are culturally produced. If I focus more on masculine subjectivity, it is both for theoretical reasons (this is where gender studies is in greatest need of development) and empirical reasons (the vast majority of firm owners in the Como silk industry are men). Rather than assume that men are naturally motivated to accumulate wealth, power, and prestige and that their actions are the outcome of logical or rational strategies, I ask what men want and why they want it. This leads me to the link between Italian bourgeois men's pursuit of capital accumulation and their desires as fathers for the continuity of their families and the independence of their sons. Bringing gender into my analysis of Italian family capitalism enables me to denaturalize both bourgeois masculinity and capital accumulation.

The marginalization of family and kinship, gender, sentiment, and identity in studies of capitalism is intertwined with key aspects of the theoretical approaches that have dominated the analysis of capitalism in the twentieth century. To understand how this came about and how we might move toward a more encompassing theoretical approach to capitalism, we need to turn to the two major social theorists of capitalism: Marx and Weber.

Marxist Reification and the Consciousness of the Bourgeoisie

Marx's analysis of the emergence of modern Western capitalism out of European feudalism is a compelling history of cultural transformation. His discussion of the historic formation of the European bourgeoisie, for example, includes a culturally nuanced analysis of how competition arose out of the bourgeois desire for independence from the fetters of feudal society and came to be experienced as a form of enlightenment (Marx and Engels 1976, 434). In arguing that societies characterized by an "Asiatic mode of production" lacked the requisite elements for the emergence of modern capitalism, Marx incorporated, albeit crudely, cultural analysis in his historical materialism (Marx 1970). He made it clear, moreover, that he was aware of the cultural specificities of British capitalism, which supplied the primary material for his model of capitalism.

Marx was primarily interested, however, in the systemic character of capitalism as a mode of production. For the sake of constructing a "pure" model of capitalism, he intentionally disregarded the historical particularities of the British case (1968, 23). According to this abstract model, once capitalism has emerged, it is self-perpetuating and requires no culturally motivated agents — either bourgeoisie or proletariat — to reproduce it. In contrast to his rich, complex analysis of the motives and strategies of the various fractions of the French bourgeoisie in their counterrevolution in the mid-nineteenth century (Marx 1963), in *Capital* the bourgeoisie are reduced to being the agents of capital.

Marx's powerful theory of the formation of proletarian subjectivity is not matched by an exploration of capitalist subjectivity. His brilliant discussion of the commodification of labor and the fetishism of commodities continues to stand as a compelling cultural analysis of how people, in this case an abstract proletariat, make sense of and come to accept their exploitation and their place in a social hierarchy.[10] But this deft analysis has no parallel in his discussions of the bourgeoisie. Indeed, Marx's lack of interest in developing a conceptual apparatus to understand how capitalist goals, actions, and subjectivities are produced and reproduced over time has the effect of naturalizing capitalist desire and action. For Marx, the capitalist has only one motive: namely, the desire for capital accumulation — "the ceaseless argumentation of value" (1976, 254). The capitalist's aim is never use value or the profit on any single transaction, but always the "passionate chase after value" (254).[11]

The first time the term *capitalist* appears in the main text of volume 1 of *Capital* is when Marx writes

> As the conscious bearer [Träger] of this movement [i.e., the circula-tion of money as capital], the possessor of money becomes a capital-ist. His person, or rather his pocket, is the point from which the money starts, and to which it returns. The objective content of the circulation we have been discussing — the valorization of value — is his subjective purpose, and it is only in so far as the appropriation of ever more wealth in the abstract is the sole driving force behind his operations that he functions as a capitalist, i.e., as capital personified and endowed with consciousness and a will. (254)

In short, for Marx the capitalist is merely the medium for the circula-tion of money. He is Capital with consciousness, the personification of Capital, compelled by the "immanent laws of capitalist production" to accumulate capital and reinvest it (739). The capitalist, no less than the worker, is enslaved by capitalism.

> The self-valorization of capital — the creation of surplus-value — is therefore the determining, dominating and overriding purpose of the capitalist; it is the absolute motive and content of his activity. And in fact it is no more than the rationalized motive and aim of the hoarder — a highly impoverished and abstract content which makes it plain that the capitalist is just as enslaved by the relationships of capitalism as is his opposite pole, the worker, albeit in a quite differ-ent manner. (990)

Marx's analysis of capital accumulation sheds light on its fetishism of value:

> Capital is money, capital is commodities. In truth, however, value is here the subject [i.e., the independently acting agent] of a process in which, while constantly assuming the form in turn of money and commodities, it changes its own magnitude, throws off surplus-value from itself considered as original value, and thus valorizes itself inde-pendently. For the movement in the course of which it adds surplus-value is its own movement, its valorization is therefore self-valoriza-tion [Selbstverwertung]. By virtue of being value, it has acquired the occult ability to add value to itself. It brings forth living offspring, or at least lays golden eggs. (255)[12]

Although he endows value with the agency to bring forth living off-spring in order to display the perversity of capitalism and its subversion of the natural world, Marx falls prey to his to his own irony.[13] Nothing is mentioned about the agency or desire of capitalists to accumulate capital. Instead, the social relations of capitalists, both their relations with members of their own class as well as their relations with those of others, are determined by the agency of value. A reified analytic abstraction supplants the consciousness of the bourgeoisie. Marx thus denies capitalists what he claims distinguishes human beings from animals — the ability to express a purpose or plan raised by one's own imagination (projective consciousness).

> For him [the bourgeoisie], only one relation is valid on its own account — the relation of exploitation; all other relations have validity for him only insofar as he can include them under this one relation; and even when he encounters relations which cannot be directly subordinated to the relation of exploitation, he subordinates them to it at least in his imagination. (Marx and Engels 1976, 434)

Given his focus in volume 1 of *Capital*, on the material and ideological processes by which surplus value is converted into capital, Marx is explicitly not concerned with any *other* uses the capitalist makes of surplus-value, let alone the broader range of sentiments and desires that inform those uses. In discussing the transformation of surplus-value into capital, he states:

> We leave out of account here the portion of the surplus-value consumed by the capitalist. We are also not interested, for the moment, in whether the additional capital is joined on to the original capital, or separated from it so that it can valorize itself independently. Nor are we concerned whether the same capitalist employs it who originally accumulated it, or whether he hands it over to others. (728)

Marx was well aware, of course, that the drive for profit and capital accumulation was neither natural, universal, nor always socially acceptable. Indeed, one of his major contributions was showing how capitalist relations that were an assault on preexisting ideas and social relations came to be accepted and glorified. Lust for money, after all, had been denounced by Saint Augustine as one of the three principal sins of fallen man (lust for power and sexual lust being the other two), and in the sixteenth and seventeenth centuries social philosophers condemned moneymaking pursuits as a form of avarice (Hirschman 1977). By endowing capital with social agency, however, Marx did not help us to understand how and why people become capitalists.

Max Weber, on the other hand, undertook to do just that.

The Iron Cage of Weberian Binaries

In his most influential and broadly cited work, *The Protestant Ethic and the Spirit of Capitalism*, Weber set out to answer the question of how activity that had been barely tolerated in Europe before the seventeenth century came to be seen as a lofty calling. In sharp contrast to Marx's willingness to sacrifice historical specificity for the sake of discovering the generic mechanisms of capitalism, Weber's analytic project was decidedly historical. His attempt to identify the distinctive characteristics of modern capitalism was in keeping with his commitment — in contrast to the approach of the British political economists — to understanding economic action within a broader cultural history (Giddens 1992, viii). Like Marx, Weber underscored the distinctiveness of modern Western capitalism from other forms of capitalism — for example, the pariah capitalism of European Jews and medieval Italian capitalism. But he went further in locating the origins of modern Western capitalism with its ethos of rational calculation within a historically and culturally specific conjuncture.[14] In characterizing the Protestant capitalist's striving for the continual accumulation of wealth as the unintended consequence of the Calvinist doctrine of predestination, Weber built a historical link between capitalist subjectivity and economic action that is missing in Marx. Rather than being the agent of capital — itself the fetishized effect of an abstract process — the Protestant capitalist is impelled by deeply felt moral sentiments to pursue a distinctive mode of economic action that integrates ascetic self-control with disciplined accumulation.

At the same time, however, Weber shared Marx's vision of capitalism as a self-reproducing institution that, once established, is independent of the historical forces that created it (Weber 1992, 181). Once capitalism is in place as the "modern economic order," it quickly becomes detached from the specific religious motivations that initially produced it. What was once an entrepreneurial practice driven by a spiritual ethic becomes an "iron cage" that determines the lives of all those born into it. Even by the time of Benjamin Franklin, the religious basis of the spirit of capitalism had died away (180). The rationalization of a religious ethic produced a secular logic of rational calculation and "in the field of its highest development, in the United States, the pursuit of wealth, stripped of its religious and ethical meaning, tends to become associated with purely mundane passions, which often give it the character of sport" (182). According to Weber, "The Puritan wanted to work in a calling; we are forced to do so" (181).

By the end of the *Protestant Ethic*, Weber has offered a provocative and ironic cultural history of how a religious sentiment produced a purely "economic action." But he leaves us without an adequate theoretical framework for understanding how capitalist goals and actions are produced in subsequent historical periods among specific cultural actors. He makes it clear that once modern capitalism had taken hold in Europe, the Protestant ethic was no longer necessary for its continued practice and dominance. Weber's project was to explain the *origins* of modern capitalism in Europe, not its subsequent adoption and diffusion to other areas of the world. His concept of institutionalization allows those lacking the preconditions to have been the original creators of modern capitalism to adopt it. In other words, capitalism and its techniques of formal rationality and diligence can be appropriated, practiced, and even developed to a higher level of competitiveness by people entirely unfamiliar with Protestantism or who lack any parallel religious ethic — whether they are German Catholics or Chinese. At the end of the *Protestant Ethic*, Weber concludes, "No one knows who will live in this cage in the future, or whether at the end of this tremendous development entirely new prophets will arise" (192).

The idea that a Russian or Indonesian must internalize the Protestant ethic or its functional equivalent in order to become a modern, rational capitalist rests on a fundamental misunderstanding of Weber's thesis. Only an "Occidentalist" version of his historical argument would claim that the Protestant ethic is an essential element of modern capitalism. A good deal of the scholarship documenting the success of Buddhist, Confucian, Islamic, and Catholic capitalism in order to refute Weber's thesis has misplaced its critique in focusing on the link between Protestantism and capitalism rather than on his failure to provide an analytic framework for understanding how people from diverse cultural "traditions" might practice heterogeneous forms of modern capitalism.[15]

A more fundamental theoretical dichotomy, however, gets in the way of Weber's formulation of an analytical framework for understanding the cultural production and reproduction of capitalist meaning and action. This dichotomy is one that Weber laid forth most clearly in his major work, *Economy and Society*. At the core of this treatise is Weber's concept of "economic action."

> Action will be said to be "economically oriented" so far as, according to its subjective meaning, it is concerned with the satisfaction of a desire for "utilities" (*Nutzleistungen*). "Economic action" (*Wirtschaften*) is any peaceful exercise of an actor's control over resources which is in its main impulse oriented toward economic ends. (63)

> "Rational economic action" requires instrumental rationality in its orientation, that is, deliberate planning. (Weber 1978, 63)

Weber's definition of "economic action" rests on the distinction between action oriented toward the satisfaction of a desire for utilities and action oriented toward the satisfaction of other desires (68). He defines utilities as "the specific and concrete, real or imagined, advantages of opportunities for present or future use as they are estimated and made an object of specific provision by one or more economically acting individuals" (68). In addition to "goods" (nonhuman objects that are the sources of potential utilities) and "services" (utilities derived from a human source, so far as this source consists of "active conduct"), "social relationships . . . valued as a potential source of present or future disposal over utilities are . . . also objects of economic provision" (69). This definition of utilities opens up his definition of "economic action" to a much broader range of actions than might be initially surmised. Indeed, it makes it difficult to distinguish "economic action" from other social actions, including those oriented toward establishing and maintaining kinship relations and friendships. Thus, what seems at first glance to be a rigorous and narrow definition of economic action turns out, on closer scrutiny, to rest on concepts that blur the boundaries of the definition. The problem is not that Weber's definitions are not sufficiently rigorous, but that his analytic strategy of differentiating economic action from other social actions is ill conceived.

On the other hand, Weber makes it unambiguously clear that it is the subjective meaning that processes and objects have for human action that determines whether they are economic actions. While he recognizes that actions may be oriented toward multiple ends and shaped by multiple considerations, Weber assumes that they can be classified on the basis of their "conscious, primary orientation" (64). Indeed, his confidence in our ability to discern the primary orientation of social actions is so great as to lead him to distinguish economic action from economically oriented action.

> As distinguished from "economic action" as such, the term "economically oriented action" will be applied to two types: (a) every action which, though primarily oriented to other ends, takes account, in the pursuit of them, of economic considerations; that is, of the consciously recognized necessity for economic prudence. Or (b) that which, though primarily oriented to economic ends, makes use of physical force as a means. It thus includes all primarily non-economic action and all non-peaceful action which is influenced by economic considerations. "Economic action" thus is a conscious, primary orientation to economic considerations. (64)

Modern capitalism, with its calculative spirit and singular goal of profit and accumulation, is accordingly distinguished from the economically oriented actions undertaken by the large capitalist households in the medieval cities of northern and central Italy (359). Because these households were committed to a principle of solidarity in facing the outside and to a "household communism"—that is, a communism of property and consumption of everyday goods (359)—Weber considered them to be based on "direct feelings of mutual solidarity rather than on a consideration of means for obtaining an optimum of provisions" (156). Hence, he concluded, they have a "primarily non-economic character." According to Weber, "Willingness to work and consumption without calculation in these communities [the family, comrades in the army, and religious communities] are a result of the non-economic attitudes characteristic of them" (154).

Weber's concept of economic action—which lies at the core of his notion between "modern capitalism" and other forms of capitalism and profit seeking—relies on the boundary between actions oriented toward the satisfaction of a desire for utilities and actions oriented toward the satisfaction of other desires. But few social actions are so singularly oriented as to be easily classified according to such a scheme. Indeed, Weber's general theory of economic action and his definition of modern capitalism are at odds with his own analysis of Puritan capitalism. According to his general theory, the Puritan capitalism out of which modern capitalism developed was not a form of economic action because its primary orientation was spiritual affirmation and not the satisfaction of a desire for utilities.

In Weber's scheme, "modern family capitalism" is an oxymoron because its orientation toward communal commitments of family unity and continuity disqualifies it from his definition of modern capitalism, which is oriented exclusively toward the rational, calculated pursuit of profit and accumulation. In the chapters to follow, I show that Italian capitalists engage in both the deliberate, calculative pursuit of profit and the fulfillment of other culturally meaningful desires. These include both the "communistic" desires that Weber associates with "household communism" and "individualistic" desires for self-realization and independence. In challenging Weber's binaries of economic action versus "other" social action and modern Western capitalism versus "other" capitalisms, I hope to clear the way for a cultural theory of economic action that treats all social action—including capital accumulation, firm expansion, and diversification—as constituted by both deliberate, rational calculation and by sentiments and desires: in other words, as cultural practices.

Weber's early work on medieval Italian capitalism led him to conclude that the legal and accounting separation of the business enterprise from the household was crucial for the emergence of modern Western capitalism. While this separation may have been a significant innovation, Weber's error was to misconstrue the *legal fiction* of separation—which was put in place for the purpose of limiting individual and familial financial liability—as a *de facto* separation of family relations from business relations. In other words, Weber turned a legal fiction of the separation of the family from the firm into a social theory in which the family and economy in modern capitalist society were cast as distinct institutions. In doing so, Weber appears to have fallen victim to the illusions of a bourgeois legal apparatus.

Other Capitalisms: A Cautionary Tale of Orientalism

Weber's distinction between "modern Western capitalism" and other capitalisms has had a profound impact on the ways in which capitalism outside the West continues to be perceived today. His emphasis on the "individualistic" desires for self-realization and independence of Puritan capitalism has encouraged a cultural essentialist theory of capitalism in which "non-Western culture" is viewed as either an impediment to modern capitalism or the basis for a different species of capitalism. "Asian capitalism" has been the prime candidate for these kinds of characterizations of "non-Western capitalism" in both scholarly and popular discussions. The current discourse about the global competition between Asian capitalism and Western capitalism for international markets and economic hegemony depicts each side as employing a distinctive mode of capitalist organization and being driven by a distinctive cultural ethos.[16] Whether the claim is that Japanese capitalism draws its inspiration from deep-rooted traditions of Confucian and Buddhist morality (Coates 1987; Yamamoto 1992) or that the rapid economic success of East Asia's four "mini-dragons" (Hong Kong, Korea, Taiwan, and Singapore) and of diasporic Chinese entrepreneurs is due to a "Confucian ethic" that is the functional equivalent of the Protestant ethic (P. Berger 1988; Chan and Chiang 1994; Kao 1993; Yao 1991), culture is envisioned as a static tradition in which distinctive values of communalism, group orientation, hard work, social discipline, harmony, and the centrality of the family have produced an Asian capitalism to rival that of the West.

If we are to avoid the pitfalls of this popular version of an essentialist theory of capitalism and culture, we need to consider the implications of current representations of "Asian capitalism" for the analysis of "Western capitalism." In these discussions, "Asian capitalism" is the marked category that carries culture, while "Western capitalism" is the unmarked category—the normal, rational, logical capitalism. Hence, crucial to representations of "Asian capitalism" are assumptions about "Western capitalism." Understanding these representations is a necessary step toward a cultural analysis of capitalist practices in Italy as well as in other European sites.

The replication of an older Orientalist discourse (Said 1978) in contemporary celebrations of an Asian spirit of capitalism, which lauds precisely the features that in the past were identified as obstacles to Asian modernization, has been roundly and deservedly criticized by anthropologists and other East Asian studies scholars (Hamilton and Kao 1991; Greenhalgh 1994; Ong 1999; Rofel 1999; Wei Ming 1996, 1998). Beyond its oversimplification of Weber's thesis of the origins of modern capitalism and the failure to demonstrate how the Confucian ethic is manifest in actual entrepreneurial organization and behavior (Wei Ming 1998), the thesis of the Confucian ethic treats values and beliefs as if they have a life of their own apart from the people who embody and enact them in historically specific circumstances.[17] To move beyond such portrayals of capitalist difference, we need guidance from a cultural theory that will steer us clear of essentialist models of culture.

Theorizing the relation between culture and capitalism turns out to be no simple task, however, and it is easy to run aground on an unanticipated set of shoals while trying to maneuver around others.[18] Attempts to refute essentialist models of culture and capitalism often lead back to acultural models of a universal "capitalist logic" of the sort proclaimed by Harvey. Antiessentialist approaches to Chinese capitalism provide a useful case in point. In challenging the Orientalist characterizations of Chinese capitalism promulgated by both Western observers and the transnational Chinese corporate elites she studied, Ong argues that claims about insurmountable cultural differences between East and West "can occur in the context of fundamentally playing (and competing) by the rules of neoliberal orthodoxy" (1999, 7). She contends that discourses of the distinctiveness of Asian values "disguise common civilizational references in a world where the market is absolutely transcendental" (7), thus suggesting that homogeneous rationalities and modes of action are demanded of those who wish to be effective players in the global economy. Along these lines, Ong suggests that "there may not be anything uniquely 'Chinese' about flexible personal discipline, disposition and orientation" or in the "mix of humanistic relations and ultrasentimentality" that she observed among diasporic Hong Kong Chinese capitalists (136). At the same time, however, Ong defines their kinship and *guanxi* networks as a "historically evolved regime of kinship and ethnic power" fashioned by subjects accustomed to "living on the edge of political and capitalist empires" (111). Rejecting cozy images of Confucian family harmony and collectivism, she characterizes these kinship and fraternal networks in Foucauldian terms as regulatory regimes that facilitate the accumulation of wealth while controlling and trapping women and the poor (116).

Ong's critique — which shares much with Greenhalgh's (1994) analysis of Taiwanese family firms — is a welcome antidote to the naïve glorification of the "benevolent paternalism" and "collectivism" of Chinese family firms. In their attempt to refute the Orientalist thesis that attributes the "utilitarian familialism"[19] of Chinese entrepreneurs to traditional values, however, Ong and Greenhalgh overcorrect in characterizing them as instrumental appropriations and reinventions by entrepreneurs adjusting to the demands of the world economy and state policies (Greenhalgh 1994, 75; Ong 1999, 136). The characterization of Chinese capitalist families as governed by "family strategies of regulation" that are "expressions of a habitus that is finely tuned to the turbulences of late capitalism" (Ong 1999, 117, 136) reflects a utilitarian theory of subjectivity in which people's goals follow from their strategies. Family sentiments and commitments are discursively constructed and legitimated simply, it seems, because they are the most effective means toward economic ends..

The language employed by Ong and Greenhalgh conveys an analytic preoccupation with the regulation and constraint of action. In Taiwan, "powerful family patriarchs" were "constrained to build their firms out of their families by powerful currents in the domestic and global political economies" (Greenhalgh 1994, 748) "because they faced intense pressures from the global and national political economies that left them with few alternatives" (764). Among diasporic Chinese capitalists, "the disciplinary norms of capitalism and culture also constrain and shape strategies and flexible subject making" — including flexible attitudes toward citizenship (Ong 1999, 19).

An adaptationist model of people struggling to adjust to the economic and political exigencies of a global political economy is not unfamiliar in anthropology, especially in light of our discipline's historic focus on less-powerful communities and societies as they are pulled into the orbit of European colonial and postcolonial states. But we have come to realize that even in the case of colonized and subaltern communities, an adaptationist scheme that fails to trace how cultural sentiments and subjectivities have shaped the path taken has serious limitations (Tsing 1974). When such an approach is applied to "powerful family patriarchs" and "Chinese corporate elites," its shortcomings are amplified. It is not that the powerful and wealthy are free from the constraints and pressures of forces that are not of their own making. But those forces open up and make possible, as well as constrain, goals and strategies. Among both wealthy elites and the subaltern they incite desire and enable action, not just suppress them. While it may seem a minor quibble whether we employ a vocabulary of constraint and regulation or one of enablement and incitement, the analytic consequences, I would argue, are significant. The former tends to lead toward economically reductive, utilitarian interpretations of strategies of action, the latter toward an understanding of the culturally meaningful ways in which people fashion strategies and, in the process, reformulate their desires and commitments. The former may be useful for understanding changes in the means people employ, but the latter enables us to understand the unfolding dialectic through which both means and ends are transformed. It prods us to ask how people reformulate ideas and sentiments of family and personhood, masculinity and femininity, parental commitment and filial loyalty, as they confront political, economic, and cultural shifts.[20]

From the perspective of an anthropologist studying Italian capitalism, these critiques of Orientalist portrayals of "Asian capitalism" have an additional blind spot. They fail to challenge the other half of the essentialist dichotomy — the representation of "Western capitalism." This leaves in place a vague and monolithic model of "Western capitalism" that appears to be imagined roughly along the lines of a Weberian individualistic, rational capitalism.[21] The critics of the Confucian-ethic thesis may be forgiven for this oversight, as their concern is to counter the West's representation of the East. As Said (1978) made clear, however, Orientalism is a discursive practice through which the West constructs itself as the modern antithesis of the Orient. It follows that a thorough critique of Orientalism requires a critical examination of both representations of "Asian capitalism" and representations of "Western capitalism."[22]

Italian Capitalism

In the mid-1990s newspapers in Tuscany published several investigative stories describing the alarming labor practices of small Chinese family firms that had moved into the lower end of the leather industry in Tuscany. Replete with allusions to shadowy "secret societies" that controlled the flow of illegal immigrants from China, these newspaper accounts honed in on the long hours that family members put in at low pay and under oppressive work conditions. In the context of the rising antiimmigration sentiments throughout Italy in the 1980s and 1990s, as the country for the first time faced a greater influx of immigrants than outflow of emigrants, sensationalist stories about the un-Italian cultural practices of immigrants were not surprising. What I did find surprising was the absence of any hint of self-recognition in these stories. Why was it, I wondered, that the journalists writing these accounts did not comment upon the similarities between these immigrant subcontracting firms and the small Italian family firms that have been the mainstay of numerous manufacturing industries in the country? After all, a common complaint I had heard voiced by the owners of subcontracting firms in Como was that even smaller (local) family firms were undercutting them by offering their services at costs so low that it was clear they were exploiting family labor.

During the same period, the popular press in the United States occasionally featured stories of the internecine squabbles over succession and control of famous Italian capitalist families such as Agnelli, Gucci, and Benetton. Over the years, I accumulated a file of clippings sent by friends and colleagues in Italy and the United States who knew of my research project. Family conflicts among the rich and famous in the United States, of course, also entice the interest of U.S. readers, but those involving Italian capitalist families seem to have the added appeal of a genre in which passionate family battles conjure up the drama of the *Godfather*. Clearly, these conflicts are read as emotional psychodramas much more enticing to follow than corporate takeovers in U.S. capitalism.

In this popular discourse, Italian capitalism sits awkwardly in the cultural essentialist divide between "Eastern" and "Western" capitalism, and a consideration of why this is so raises important questions both about Italian capitalism and about "Western capitalism" itself. As will be seen in the chapters to come, Italian capitalism is shaped by commitments to forms of collectivity, filial loyalty, and patriarchal authority—all features associated with "Asian capitalism." At the same time, however, it is influenced by commitments to individualism, independence, and rationality. It is not my intention to turn the tables on the West and subject "Italian capitalism" to an Orientalist analysis that characterizes its motivations and orientations as irrational expressions of cultural "tradition." This, of course, would merely recycle the analytic dichotomies that have impeded our understanding of the multiple commitments and desires that shape all "economic actions" and of the complex sentiments, orientations, and relations that make up "Western capitalism."

The familial character of Italian capitalism has contributed to its "othering" in the West. But it is not the only reason for its reputation as a "culturally traditional" form of capitalism. For one, Italy, along with other Mediterranean societies, has been viewed by northern Europeans and North Americans as more closely linked to the agrarian, preindustrial past of Europe. Until recently Italy, like Greece, signified both Europe's glorious "classical" past and its more recent, premodern backwater.[23] The anthropology of Mediterranean societies has reflected this view in its near exclusive focus on rural or small-town life in the least industrially developed regions of Italy. Ethnographic studies in Italy have tended to focus on the south (e.g., Davis 1973; Schneider and Schneider 1976) and other less industrialized areas (Silverman 1975; Holmes 1989; Pitkin 1985), and there have been almost no studies of the urban north.[24] The "honor and shame" complex and its associated gender hierarchy came to be the marker of Mediterranean society just as caste has been for India, lineage for Africa, and the closed peasant community for Mesoamerica.

Italy's relatively late transformation in comparison to other Western European nations from an agrarian society to an urban-industrial one, of course, contributed to the characterization of its social and economic institutions as holdovers of a preindustrial, southern European folk society. Industrial development did not get underway in Italy until the 1880s, and its timing and sequence has had a long-lasting impact on its place in the international market and its national politics. Confronting a regional and international market already dominated by more industrially developed nations, the northern Italian bourgeoisie had to ally itself with agriculture-estate owners in the south to create a national market sheltered by tariffs (Piore and Sabel 1984, 151). The result was the dependence of the bourgeoisie on the newly formed state and its concession of considerable political power to other social classes (Martinelli and Chiesi 1989, 110).[25] Although the political legitimacy of the bourgeoisie has been significantly strengthened in Italy over the last quarter-century, their earlier lack of clear-cut political hegemony led other advanced industrial-capitalist nations to view Italy as politically unstable.

Weber's thesis of the lack of "affinity" between Catholicism and the regularized investment of capital contributed as well to the relegation of Italian capitalism to the margins of "Western capitalism." Although Weber considered the medieval cities of northern and central Italy the source of the "uniquely Occidental" innovations that eventually led to the development of modern capitalism, he concluded that Catholicism lacked the "this-worldly asceticism" of Puritanism and the moral energy and drive to generate modern capitalism (1978, 359). The impact of Weber's thesis has been great, despite its basis in his misunderstanding of Catholic doctrine (Giddens 1992, xxiii) and his failure to study the actual workings of Catholic and Protestant capitalism. Whether we regard "Western capitalism" as an essential, stable practice of the West or as a discursive construction, Weber's thesis of its Protestant origins has had the effect of marginalizing Italian and other non-Protestant European capitalisms in models of "Western capitalism."

Finally, the predominance of family firms and the weaker development of public joint-stock companies in Italy in comparison to other Western European capitalist nations has contributed to the view that Italian capitalism has yet to mature into advanced capitalism. The persistence of communal values in family capitalism is problematic for both Marxist and Weberian theories of capitalism, as both Marx and Weber assumed family firms would eventually decline and be replaced by joint-stock corporations. The Parsonian model of capitalist modernity that has dominated sociology in the twentieth century elaborates the Weberian thesis into the theory of structural differentiation (Parsons and Bales 1955). According to this social evolutionary theory of increasing functional specialization, the spatial and institutional differentiation of family and work is central to capitalist-industrial society. A functionally reduced family that specializes in the reproduction functions of child care, nurturance, and socialization evolved out of the multifunctional, preindustrial household (Parsons 1943; Parsons and Bales 1955; Smelser 1959). This theory of capitalist modernity renders those for whom family relations are productive relations an anachronistic vestige of precapitalist society. The family, after all, is supposedly an insufficient basis of accumulation, and the dynastic character of entrepreneurial families is considered incompatible with the meritocratic values of modern bureaucracies and technostructures. Consequently, where family firms have been crucial to the industrial dynamism attributed to flexible specialization and flexible accumulation in economically successful nations such as Japan and Italy, their persistence is seen as calling for explanation.[26]

In Italy's case, these explanations have focused on the political-economic forces that have created a large entrepreneurial middle class engaged in small family enterprises. Most scholars agree that Italy's place in the global economy has been crucial in the creation of this family business sector, but they do not agree as to how. Suzanne Berger (1980) contends that this sector fills a shock-absorbing function in an international market with its ups and downs, while Pizzorno (1981) emphasizes the ruling Christian Democrat party's political motives for supporting it, arguing that its strength is crucial to continuing the party's political hegemony. Martinelli and Chiesi (1989, 123) add that the big capitalist families in Italy have been able through adept financial strategies to counteract the difficulties posed by state managers, insufficient accumulation, a progressive tax system, and inheritance taxes.[27] All agree that whatever the multiple causes of the persistence of family firms in Italy have been, there is no indication that the system is in decline (Chiesi 1986).

The paucity of empirical studies of family firms makes it difficult to assess these explanations of the continuing vitality of family capitalism in Italy. Sociological research has yielded useful information on family firms in a number of regions and sectors (Martinelli, Chiesi, and Dalla Chiesa 1981; Paci 1982; Frigeni and Tousijn 1976), and there have been a few historical studies of dynastic families (e.g., Bairati 1988; Scassellatti 1994). The one ethnographic study of family firms by Blim (1990), which does a superb job of locating these firms in a regional political-economic history, is focused on small firms primarily in the shoe industry of the Marche region. Given the paucity of ethnographic research on

Italian family firms, we lack an understanding of the processes through which individuals and families create, develop, expand, reproduce, and divide firms. As a result, attempts to bring culture into the analysis of Italian family capitalism have tended toward what could be labeled a "culture resource" model. I discuss this model in chapter 4, where I review the literature on Italian family capitalism. Here it is worth noting the parallels between this approach and the Orientalist analysis of Asian capitalism. Several researchers (Paci 1982; Frigeni and Tousijn 1976; Blim 1990; Piore and Sabel 1984) trace the formation of small firms in Italy to the family traditions that have facilitated the pooling of labor and capital in various regions of Italy. Like Confucian communal values of filial piety and family unit, the communalism of agrarian households and other preindustrial kinship formations in Italy are presented as stable resources that have been drawn upon to develop efficient capitalist enterprises. Family and kinship, indeed culture in general, are treated as institutional resources that are distinct from capitalist enterprise and as means that can be useful for capitalist ends.

Family + Kinship

The Silk Industry of Como

Even before the proximity of hydraulic power from Como's many rivers and streams made it one of Italy's first industrial manufacturing industries in nineteenth century, silk production in Como was spread over a loosely organized network of production units.[28] As in the early development of the northern European textile industry (E. Goody 1982), merchants functioned as the industry's entrepreneurs by taking on both supply and marketing functions. Instead of grouping weavers together in factories, merchants bought the thread that had been spun in the homes of farmer-artisans, who often raised silkworms and cultivated mulberry trees along with other agricultural products. The merchants then had the thread woven by artisans who owned their own looms. Even after the industrial transformation of the industry led to the concentration of the spinning of thread in large factories (*filature*) and the adoption of mechanical looms, production continued to be dispersed. Although there were a few vertically integrated firms, the vast majority of firms operated in only one phase of the production process. After the 1930s, the cultivation of silkworms declined rapidly in the region and the industry came to rely entirely on raw silk imported from China. But the other phases of the production process — including the twisting of the silk thread, its preparation for weaving, the dyeing, weaving, and printing of the fabric, the preparation of screens for printing, and the packaging and marketing of fabric — continued to take place in different firms.

In the late 1950s and 1960s—the period considered the "miracle years" of rapid economic development and growth in Italy—there was a move to centralize production in vertically integrated firms. But the decentralized industrial structure of production was reinvigorated by the labor conflicts of the late sixties and the rising labor costs and world recession of the early seventies—all of which underscored the advantages of decentralized, but coordinated, networks of small firms. Firms called "converters" put the production process in motion by deciding what kind of fabric should be produced and then ordering the spinning and twisting of thread and the weaving, dyeing, and printing of fabric by other firms.

During the 1970s and 1980s, there was a decline in the total number of firms and employees in the industry along with an increase in output per worker, but the size distribution of firms was fairly stable, with 68 percent of the firms having fewer than ten workers, 18 percent having between eleven and fifty workers, and 14 percent having fifty-one or more workers. In 1985 the industry employed about thirteen thousand workers in the province of Como, thus constituting its leading manufacturing industry.

Throughout its history, the industry has been characterized by the overwhelming predominance of local ownership by Como families. In 1985, out of the approximately four hundred firms in the industry, there was only one joint-stock company that had been started by investors outside of Como and there was no multinational ownership. Local ownership does not mean, however, that the industry is, or ever has been, an autonomous local system of production and distribution isolated from international flows of capital, technology, and labor or from international markets. During its industrial beginnings in the last two decades of the nineteenth century, the industry depended on German and Swiss finance capital, German textile machinery firms, and French textile firms—for which it performed many of the earlier stages of production, leaving the final, and greater valued-added, phases to the French firms. Since World War II, moreover, Como has not produced any raw silk and instead has relied entirely on China for its supply. With Italy's increasing industrial success, Como's firms have come to be tied in more with Italian finance capital, but they are still integrally linked with transnational industrial and commercial networks.

Como's silk industry is commonly described, by both outsiders and insiders, as a "provincial" industry rooted in local entrepreneurial values. One of the frequent complaints voiced to me, especially by the owners of larger firms, was that the industry was being kept from achieving its true potential by the "conservative" "closed," and "provincial" mentality of the small firm owners. In the last chapter of this book, I argue that the "provincial" character of capitalism in Como is

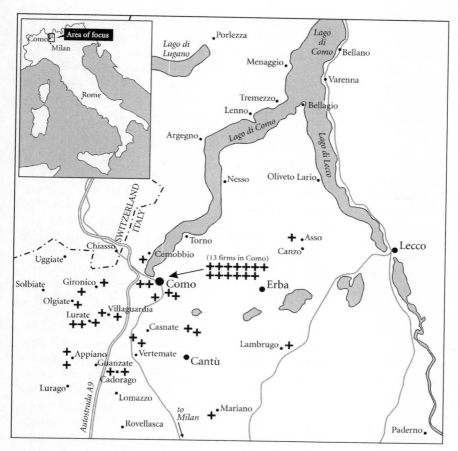

FIG. 1.1. Location of Firms in Study

not merely the expression of a unique local culture of entrepreneurship or, as some Comaschi claim, of a personality type wrought by the province's northern exposure to the Swiss. Rather, it is the discursive and material outcome of the relations of production among fractions of the Como bourgeoisie which have been historically constituted by sentiments of kinship and gender, regional and international political economies, and the Italian state.

The Scheme of This Book

This introductory chapter sets the stage for what is to follow: an ethnographic study of Italian family capitalism that treats capitalist action

Capitalism w/cultural value

as culturally produced and, therefore, always infused with cultural
meaning and value. My critique of the concept of economic "interest"
has led me to propose an alternative theory of capitalist motivation in
which sentiments operate as forces of production that incite particular
kinds of capitalist action. I have argued that the productive capacities of
the bourgeoisie are, like those of workers, produced and reproduced
through cultural processes in which kinship and gender are crucial. The
marginalization of kinship and gender, sentiment and subjectivity in
models of capitalist action was traced to the ways in which the two
major theorists of capitalism—Marx and Weber—conceptualized capitalist agency. This was followed by a cautionary tale of the way in
which a Weberian binary between "modern" and "premodern" capitalism has been replicated in recent popular and academic discussions of
the struggle between "Western capitalism" and "Asian capitalism." My
discussion of the adaptationist reductionism of some anthropological
critiques of this essentialist model of culture and capitalism led me to
question both halves of this binary. Finally, I have attempted to consider
the challenges that an ethnographic study of Italian capitalism confronts
and to provide the reader with an abbreviated history of the silk industry of Como.

In chapter 2, "The Generation of Firms," I mine the "official" histories of firms, treating them as origin narratives that tell us a good deal
about Como entrepreneurs' concepts of personhood, entrepreneurial
success, family, firm, and society. All "official" firm origin narratives
recounted to me by the current owner-managers of firms identify a beginning and a founder who is represented as having used his creative
energy to generate his own firm, his own family, and his own destiny.
Fathering a family and fathering a business are mutually interdependent
projects of creation in Como firm owners' cosmology of kinship and
business, family and capitalism. The interpretation of these "official"
firm histories leads me to consider issues of representation that have
been raised by recent challenges to ethnographic authority. I extend the
reflexive critique of ethnographic accounts to argue that the stories our
informants tell, like the stories the anthropologist tells, must also be
situated within the broader context of the stories told by other people.
Accordingly, I draw on alternative histories provided by other family
members and on the "stories the state can tell" contained in the archives of the Camera di Commercio (state-sponsored chamber of commerce) to verify, supplement, challenge, and raise questions about "official" firm histories. My investigation reveals systematic exclusions of
the flow of capital from founders' wives' parents, which suggests a comparison to the gender amnesia that Evans-Pritchard discovered among
the Nuer. This leads me to conclude that the sentiments and commit-

ments shaping capital and kinship investments among the Como bourgeoisie are more complex and more compromised than those portrayed in official firm histories.

Having shown that founding a firm and founding a family are integral achievements of male adulthood among the Como bourgeoisie, I address the challenges facing the sons of founders, who cannot claim to have created their own businesses and, thereby, their own destinies. In chapter 3, "Reproducing the Firm," I bring into dialogue the concerns about continuity expressed by bourgeois fathers in Como and those expressed by British kinship theorists to question the notion that law, rather than sentiment, ensures the continuity of the social order. The distrust of sentiment and the abiding faith in law as the basis of corporate continuity, which characterized the work of British kinship theorists, is not borne out by Italian family firms. More than law, the patriarchal desire of fathers to endow their sons with the means of independence from subordination to other men operates as a force for the continuity of firms. The question of how likely it is that sons will successfully continue the firm leads, at the end of the chapter, to a discussion of social mobility and internal differentiation among the Como bourgeoisie. In order to understand the strategies and struggles for firm continuity and mobility among the Como bourgeoisie, I need first to address the issue of what they share as a class and what differentiates them internally. I divide the Como bourgeoisie into three fractions on the basis of their effective control over the means of production, their class trajectories, and their strategies of class reproduction and social mobility. This lays the groundwork for my analysis in chapters 4 and 5 of the different configurations of capital and kinship that shape the development and demise of firms in different fractions.

Chapter 4, "Betrayal as a Force of Production," begins by contrasting the distrust of kin voiced by Como firm owners with what scholars have written about the key role that collectivity and commitment to extended family ties have played in the success of Italian capitalism. I ask why Como firm owners' descriptions of their collaboration with other firms and the constraints on innovation diverges from the rosy picture of flexible specialization touted by some scholars. I show that betrayal and estrangement are as much a part of the experience of the lower fraction of the Como bourgeoisie who own and manage small subcontracting firms as are trust and collaboration. Moreover, the histories of these firms and their relation to other firms reveals that the decentralized structure of production of the silk industry of Como was not an "accidental discovery" of the postwar years, but the reinvigoration of a long-standing system in which larger firms rely on small firms for manufacturing services. The metamorphosis of some employees, including relatives, into competitors connects trust and betrayal to issues of control of technical knowledge and clients, which are the primary means of production among small subcontracting firms.

Where chapter 4 focused on the lower fraction of the Como bourgeoisie, chapter 5, "Capital and Gendered Sentiments," describes the processes of family and firm reproduction and division among the upper and middle fractions of the Como bourgeoisie. The struggles over the concentration and fragmentation of capital in these families parallel those over the control and deployment of technical knowledge among families of the lower fraction. In the upper fraction, family maturation and segmentation are anticipated and managed by strategies of capital diversification that often begin with the division of management labor among children. New firms may be created in allied sectors of the industry rather than in the same sector, thus complementing the work of the original firm and avoiding direct competition with it. Families in the middle fraction, however, generally do not have sufficient capital to support this process of diversification and, as a result, some siblings leave the firm. The eventual conflict between the divergent class reproduction strategies of siblings divides the family, some of whose members move into other fractions of the bourgeoisie. My investigation of the struggles over inheritance and succession among these upper- and middle-fraction families is set in the context of the 1980s as the demographic, cultural, and legal shifts initiated in the 1960s and 1970s began to be felt by the Como bourgeoisie. This brings to the fore issues of gender and the inclusion of daughters, as family members rethink and reconsider sentiments and strategies of capital accumulation, firm reproduction, and family continuity.

In the concluding chapter, I argue that the struggles within the families of the Como bourgeoisie not only shape family and firm processes; they are also processes of class making and self making. Thus, the making of the Como bourgeoisie cannot be understood without considering kinship processes. Having shown that entrepreneurs who share cultural sentiments, meanings, and desires can have capitalist ethics as different as those labeled "provincial" and "global" in Como, I circle back to the theoretical issue that I raised in the introduction to this book—the relation between culture and capitalism. The answer I propose lies in an approach to culture and capitalism that enables us to understand the connections between the diverse capitalist orientations and practices that not only coexist in an industry, but that are constituted in relation to each other.

꩜

CHAPTER TWO

THE GENERATION
OF FIRMS

The Barbieri firm was mentioned frequently by firm owners as one of the most prominent in the industry.[1] Its prestige derived not only from the fact that it was one of the largest and oldest firms in the industry — founded over ninety years ago — but from the recognition that it was being managed by the third generation of the family. Having been handed down from founder to sons to grandsons, the firm had escaped the demise predicted by the local adage "The grandfather founds the firm, the sons develop it, and the grandsons destroy it." Generational time, even more than historical time, endowed it with social distinction.

Mario Barbieri, one of the three cousins who had been managing the firm since the 1970s, was the first member of the family whom my research assistant Simona Segre and I interviewed. We were especially interested in meeting him because he had served recently as the president of the Italian association of silk-weaving firms. As in all first interviews, my initial question to Signor Barbieri, once we had settled into his office and had gone through the introductions and pleasantries, was "Ci può raccontare la storia della ditta?" (Can you tell us about the history of the firm?) He responded:[2]

Yes, this firm was founded in 1898 by Signor Renzo Barbieri, who was my grandfather; therefore, we are now in the third generation. My grandfather started by taking over a small weaving factory that already existed and developing it substantially over the years. The firm survived the vicissitudes of different historical periods, including the two world wars, to arrive to where we are today.

This skeletal outline of the firm's early history, which Signor Barbieri then went on to flesh out, included three elements that were common in owners' narratives of the beginning of firms: the date of the founding of the firm, the name of the founder and his relation to the speaker, and the number of generations the firm had survived. Information about other initial characteristics of the firm — such as its technology, organization of production, financing, site, factory, and market relations — also appeared frequently in these histories. But these technical and financial details were decidedly optional and, with a few notable exceptions that I will discuss later, provided the backdrop to the central drama that unfolded in these narratives — the drama of generational succession.

It was this history of succession that Mario Barbieri went on to describe:

The founder was my grandfather, who was the only member of his family actively involved in the management of the firm, even though some of his brothers were partners in the corporation that was formed when the firm was begun. In the beginning there were about fifty employees, but by the period between the two wars there were fifteen hundred in three factories of which the main one was the original one. The others were in nearby towns.

Then my grandfather's two sons, Bruno and Carlo, joined the firm, but Bruno, who was older and had entered the firm first, died young in 1937. His younger brother, Carlo, entered the firm and together with his father Renzo managed the firm until 1963, when Renzo died. By then Bruno's two sons (Paolo and Stefano) and then I [Carlo's son] had entered the firm. Paolo and Stefano had entered around the end of the 1950s and I, who am younger than them, entered the firm in the 1960s. At present, the three of us manage the firm. The life of this corporation has been continuous, without any substantial changes in its foundation. The partners are all the descendants of Renzo Barbieri, children and grandchildren. The three of us [Paolo, Stefano, and Mario] own shares in the corporation as well as manage the firm.

I soon came to recognize Mario Barbieri's account as the oral version of the "official" history the firm had published on the occasion of its eightieth anniversary.[3] Both versions celebrate the theme of generational succession, although the anniversary publication recognizes a parallel drama of generations.

The text of the Barbieri eightieth anniversary publication, which is replete with glossy color photographs of the factory, its state-of-the-art machinery, and its products, opens with a history that Mario Barbieri, like the other firm owners interviewed, did not mention — the history of the firm's workforce. In the introductory paragraphs of the first chapter of the anniversary volume, which is entitled *Three Generations of Labor*, the social history of the town and the surrounding region in the last decade of the nineteenth century sets the stage for the founding of the firm. A description of the social life of the community and the occupations (farmer, bricklayer, housewife) of its two thousand or so inhabitants just before the opening of factory draws attention to the close ties between the firm and the town from which it has drawn its workforce over the past eighty years. A day-long celebration attended by seven hundred current and former workers is documented by photographs and a journalistic depiction of the event.

In spite of its opening homage to the generations of workers in the firm, however, the anniversary text shifts quickly to the generations to which it attaches primary significance — the three generations of the Barbieri family. The report of the eightieth anniversary celebration concludes with a note that the profits from the day's production were donated to the local church and to the municipality — in other words, to the sacred and secular welfare of the town. However, the text then continues,

> Is this exhibitionism? Paternalism? No. It is a tradition of solidarity that blooms in an extraordinary occasion, but that is an ordinary part of the Barbieri firm and the life of Lomazzo of which it has been an integral part for the past 80 years. The life of a person, the life work of three generations.

> After Renzo Barbieri arrived in Lomazzo in the last years of the nineteenth century came his sons Bruno and Carlo; the first dedicated three shining years to the firm before dying prematurely in 1937, the second accompanied the development of the firm until 1973, helping with the entry into the factory at Lomazzo the education of the third generation.

Any ambiguity about which generations are being celebrated by the chapter's title vanishes at this point. The "three generations of labor" referred to are not, as we might first have expected, those of the workers, but those of the Barbieri family. The "tradition of solidarity" be-

TABLE 2.1
Distribution of Firms by Kin Relation between Current Manager(s) and
Founder ($N = 38$)

Grandfather	Father	Other Relative[a]	Nonrelative	Self
2	20	5	3	8

[a]"Other relative" includes grandmother, father-in-law, mother-in-law, great-uncle, cousin, and sister's husband.

tween the firm and the community that provided its labor force fades in comparison with the "lifework" of the three generations of Barbieri.

By the second chapter of the volume, the town and its population have become the setting for the key dramatic moment in the origin narrative: the arrival of the founder.

> On the first of August 1898, Renzo Barbieri, a young man of thirty who was an ardent worker, arrived in Lomazzo from his native Milan to found under the name "R. Barbieri & C." what would become one of the most solid and growing silk weaving firms not only in the province of Como, but in all of Lombardy.

Not all firm histories begin with grandfathers. Indeed, the social distinction of the Barbieri firm is greatly enhanced by the fact that it is one of the few that can claim a grandfather as its founder. Only two of the thirty-eight firms in my sample had been founded by the grandfather of the current generation of owner-managers, and in only two more had grandsons even begun working in the firm. Table 2.1 shows the distribution of firms in the sample according to the kinship relation between the current owner-manager(s) of the firm and the founder. Whereas only two of the thirty-eight firms were headed by grandsons of the founder, more than half were headed by a son or sons. Thus, while the adage predicts the destruction of firms by grandsons, it appears that the vast majority of firms do not survive long enough for grandsons to take over their management. Few survive even long enough for grandsons to begin working in them.

Firm histories that begin with the founding of the firm by the father of the current owner-manager, consequently, are by far the most common, followed by those that begin with the founding of the firm by the current owner-manager himself. Yet these differences in the generational depth of firms do not yield significant thematic variations in official firm histories. Whether they are describing grandfathers, fathers, or themselves, founders are depicted in very similar terms: as men of strong character who had the will, initiative, and discipline to successfully initiate an enterprise—in a word, entrepreneurs.

Firms' Histories as Origin Narratives

The official histories of firms recounted to us by firm owner-managers constitute narratives of origins not dissimilar to the stories of coming-into-being that have been the conventional object of analysis of anthropologists studying oral traditions in preliterate societies. In our introduction to the volume *Naturalizing Power*, Carol Delaney and I wrote:

> Origin stories are a prime locus for a society's notion of itself — its identity, its worldview, and social organization. Anthropologists often include origin stories of the peoples they study, recognizing, after Malinowski, that "an intimate connection exists between the word, mythos, the sacred tales of a tribe, on the one hand, and their ritual acts, their moral deeds, their social organization, and even their practical activities, on the other." Yet these same anthropologists hesitate at the threshold of their own society, reluctant to explore their own origin myths (whether religious or scientific) as these have naturalized their own world view. They have treated their own origin myths as taboo — set apart and sacred — under the notion that their stories of origin are, in some sense, real and true while those of others, especially primitive others, are myth and superstition. (Yanagisako and Delaney 1994, 2)

I use the term "origin narratives" to draw attention to the mythic significance of these accounts of the beginnings of firms. I do not, however, intend to imply that these narratives are "false" stories or purely fanciful tales ungrounded in historical fact. Rather, I mean that these narratives constitute a discursive practice that can tell us a good deal about Italian bourgeois concepts of self, family, firm, and society. In other words, they are a rich source for a cultural analysis of Italian bourgeois theories of capitalism and kinship. As part of the "story people tell themselves about themselves" (Geertz 1973), these narratives anchor people's motives and actions within meaningful social histories. They display the cultural models of personhood, firm, and family through which firm owners interpret their entrepreneurial histories, including where they have come from and where they are going. As we shall see in the chapters to follow, family members do not necessarily share the same cultural models. Nor are these models fixed and unchanging. New contexts, altered circumstances, and new opportunities continually present novel challenges to the Como manufacturing bourgeoisie, as they do to people everywhere. In meeting these challenges, people reformulate their strategies and goals and, at the same time, their interpretive models and modes of understanding.

Founders as Creators

With a few exceptions, the family firm is represented in owners' origin narratives as the creation of an individual man. The exceptions are the firms started by couples in which both husband and wife continue to be active in management. The contradiction inherent in this representation of a family firm, which firm owners at other times characterize as a collective enterprise, is evidenced in telling omissions in origin narratives. As we saw in the Barbieri firm's eightieth anniversary volume, the dramatic moment in the origin narrative is the arrival of the founder in the town where the factory is to be located. The focus is on the character and the agency of one man, the generator of the firm and the genitor of the sons and grandsons to follow. Missing from this official firm history are the siblings of the founder who were partners in the founding of the firm. Mario Barbieri mentioned them in passing, but minimized their significance by explaining that the founder was the only one among them actively involved in the management of the firm. Later in the chapter, when I discuss alternative narratives of origin, I will show that the financial and family origins of the Barbieri firm were even more complex than was hinted at in Mario Barbieri's account.

Regardless of whether the founding of a firm was made possible by several investors, founders are described in terms that attribute the creation of firms to their intentions and actions as individual agents. Ovidio Colli put it in the following incisive terms:

> I consider my father the founder of the firm, even though there were other investors involved. The firm was born because he conceptualized it, he initiated it, and so I see him as the initiator of the firm.

"Initiative" is a key symbol of the essential character that enables founders to carry out their visions—in other words, to create what they can imagine. It describes both an internalized attitude and a way of acting in the world. Hence, for Renata Barbieri, what distinguished her father, the founder of the Barbieri firm, from his identical twin brother was her father's initiative and enthusiasm. The twin brother, she claimed, had nowhere near the creative initiative of her father, Renzo; like his other siblings, he simply followed along in the footsteps of his own father. This, she explained, was why her father was the son chosen by his father to study textile manufacturing abroad in Germany.

A corollary to the initiative of founders is their openness to novel ideas and changing circumstances. Founding fathers are frequently described as having been very modern and up-to-date; indeed, they are said to have been ahead of their time. Whether they were the first in Como or Italy to try a new type of loom, buy a car, own a radio, or computerize their production process, <u>their eagerness to modernize and</u> <u>innovate both in their businesses and their daily lives is viewed as key to</u> <u>their entrepreneurial success.</u>

Above all, <u>founders exhibit a work ethic that distinguishes them from</u> <u>the norm.</u> The son of one founder described him as having a "monstrous capacity for work." The daughter of another said that he had "endless ideas, endless energy and worked twenty-six hours a day." Both admitted they did not have half the work capacity of their fathers. Whether metaphors of machinery ("my father is the motor that drives everything in the firm") or animality ("the founder of this firm was a beast for work") are employed, founders are depicted as extraordinary.

The characteristics that make founders successful entrepreneurs are not without their drawbacks. Many founders are also described by their children as domineering — of being *accentratori* (people who insist on making all the decisions themselves), and several founders readily admitted that they were strong-willed and difficult to get along with. The endless energy and drive of founders also has its dark side. The daughter who described her father as having endless energy added:

> All the entrepreneurs are a bit obsessive, pathologically obsessive; they find an outlet in their business activities.

Just as they are depicted as the creators of firms, founders are often represented as the creators of themselves. A parallel narrative of the construction of the self is commonly embedded in firm origin narratives. This theme of self-manufacturing is strongest in the firm origin narratives of founders who have experienced significant social mobility, especially those who moved from employee to employer. For these men, starting a firm marks a decisive break with the past. It constitutes the enabling moment after which they were able to fully realize their talents and ambitions. As Franco Scotti described his father:

> My father is a classic figure of the "self-made man."[4] He taught himself everything through practical work, studying whatever he could. He started working when he was nine years old, transporting wine in a horse-drawn cart. He started smoking when he was nine years old, because he didn't have enough to eat, and so he had to smoke. He was an exceptional person.

The founder of a photoengraving firm described himself in similar terms:

> I began fifty years ago, during a period of great unemployment. I applied to work in the third photoengraving firm that began after the technique was imported from Lyon. I didn't know anything, I just asked for work. After they hired me I enrolled in an evening course in design and after a little they put me to work in making designs.

After four years, because I wanted to improve and learn all the techniques of photoengraving, I went to work for another firm and worked for them for six years. I was intent on robbing all the techniques from everyone. In 1948 I felt I was ready to go on my own and start my own business. No one encouraged me to do this. In fact, my mother was against it, and I had to hide from her the fact that I had opened my own firm.

Trajectories of Social Class

As my discussion of the theme of self-manufacturing suggests, the most significant variations in origin narratives are linked to social mobility — that is, to the social class trajectories of founders and their successors. One son recounts the origin narrative of his father, who came from a family of sharecroppers but founded a firm that seventy years later was among the top twenty in the industry. The story anticipates and lays the foundation for the upward mobility the firm and the family subsequently achieved.

> My father was born in 1898 in a small town on the outskirts of Como. His family were sharecroppers — they worked a piece of land and as rent gave a certain share to the landowner. My father was the second eldest of four brothers and one sister.
>
> When he was eighteen years old, the first industrial weaving firms opened in the province of Como. My father was tired of being a farmer, so he went to work as an assistant to the chief technician of looms for a firm At the same time, he went to the Setificio [silk industry technical school] at night for several years, although he never earned a diploma. He only finished elementary school.
>
> After working in this firm for a few years, my father, [when he was twenty-six years old], was given about a dozen looms by a firm called Meda in Fino Mornasco, which had come to know him and his work while he was an assistant to the chief technician. Those first looms were mechanical, but not automatic. My father's arrangement with Meda was that in exchange for the use of the looms, which Meda continued to own, he produced fabric for them. He was paid a fixed price per meter of fabric. It was an exclusive relationship — that is, he was not allowed to use the looms to produce fabric for any other firm than Meda. He produced primarily linings of acetate for them.
>
> Because my father did not have a factory where he could put these looms, he arranged to spread them among several families in small towns around Fino Mornasco and in Fino Mornasco itself. Those

families were then responsible for weaving the fabric that my father assigned to them. This relationship went on for many years, and Meda continued to give old looms to my father. He was an expert technician, so he was able to adjust these looms, which he then passed on to the families which worked them for him. His relationship with Meda went on like this until 1956, when he had accumulated about one hundred looms.

The son goes on to describe his father's rise from these humble beginnings as a subcontractor, who was little more than a shop foreman whose "shop" was dispersed throughout the countryside. After accumulating enough savings to buy his own equipment, the father was able to free himself to work for a larger number of clients, thus increasing his bargaining power with Meda. Later he began to produce and sell his own finished fabric to converters, and his business grew until it eventually became a firm that itself employed thirteen subcontracting firms. Like the shift from subcontractor to owner of the firm that farms work out to subcontractors, the shift from employee to employer lends an ironic tinge to origin narratives. Pietro Casati, who had gone from working as a director in his uncle's printing firm to opening his own printing firm, spoke of the "moral satisfaction" of becoming what he could not be as long as he remained an employee rather than a firm owner.

> I was the director of a middle-sized printing firm from 1956 until 1969. Actually this firm was owned by my uncle [the husband of my father's sister]. In a short period of time I had become director of the firm. But then I realized that I wasn't going to be able to advance in the firm. Just before I decided to start my own firm, my cousin [the owner's son] had begun to take on a managerial role in the firm and we soon found ourselves in competition, given that we both had very strong characters.[5]
>
> In 1969 I started my own firm, and in 1973 I constructed this factory here. I did it more for moral satisfaction than for any material goal.

The opening of one's own firm is represented as a decisive break with the past, as I mentioned earlier, especially by founders who were formerly employees. It marks the beginning of a founder's true life project of making his fortune and his class location—in short, his social destiny. Although this theme is most strongly emphasized by entrepreneurs who were formerly employees, it is not limited to them. In the origin narratives of even those who never worked as employees, the founder's decision to start a firm is commonly associated with a break with his past. The break may have been accomplished through spatial movement away from the locale in which the founder previously lived, as when a founder left to fulfill his required military service or to apprentice with another firm for a period of time. The most dramatic of these spatial movements occurred when the founder went off to war or fled fascist persecution.

> My husband was a labor organizer who was persecuted by the fascists. He had to escape into Yugoslavia, and when he returned he had to "start from zero." He started producing ties with his sister, and then he rented some looms and had people weave in their homes until he could buy a factory with his partner.

A break with the father or independence from him through employment or other means also commonly precedes the founding moment. Another version of the founding of the firm just described by the widow of a founder was told to us by her daughter. In this version, the father's rebellion from his grandfather, rather than a flight from fascism, constitutes the decisive movement preceding the founding of the firm.

> My father was one of the *sindacalisti bianchi* [Christian Democrat labor organizers] and had organized a strike in his father's factory and had been thrown out of his father's house. His father was angry with him because he saw this as an act of rebellion against paternal authority.

The founding of firms by men who did not experience a significant shift in class location, especially those from families that were already members of the industrial bourgeoisie, is described in more fluid terms of family continuity. Here founders are situated within a family history of industrial capitalism. Several founders' sons noted that their fathers' families had already been in textile manufacturing, sometimes in others sectors of the industry. As the industry evolved, shifting to later stages of production, the family invested capital in newly emerging sectors. Attilio Bortolotti described how his grandfather had sent his father, Ernesto, to study in a textile school in Switzerland. Upon returning to Italy, Ernesto opened a firm with capital provided by his father. The children of another founder pointed to the land on which both the factory and the family home were still located as a tangible link with their family past. The land had been the site of the country home of their paternal grandparents, who were themselves owners of a weaving firm.

Women as Wives/Women as Founders

Distinctive characters and strong personalities are not attributed to the wives of founders, with the exception of women who are considered

cofounders of the firm. Wives who were raised in upper bourgeois families tended to give more elaborate accounts of their childhood and emergence into womanhood than did wives who came from families of more
modest means. But these coming-of-age stories are not linked to the
origin narratives of firms. Whether or not wives of founders have unique
skills or distinctive personalities is apparently not considered relevant to
the origins of firms. Indeed, the descriptions of wives as founders are
comparatively sparse, or at least lacking in rich detail, whether they are
told by their husbands, their children, their grandchildren, or themselves. This founder's characterization of his wife is a rather extreme
example that serves by its very exaggeration.

> My wife is a simple woman. She was a textile worker who had not
> studied anything beyond the required schooling. I married her be-
> cause I liked her.

The exceptions to this poverty of description were those few wives
who were viewed both by themselves and their husbands as collabora-
tors in the founding of the firm. In their initial responses to our in-
quiries about the history of the firm, the two women interviewed who
had collaborated with their husbands in opening a firm and who continued to manage it with them focused more on technological and marketing developments than did male founders. These responses cannot be
attributed entirely to different gender perspectives or experiences, since
the children of both of these women had only recently begun to work in
the firm, and, as a consequence, there was little by way of family history
and generational succession to recount. Still, it was striking that these
women's firm histories were all business. In answering our opening
question about the history of the firm, Carla Mainini began:

> Oh, it's a long story. It's impossible to tell you all of it . . . so here's
> the general outline. The weaving firm was started in 1962, one year
> before I got married. It was an artisan firm that was started as an
> individually owned firm by me and my husband. From the beginning
> the two of us have always been the only two partners—we each
> owned 50 percent of the firm. For about five or six years we worked
> exclusively as a subcontractor. Until about 1968 we sold undyed
> cloth to converters, and it wasn't until 1973 or 1974 that we began
> to produce our own collection, and from then on we sold directly to
> clothing manufacturers. In the beginning we were limited only to the
> Italian market, but from 1984 we also began to sell in the foreign
> market. In 1979 we expanded. We created another company in addi-
> tion to the weaving firm that specialized in tinting, and in 1983 we
> added a printing firm. From last September, that is, very recently, we

opened a new firm outside the textile industry which makes rubber products. We'll see how that goes.

Only after we asked explicitly about their motives for starting a firm and their experiences as women in the industry did these two women discuss their personal and family histories. Once they began to do so, the terms in which they described themselves echoed those of male founders. Carla Mainini explained:

I was very young; I was only eighteen years old when I married my husband, so starting a firm wasn't a decision I made, but was something that I was just confronted with.

I began from zero, I knew absolutely nothing. I had gone to the science high school, so I had not learned anything about textile manufacturing. I learned it all through experience. And now I have a lot of experience. . . .

What pushed me from the beginning was the will to succeed, to change my life; while today what pushes me is more a sense of responsibility. In the beginning we were small; now we have expanded. I wouldn't say that what motivates me is the desire to earn more; it's not the money, but really it's for personal satisfaction. I really want to emphasize that because personal satisfaction is perhaps what motivated me the most to push on, more than anything else.

I have a heavy curriculum vitae, made by sacrifices and very hard work . . . . and I think I have passed that on to my children.

Like her male counterparts, Carla Mainini characterized herself as a diligent entrepreneur who learned by hard work and experience and whose pursuit of entrepreneurial success and personal satisfaction had required considerable sacrifice. The other woman who founded a firm with her husband, Benedetta Carbone, also described herself as industrious and committed, and as an autodidact.

I am from Mariano Comense, so I'm from Brianza [a province adjoining Como]. My husband is from Como. My family instead are all Brianzoli, which is an important difference to note. Brianzoli are more industrious, harder workers, and, another thing, if someone from Brianza starts a job, even if the world collapses, he will finish it, whatever adversity he encounters. Like me—I ran into a lot of adversity, including two firms which went through very bad times, but I always finish what I start.

I worked first in a weaving firm. There I realized that I didn't understand anything that was going on; it was like hearing Arabic if someone used a technical term to ask me to do something. So I enrolled in a night course at the textile college. But I learned a lot by myself, at night, and then by making mistakes. Other people's experiences aren't useful because you don't want to take their word for it. You always think, I'm different from them.

What the two women founders add to male founders' tales of hardship and sacrifice is what they gave up as mothers. As Benedetta Carbone went on to say:

At times I say to myself, if I were to do it all over, perhaps I wouldn't have done it the same. You see your children grown and you think, I never had time to spend with my children. I was always on the run. I was just there to tuck them in bed at night, wake them up early in the morning and get them dressed and drop them off at preschool or school, go to the office, and then pick them up at the end of the day. I took my children with me on a lot of my business trips. I had to travel a lot, both in Italy and outside Italy. At that time children could travel on airplanes free until they were fourteen years old. So I took them with me: first the older one and then the younger one. My daughter still remembers how we used to travel with all the fabric samples and how she used to organize them in the suitcase. What a sacrifice it was!

I remember that once I had to leave suddenly for Frankfurt and my son had an exam the day after. I took him with me anyway and he studied in the airplane and at the airport. He told me it would be my fault if he failed, and I told him that if he failed, he should be patient and just repeat the year of school. How many sacrifices we made!

Interpreting Authoritative Histories

The critique of anthropology and its privileged position in a past and present global system of unequal economic, political, and cultural power has called into question the ethnographic authority we once enjoyed as the disinterested professional interpreters of culture. In the wake of the so-called postmodern crisis of representation, the characterization of anthropology's mission as the interpretation of "the stories people tell themselves about themselves" (Geertz 1973) seems to belong to a past age of epistemological and political innocence, before suspicions arose about our representations of Others. One response to this crisis was an attempt to let our ethnographic subjects "speak for themselves."[6] Another has been to reduce the knowledge claims of ethnography and to situate ethnographic representations in the system of political and cultural inequality in which the anthropologist and her subjects are located (Haraway 1991). Unfortunately, many of the recent efforts by ethnographers to "locate" themselves in relation to their subjects are not accompanied by efforts to locate the particular subjects studied in relation to others in their social world. In other words, the reflexivity of the ethnographer usually does not extend to a critique of the knowledge claims of the subjects.[7]

As we confront new issues of representation, ethnography is still plagued by old ones. In the past, critiques of representation in anthropology were focused more on the subjects than on the ethnographer, as in the commonly raised question of the "representativeness" of the particular subjects chosen for study and the extent to which others in their social community shared their ideas and modes of action. But this seemingly objectivist issue of "representativeness" was, I suggest, also the metonymic expression of a broader cluster of methodological anxieties anthropologists felt about their lack of critical methods for interpreting the representations of their subjects. Questioning whether the representations of particular members of even small-scale, local communities were "typical" of the rest of the community both challenged assumptions of cultural homogeneity and called for critical methods of interpretation. The issue was not whether those particular "natives" appearing in ethnographies lived "typical" lives and expressed "typical" beliefs, but how we were to use our knowledge of the particular character of their atypical lives and atypical beliefs to interpret their representations and actions.

Critical methods for interpreting individuals' accounts of their lives and histories must be part and parcel of cultural anthropology's reflexive critique of ethnographic representations. To engage in the latter without the former runs the risk of merely shifting the burden of representation from the anthropologist to the subject. Naïve attempts to "give voice" to subjects without adequately locating them within a social landscape that encompasses both "their" society and "ours" can reproduce the illusion of objectivity of ethnographic representations. In place of the anthropologist's representations, those of her subjects — and of particular ones at that — become the privileged "reality," as one authoritative voice is replaced by another.

To avoid reproducing a subjectivist version of an objectivist error, the stories people tell about themselves, like the stories the anthropologist tells, also must be situated within the broader context of the stories that are told by other people. In ethnographic studies such as this one, where the subjects are endowed with sufficient financial and cultural resources to make themselves well heard, the challenge is less how to give them voice as it is to let others speak as well. Given our discipline's preoccupation with studying less powerful Others, anthropologists have only begun to confront the question of how we are to represent elites who are not disadvantaged in the means of self-representation.[8]

One of the few anthropologists to study elites in American society,

George Marcus, has written perceptively of the need to deconstruct the authoritative histories of wealthy, dynastic families. Marcus (1988) employs the "alternative" histories of "marginal" family members to subvert and thereby shed light on "authoritative" family histories.[9] He does not, however, identify the specific sources of these alternative histories. That is to say, we are not told the structural locations or personal histories of the marginal family members who have provided specific alternative accounts. This makes it difficult to interpret them. The dichotomy between authoritative and alternative family histories, moreover, oversimplifies what is usually a more complex cacophony of voices. Among Como entrepreneurial families, in any family where there is more than one person "in charge," there is often more than just one authoritative family history. In addition to founders, sons, and grandsons in the direct line of succession, there are wives, daughters, managers, lawyers, notaries, priests, and judges who can provide family histories that, depending on the context, carry considerable authority. Indeed, what constitutes an authoritative history depends on who is granting authority and in what context. Narrators of firm and family histories do not have inherent authority but must be granted it, if only provisionally, by specific listeners. For example, in the context of an inheritance dispute or a disagreement over contracts, judges have the final narrative authority. In family therapy sessions, a psychiatrist may be granted narrative authority. In an ethnographic text, the anthropologist cannot escape the representational power she wields as writer and ultimate arbiter of narrative differences.

In the section below and the chapters to follow, I use the accounts of other family members to supplement, challenge, and interpret the "official history" of a firm provided by the current head of the firm — usually the founder or his son. In addition, I draw on another source of "official histories" — the records of the Italian state.

Stories the State Can Tell

One of the legacies of Mussolini's fascist government was the transformation of the Camera di Commercio (chamber of commerce) from a civic association for the promotion of commerce into a state agency to regulate it. David Horn (1994) has traced the ways in which the Italian fascist state both created a national social body and disciplined its citizens as it developed a state apparatus to promote the physical and mental health of the Italian population. The expansion of the Italian state's efforts to promote commerce and industry likewise resulted in increased surveillance and regulation. After 1926, the Camera di Commercio, which had been introduced in Italy by Napoleonic legislation, was no longer a voluntary association, but a state regulatory agency charged with both promoting and compiling information on commercial, industrial, and agricultural enterprises at the provincial level.[10] Since 1925, all businesses have been required to register with the Camera di Commercio in the provinces in which they conduct their commercial, industrial, or agricultural activities.

Within thirty days of the initiation of any of these economic activities or the establishment of a business partnership or corporation, businesses must register and submit the following information: name and location of the business, name of owner (if it is an individually owned firm), type of activity, products, date of initiation, preceding firm (if it is a continuation of an earlier firm), type of legal status (including a copy of the incorporation document), the amount of the *capitale sociale*,[11] the names of the partners and their respective proportion of shares (if it is a partnership), and the names of the legally responsible administrators. All changes in any of this information must be reported within fifteen days. Each firm's file also includes the industry survey form all firms are required to fill every ten years, which includes information on number of employees, equipment, factory size, gross product, and net profits.

Files of all firms that have ever registered with the Camera di Commercio are kept at the provincial offices and are available to the public, including researchers. One need only request a firm's file and wait a couple of days if it is in storage to be allowed to examine it in the provincial office, which in Como is located close to the center of town. The files contain a continuous record of the firm, from its initial registration (or from 1925, if it was founded earlier than that) to the present — a wealth of information that my research assistants and I spent over a hundred hours extracting for all the firms in the sample.[12]

I call the firm histories I gleaned from these records "Stories the State Can Tell." These stories, of course, have been reconstructed from the "facts" reported by firm owners to the state. Just as the officials of the Italian state are not so naïve as to assume that these reports are wholly accurate reflections of a firm's characteristics over time, neither am I. Firm owners have numerous reasons for reporting facts that reduce their tax burdens, lessen obligations to employees, and avoid a host of other state regulations. On the other hand, owners are discouraged from misreporting by the threat of state sanctions — a coercive check on reality that the anthropologist does not wield. Whether these pressures yield firm histories that are more accurate than the histories recounted to the anthropologist is unclear. Both, I suspect, have their respective omissions and distortions, as well as their respective accuracies. What, above all, distinguishes the "stories the state can tell" from the "stories told to the anthropologist" is that the former are culled from facts reported to the state over a longer span of time, usually by different individuals—none of whom was trying to impart a coherent history of intentions and actions to the anthropologist. Hence, the stories the state can tell, while undoubtedly also shaped by self-interest, are shaped by a different kind of self-interest. As such, they constitute a distinct genre of official history which can be used as a resource for interpreting other firm histories.

Like the stories told to the anthropologist, the stories the state can tell are incomplete. For one, they begin only with the official registration of the firm. In some cases, this may have been preceded by months or even years of unofficial activity—planning, development, and even actual production. In addition, firms sometimes begin operations under one name and then switch to another, leaving no way to trace the original firm through the state's records. Finally, the information firms are required to report is selected for the state's interests in industry oversight and regulation, not for the anthropologist's research objectives. The state is not, for example, interested in whether a son who is the legal owner of half the firm's shares has 50 percent de facto control over the firm. The anthropologist is.

Even though they are incomplete, the stories the state can tell can be usefully employed to verify, supplement, raise questions about, and challenge other narratives. The great majority of the information extracted from the Camera di Commercio files fell into the first two categories: it confirmed the oral histories provided by informants and supplemented them with noncontradictory information, providing more detailed data about amounts of capital invested, changes in the firm's legal status, acquisitions of equipment, and the specific dates of these changes. These discrepancies pertained to details that could easily have been forgotten, and the discovery of them in the firm files did little to alter my informants' versions of firm histories.

There were, however, other discrepancies between the official firm history and the story told by the state that were both more systematic and more revealing. The most significant were telling omissions. The histories provided by family members other than the founder and his successors and by employees also brought to light certain kinds of information commonly left out of the official history of firms. The most common of these was the involvement of relatives and nonrelatives as partners and investors in the firm.

I treat these omissions as systematic exclusions that were motivated by the discursive interests of firm owners. In other words, they arise from narrative conventions that are themselves forged by a dominant bourgeois model of capitalism and kinship. By omitting facts that do not conform to this model, firm owners simultaneously claim success for their firms and affirm the model. Whether these acts of exclusion are deliberate is a question I am unable to answer, nor do I think it analytically productive to do so. Regardless of the conscious intentions of the narrators, these systematic exclusions can tell us a great deal about bourgeois models of the success of individuals, families, and firms.

Other Founders/Other Investors

In the official history of the Barbieri firm that appears in the firm's eightieth anniversary volume, the arrival of Renzo Barbieri in the small town of Lomazzo on the first of August 1898 decisively marks the beginning of the firm. Once the precise date of origin has been established, the characterization of Renzo Barbieri as a "young man of thirty who was an ardent worker" completes the narrative elements necessary to launch the history of a successful firm. Absent from the anniversary text are Renzo's parents and siblings. Mario Barbieri mentioned them, but — it will be recalled — minimized their significance by noting that none of them had been actively involved in the management of the firm.

The Camera di Commercio records show that when the firm was founded in 1898, Renzo's six siblings (three brothers and three sisters) owned 24 percent of the firm. Renzo owned 16 percent. The remaining shares (60 percent) were distributed among six other partners, only one of whom was a relative (the husband of one of Renzo's sisters). Like the other partners whose names appear and then disappear from the Camera di Commercio records during the firm's long history, many were members of well-known Milanese industrial families. Mario Barbieri not only failed to tell us that non–family members held the majority of shares in the firm in the beginning, but he also never mentioned that his grandfather's siblings continued to own shares in the firm until 1950, when the last brother was bought out. In other words, it took over fifty years before the firm became the exclusive property of Renzo Barbieri and his descendants. By then the grandsons had taken over the management of the firm.

A trace of the more complex family entrepreneurial history leading up to the founder's arrival in Lomazzo can be found in the anniversary volume's description of Renzo as a native of Milan. What the volume does not reveal, however, is that Renzo's father was a Milanese industrialist who owned four silk-thread spinning factories in the region. While his older brothers were taking over the management of their father's spinning factories, Renzo was sent to study textile industrial engineering in Germany. He then worked as the director of the Italian branch of a Swiss textile firm. This provided him with invaluable knowledge and experience to bring to the management of the new weaving firm, which his family furnished with thread produced by the Barbieri spinning firms.

While it is true, therefore, that Renzo was the only member of his family actively involved in the management of the new firm, it is also true that the firm was an extension of his family's industrial enterprise. By financing one of its sons to open the weaving firm, the Barbieri family expanded its manufacturing capacity into the next phase of production. This has been a common capital diversification strategy among families in the Como silk industry; over the past hundred years the industry has continually shifted to later, and more profitable, phases of production. It is also common in other regions of Italy and Europe (see the discussion in chapter 4 on the *systeme Motte* in nineteenth-century Lyon and the twentieth-century textile industry of Prato, Italy).

An alternative origin narrative can be constructed from the state's records and from the information provided by family members that contrasts significantly with the official origin narrative of the firm. Rather than the tale of the founding of the firm by an enterprising young man, it is an account of the capital diversification strategy of an enterprising Milanese industrial family and their network of bourgeois allies.

While the sheer number of investors involved in the Barbieri firm is unmatched by all but a couple of the largest firms, the existence of "silent partners," both relatives and nonrelatives, who are unmentioned in the official history but who appear in the state's records is common. Some of these minor partners may have had little or no impact on the firm's management or on the major partner's productive and financial strategies. Others undoubtedly did, and their inclusion in official firm histories would yield significantly different narratives of origin.

Pedretti, a small dyeing firm, presents another such case. As one of the smallest subcontracting firms in my sample, Pedretti would seem to have very little in common with the Barbieri firm. Yet the owner-manager of Pedretti, like Mario Barbieri, excluded from his official firm history the more complex configuration of family collaboration and investment entailed in the creation of the firm. Indeed, after the first interview with him, I was prepared to categorize Pedretti as one of the few firms in the industry that was not a family firm. The affable and outspoken owner-manager, Piercarlo Venturini, was unmarried and had no siblings or other kin working in the firm. He had not inherited the firms from his parents or any other relative, but had bought it from its previous owners. In addition, Venturini's parents had never been involved in the industry, nor had any of his grandparents. His father had been a commercial agent for food products,[13] and his mother was a housewife. He had one sister, a widow, who he said had never worked in the firm.

Venturini's work history read like that of the paradigmatic self-made firm owner. After obtaining a degree as a chemical technician from the Setificio, he held a series of technical and management jobs in a number of different firms in the industry. These jobs brought him a wealth of experience in color design, organization of production, personnel management, and printing techniques. He had become the manager of the printing section of a major firm when he decided to buy the dyeing firm Pedretti.

Venturini explained that when he took over the firm in 1965, he bought only the machines and the rights to the firm's name and productive capacity. He could not afford to buy the building and the land, so he arranged to rent them from the firm's former owners. In our first interview, Venturini stated that the money for the purchase of the firm came from the severance pay from his previous job,[14] from his father, and from a bank loan backed by his father. However, in the second interview, when we asked him whether he had paid back his father, he said,

> Actually, now that I think about it, I realize that I was wrong — it wasn't my father, but my mother. My father died in 1964 and left the entire estate to my mother. At that point, since I wasn't married and still lived with my mother — and I am not married now either — the effective administration of the family's money became my responsibility. My mother had never been particularly interested in that sort of thing. In effect, therefore, the money which I used to start the business, beyond that which I had from my severance pay and that which I got from the bank, was money from the common fund of me and my mother. Thus, the question of paying it back never presented itself in those terms. My mother and I still live together and have our money together.

Italian inheritance law, which I discuss extensively in chapter 5, did not permit, in the 1960s a man with two legitimate children to leave his entire estate to his wife. It prescribed that at least two-thirds of it would be inherited by the children, with each receiving an equal share regardless of gender. Hence, Venturini's father could not have willed his entire estate to his wife. It is more likely that part of Venturini's parents' wealth came from his mother's parents, in which case she would have retained control of it. Whatever the precise inheritance provisions left by Venturini's mother and father, it was his parents' capital that enabled him to purchase the firm. When we asked him to clarify his sister's relation to the firm, Venturini told us that in 1978 he had changed the firm's legal status to a *società a responsibilita limitata* (a limited corporation)[15] in order to pay lower taxes than when it had been classified as an individually owned firm. To establish this corporation, there had to be at least two partners. Consequently, Venturini gave half the shares in the firm to his sister. He was quick to point out that his sister did not purchase these shares and while, legally, she owned half the firm and was owed half the profits, in fact, she did not expect to be paid. Instead, Venturini explained, he gave his sister money "because I want to, because my sister and I have a wonderful relationship and I want her as well to benefit from the success of the firm, but not because of her position as a shareholder." His sister had been widowed since 1966 and was currently living alone. But, for several years after her husband's death, she had lived with Venturini and his mother. Even later in the interview, Venturini revealed that his sister had worked in the firm, after she was widowed at an early age. She had no children, and she came to work in the firm primarily to have something to occupy her time. After six years, she stopped working because he convinced her that it would be more help to him if she stayed home with their mother.

Venturini's claim that his sister was not really a partner, except on paper, and that he shared the firm's earnings with her only because of his fraternal generosity is highly suspect. Legally, he and his sister had equal inheritance rights to their parents' property. Since Venturini drew on this family fund to start the firm, his sister and mother shared in the ownership of the firm, whether or not they actively participated in its management. Although Venturini also invested his severance pay in the business, I later learned that this accounted for only L.2 million of the initial L.13 million investment.

Located at the opposite ends of the wealth and prestige hierarchy of the Como manufacturing bourgeoisie, Piercarlo Venturini and Mario Barbieri nevertheless shared a common discursive interest in tracing the origins of their respective firms to an individual rather than to the more complex configuration of social relations that had enabled the founding of the firms. Like the many other firm owners who omitted partners and investors, both kin and non-kin, from their official histories of firms, Barbieri and Venturini embraced not only the ideal of the individual founder but also that of *autofinanziamento* (self-financing). Another firm owner, Ovidio Colli, spelled out this ideal in describing the history of financing of his firm:

> The firm was family financed, because in the beginning the investment was relatively modest. Little by little, however, the firm needed more capital—some of this was self-financing, others came from low-interest loans from the government and also leasing of machinery. We used every form of financing to be sure that we were technologically up-to-date. This increase in financing however took place in a second phase; in the beginning the firm was entirely self-financed. It's just that after a certain point technology developed such that self-financing could not be the exclusive source of capital.

Family financing—drawing exclusively on resources inside the family— in the firm's early years has the symbolic value of rendering the firm the creation of the family. Once having established the firm as its own, the family can draw on sources of capital outside it without compromising their status as the owners of the firm, even if they may share legal ownership with a number of investors. The firm is unmistakably their project and their property.

The omissions in official firm histories that I have discussed thus far reveal the common interest current owners share in attributing the origins of the firm to an individual. Below I discuss their common practice of tracing a particular genealogical route to that individual.

Wives and the Flow of Capital: Three Cases

G. Pezzi

Our interviews with the members of the Pezzi family and a review of the state's records yielded three "authoritative" accounts of the origins of the firm. The founder's narrative was of how the son of a textile manufacturing family went off to war, returned to see where the future lay in the industry, and pursued this vision by starting a successful converter firm. His son's version differed only slightly—emphasizing a bit more his father's family's history of involvement in the textile industry. The state's records suggest a distinctly different tale. It tells of a family of textile manufacturers who set up their son-in-law in a firm in an allied sector of the industry. While their son-in-law managed the firm, the family retained the controlling shares, which they eventually handed on to their daughter and her children. All three narratives speak of the reproduction of social class and the flow of capital across generations. They differ with regard to the routes through which they trace this flow.

From his office in the elegant lakeside villa that served as the firm's headquarters, Guido Pezzi gave the founder's version of the firm's beginnings.

> I began my business in 1934 with a partner named Brambilla. The firm was called Pezzi Brambilla Società in Accomandita. In 1938 Brambilla and I split up, and I took over the firm because I made the higher sealed bid. Brambilla started his own converter firm. From 1939 the firm was called SPA [società per azioni; see n. 17] Pezzi Guido, becoming later Guido Pezzi SPA.

Over the course of three interviews, Guido linked his own career to his family's history in the manufacturing sector of the Como silk industry and to his decision to break into a different sector. He explained that he was the youngest of three sons whose grandfather had, in 1895, founded a weaving firm, which Guido's father and his father's brothers continued to operate. As a young man, however, Guido soon realized that there were too many heirs (he had two brothers and two male cousins) in his generation for all of them to take over the firm. He could see that the industry's future lay in the commercial sector rather than in manufacturing, so after he returned from the army at the end of World War II, he opened a converter firm. He was eventually proved right, as his family's weaving firm declined and was liquidated in the 1970s.

Guido explained that he knew Brambilla, his original partner in the firm, because Brambilla's older brother was the accountant in his father's firm. When he decided to open his own firm, he asked Brambilla to join him, and the latter accepted because the Pezzi name was a strong guarantee. Brambilla took charge of the accounts and Pezzi handled sales. After they dissolved their partnership, they continued to be on good terms.

The son's version, like his father's, linked the firm to his father's family's history in silk manufacturing. Both represented the founding of their firm as the independent move by a son to branch out into a newly developing sector of the industry. The son, however, brought his mother into the narrative in the later years of the firm.

> This converter firm was founded by my father, Guido Pezzi, in 1935, together with a partner named Brambilla. But my family had already been in the textile industry since the end of the nineteenth century. My great-grandfather had a weaving firm in Lurate Caccivio [a nearby town], where my grandfather, my father, and his brothers worked. Then my father left his family's firm because he believed that the commercial sector of the industry would develop more than the industrial sector; so he founded this firm.
>
> In 1939, my father and Brambilla split up. Brambilla opened another firm and my father stayed on alone in this firm. The firm was initially called Pezzi Brambilla SAS,[16] but after 1939 it was called Pezzi Guido. Around 1950 it became an SPA,[17] and my mother became one of the partners, taking charge of the design department.

The story told by the state's records does not necessarily contradict the founder's representation of the firm as the product of his vision. But its record of capital investments reveals that the fulfillment of this vision was a collaborative family project, rather than an individual one. In contrast to both the founder's and his son's accounts, moreover, the state's records link the firm to Guido's wife's family rather than to his family, conjuring up a history of matrifilial transmission of capital and social class.

When the firm opened in 1934, Guido was not listed as one of the owners. Indeed, his name did not appear until three years later, at which time he appears as one of several partners, along with Brambilla. By early 1939, Brambilla and Guido Pezzi each owned half of the firm, but later that year three people joined them on the Board of Directors: Guido's wife, Elda Pezzi Mascheretti, her mother, and two nonrelatives. The *capitale sociale* was doubled with the new shares distributed among Elda (L.40,000), her mother (L.40,000), and the two nonrelatives (each of whom owned L.10,000). A year later, the *capitale sociale* was again increased by 25 percent, with small shares going to Elda's brother. In the same year, Brambilla resigned as the delegated representative of the firm to start his own business. By 1940, Elda, her mother, her father, and her brother together owned 126 of the firm's 200 shares, while Guido owned 50. In other words, while Guido managed the firm, his wife's family owned and controlled the majority of its shares. In 1943 the firm name was changed to SPA Guido Pezzi. Still, the members of the Mascheretti family owned 78 percent of the firm's shares, compared to Guido's 20 percent. Then in the mid-1950s, Elda's parents transferred their shares to her, so that by 1957 Guido and Elda each owned equal percentages of shares, with only a tiny percentage owned by the two nonrelatives.

The state's records reveal that the Mascheretti family's capital was crucial to the "founding" of the firm by their son-in-law, Guido Pezzi. Indeed, it could be argued that the "founding moment" of the family firm occurred when the Mascheretti family bought out the original partners and installed their son-in-law as the nominal owner and director. It was their capital that enabled Guido Pezzi to outbid his partner and to make it a family firm. In sum, the "family" that owned and controlled the firm was much larger and more inclusive than the one described in the official history.

Stamperia Breva

Like most of the manufacturing firms in the industry, Stamperia Breva sits on the outskirts of one of the small towns that dot the Lombardian plain to the south of Como. The clean lines of its single-story, modern plant seem out of place in its semirural surroundings of fields, gardens, and dispersed residences. Inside the building, the sparse furnishings and unadorned hallways of the firm's offices, which are attached to the printing plant, convey the ascetic quality of a research laboratory — a stark contrast to the opulent, aristocratic charm of the lakeside headquarters of the Pezzi firm. Roberto Franchini, who was listed in the industry green book as the "legal representative" and "administrator" of the firm — but not its general director — was a man in his midfifties whose lean build matched the spare design of the building. He responded to our inquiry about the firm's history by pulling out a sheet from his desk and reading from notes he said he had prepared for a group of middle-school children who had visited the firm the year before.

> Stamperia Breva was founded in 1952. We developed a particular printing technique called [omitted so the firm cannot be identified]. When the firm was created, however, I didn't work here because I was the director of another firm, Bernini. I had begun working there in 1948 right after I received my *laurea* degree in chemistry. So in the beginning I was in charge of only the technical side at Breva. There was also my wife, who managed the accounts, and my brother, who was in charge of procuring orders.

Franchini then went on to describe the production history of the firm: its acquisition of specialized machinery, the construction of a new factory, the addition of a finishing department, and its response to changes in the textile market. He ended by returning to the subject of the family's management of the firm.

> Ours is a family firm. There are myself and my wife, and then we brought in our two children, our older boy and our daughter. My son has taken my place — he is the general director. And my daughter is in charge of the accounts with the help of an accountant.

This conclusion to the written narrative gave us the impression of having encountered yet another firm that was being transmitted from father to son, with the supporting role devolving from mother to daughter. Only later, as we reviewed our interview notes, did we realize that Franchini had never said he founded the firm. Rather, he had used the passive form of the verb and said the firm "was born in 1952." We were puzzled too by the haziness of his memory about the early years of the firm. When we had asked Franchini for the names of the original owners of the firm, he said he could not recall them.

Later in the interview, as he was explaining the fluctuations in the size of their workforce over the years, Franchini veered off into a discussion of the firm's current management structure and how his son-in-law had been brought into it. He then went on to talk about his own early career history.

> At this point there are three managers, my son-in-law, my son, and the accountant. My son-in-law was a graduate from the Setificio who needed a job, poor guy. My son and my son-in-law's parish priest insisted, so I hired him — but he had to work his way from the bottom up, just as I had to. In my case, I had worked at one firm and then after I graduated from the university at another firm. I would have become a researcher [in chemistry] but my mother-in-law had a dyeing firm and sent me to the firm Bernini in Como, where I brought about significant innovations. At that time she wasn't my

mother-in-law yet, but my mother-in-law to be. She was a partner in a dyeing firm in Como. She supplied Bernini with fabric and had recommended me to the director. Her husband worked in her dyeing firm, but he was a mechanic in charge of the boiler.

The link between his son-in-law's entrance in the firm and his own early career appeared to have been drawn by Franchini so that we would know that he too had worked his way up from the bottom. It also alerted us to other parallels between Franchini and his son-in-law. These suggest a tale of intergenerational transmission quite different from the one implied in his written history. If Franchini's future mother-in-law, who had been a partner in a dyeing firm, had found him a job in a printing firm to which she supplied fabric, how else might she have been involved in his career and the founding of Breva? The fact that her husband worked as a technician in the firm she co-owned was hardly a common marital arrangement. Indeed, it was the only such instance we came across in our study. Combined with what we knew of Franchini's own parents' occupations — his father was an accountant in a bank and his mother was a housewife — it raised the possibility that Franchini, like his son-in-law, had been recruited into his in-laws' firm.

Toward the end of the interview, after declaring that no other relatives besides his wife and brother had been involved in the firm during its early years, Franchini revealed that his wife's parents had owned a part of the firm. He could not recall the specific dates they were involved, however, and he hastily added that after 1958 he and his wife were the sole owners. Because he appeared uneasy and clearly did not want to pursue the subject, we let it drop.

In our second interview, when we asked Franchini who managed the firm while he was still working at Bernini, he gave the following version of the firm's early years.

> Before I starting working in the firm, my wife was the general director and fulfilled all managerial functions. I was a technical consultant. There were hired managers who headed the different departments, such as a foreman of printing, et cetera. My brother was a salesman for the firm. After I left Bernini, I became the general director and director of everything at Breva.

This second account granted Franchini's wife, Rosalba Tanzi Franchini, a more central role than the first one. It all but guaranteed that her parents had controlled the firm. Rosalba, moreover, had a university degree in chemistry. Having this very unusual credential for a woman of her cohort suggested that she had prepared to follow in her parents' footsteps in the printing and dyeing sector of the industry. The fact that she was an only child increased the likelihood that she was the intended successor to her mother's business projects. Rosalba was being groomed to manage Breva or, at the very least, to be knowledgeable enough to oversee its management. Intrigued by this possible case of mother-daughter succession, we asked Franchini if we could interview his wife. He put us off with a series of excuses and then finally declined for her, explaining that as his wife was no longer involved in the management of the firm, she would have nothing to add to what he had already told us.

Three years later, another research assistant, Paola Schellenbaum, returned to Breva to interview Franchini's daughter, Eleonora. By then I had received a grant to study women managers, providing us with the perfect excuse to request interviews with the women in the family. It turned out we did not need one. Less than a year after Simona and I had interviewed Roberto Franchini for the second time, he had been seriously injured in an automobile accident. During his lengthy recuperation, he had withdrawn from active involvement in the firm, which was currently being managed by his son, his daughter, and her husband.

Eleonora named her parents as the co-founders of the firm. Even more interesting, however, was her claim to a family "tradition" of women managers. As she put it,

> In my family there is a tradition of women working in the textile industry. In fact, my maternal grandmother was a partner in a printing firm that still exists.

In addition to her grandmother, her mother, and herself, she added, her brother's wife is a partner in a dyeing firm. "We call ourselves the women's factory," she joked just as her brother Sergio entered the room with his wife, Luisa, whom he had brought to introduce to me. In fact, I would have asked Sergio to join in the interview, but Eleonora told him that the interview was focused on women managers and that he should leave us to talk alone!

Despite claiming a family tradition of women managers, Eleonora did not mention her grandmother's involvement in Breva itself, perhaps because she was not aware of it. The firm's Camera di Commercio file was of little help in answering our questions about the founding of the firm, as it did not begin until 1958, six years after the firm opened. It verified Franchini's assertion that by 1958 he and his wife were the sole partners in the firm. But it revealed nothing of the firm's history before that year.

The timing and sequence of events that anthropologists have conventionally called "life-cycle" events and those considered "business" or "firm" events, however, suggest that Franchini's mother-in-law played a significant role in the founding and development of the firm. First, her daughter had managed it during her early married years, when she was only in her twenties — an extremely unusual and otherwise inexplicable choice for the position of manager of a manufacturing firm. Second, the mother-in-law's death was followed rapidly by her grandchildren's entrance into the firm and by its expansion and reorganization. It took a while for us to piece together the links between these events because when we first asked Franchini when his mother-in-law had died, he claimed he could not remember. This was surprising since, as we later discovered, his mother-in-law had lived with him, his wife, and children until she died in the twenty-fifth year of their marriage. Actually, Franchini had moved in to live with his wife in his mother-in-law's home, where they remained to raise their children. Eventually, he told us that his mother-in-law had died a couple of years after his own mother died, which would have made it 1973.

That same year Franchini's son Sergio entered the firm and the firm acquired the land on which it built its modernized plant — all of which would have required considerable capital. It seems likely that the inheritance from the grandmother financed the restructuring and expansion of the firm and, thereby, its survival and transmission to the next generation. It is notable that both Sergio and his sister Eleonora married that year, at relatively young ages: Sergio at age twenty-four and Eleonora at age twenty-one.[18] Franchini himself commented that his son had been too young to be getting married, suggesting that his children had more power in the family than usual and had been able to override his objections. Finally, at the age of twenty-seven and just three years after he entered the firm, Sergio replaced his father as general director of the firm. His father was only fifty-four years old at the time. No other firm in the study was headed by a son so young and with so little experience. The only son under the age of thirty who expected he would become the director soon after he entered the firm was one who was the clear designated successor of his maternal grandfather. His father was merely an interim director of his maternal grandfather's firm.

Adding to this telling pattern of events was the name of the firm. I had initially thought Breva was an obscure Italian word unfamiliar to me or derived from the regional Comasco dialect. I asked Paola to inquire about it during her interview with Eleonora, who explained that it was *un nome di fantasia* — a fanciful name that her family had adapted from the term used for a wind direction on Lake Como. Why, Paola went on to ask, did they not name the firm Franchini? "Because it's an ugly name," Eleonora replied, wrinkling her nose. Others might not have found her father's surname as unattractive as Eleonora did. But it had another obvious shortcoming: It was not, after all, the surname of either the grandparents who were among its original partners, nor of the grandchildren who were to carry it on. Breva was one of the thirteen firms in our sample of thirty-eight that did not bear a family name.

Seven of these had been started by a group of unrelated partners or by founders who did not have sons to carry it on.

Whether Franchini's mother-in-law founded the firm to transmit her capital to her only child and her grandchildren remains an uncertainty. At the least, the pattern of action lends support to the granddaughter's claim of a family tradition of women entrepreneurs. More precisely, the firm's history could be told as the story of three generations of women entrepreneurs, each of whom married a husband with technical expertise crucial to the firm's success: from the grandmother whose husband was a technician in her dyeing firm, to the daughter whose university studies brought her both a chemistry degree and a husband with similar credentials who could be the technical director and then the general director, to the granddaughter whose husband's training at the Setificio qualified him to be the next technical director of the firm. Whether they planned to or not, all three generations of women succeeded in recruiting through marriage what many firm owners told us was the scarcest, and the most crucial, resource in the manufacturing sector of the industry — a good technician.

Giussani

In each of the two previous cases, an alternative to the firm owner's origin narrative could be constructed by combining the state records and the accounts of other family members, as well as the information conveyed by the owners themselves. In the case of the converter firm Giussani, information crucial to an alternative account was volunteered by a longtime employee of the firm.

Pietro Targetti, the current owner-director of the firm, was very cordial and more at ease than most of the owners we interviewed. While many of them appeared to enjoy being interviewed, he seemed to find it downright entertaining, occasionally bursting into laughter at his own responses or lack of knowledge. He described the firm's early history as follows:

> Our firm doesn't have a long history of centuries. . . . It is pretty recent. It was born in 1963, — no wait, around 1960 — under another name, LGS, by my father and another partner. In 1962 it became Giussani because the two partners separated. My father opened Giussani with two other partners — there were three of them in all. During this period, however, my father didn't work here at Giussani. After 1968, Giussani belonged entirely to my father because the other partner died.

Like Franchini, Targetti used the passive verb form to describe the founding of the firm. As in Franchini's account there was also some vagueness, as well as inconsistencies, about the identities of the founders. If, as Targetti reported, his father started the firm with two other partners, and then one died, enabling the father to become the sole owner, what happened to the other partner? Unlike the gaps in Franchini's more carefully crafted account, however, those in Targetti's seemed to stem more from his lack of knowledge about the early years of the firm than from any attempt to conceal crucial facts.

Any puzzling over these gaps on our part was short-circuited by the interventions of an employee of the firm, who entered the room unannounced shortly after the interview began. After seating herself at one of the three large desks in the office and following the conversation for a few minutes, this woman began adding information about the firm and supplying precise dates of birth, marriage, and deaths in the family. Signor Targetti appeared entirely relaxed about her presence and deferred to her report of events and dates because, he explained, she had been with the firm from the beginning.

The information supplied by this woman, who was later revealed to be one of two women managers in the firm, yielded the following account of the firm's early history. From 1945, the year he married, until 1968, Davide Targetti was the director-manager at the weaving firm of Tessitura Montesi, which was owned by his wife's family. His wife's brother's son, Luca Montesi, worked with him from 1963 to 1968. In 1968, this nephew became the director of Tessitura Montesi and Davide moved to Giussani, a converter firm that had been founded around 1960 under the name LGS by Tessitura Montesi and another partner. It had been renamed Giussani in 1962 when the other partner left. Luca Montesi continued to own 35 percent of the shares in Giussani until 1979, when he was bought out and his shares transferred to the eldest daughter of Davide and his wife. She had been working in the firm for six years — one year longer than her brother had been.

The employee's account went far beyond correcting the dates reported by Pietro Targetti. It extended the firm's history back in time before its "birth" in 1960 and located its origins in another family — that of the putative founder's wife. The Montesi family conceived Giussani as a subsidiary firm to market their weaving firm's fabric. When their son was ready to direct the weaving firm, they transferred their son-in-law, who had been the interim director of the weaving firm, to the subsidiary firm. Giussani became the enterprise of their son-in-law and daughter's family only gradually as their children began to work in it. When asked later why Tessitura Montesi had continued to own over a third of the shares in the firm for nearly twenty years, Pietro Targetti explained that it took time to accumulate enough capital to buy out the

TABLE 2.2
Sources of Capital for Starting Firms (N = 38)

Fractions	Both Husband's and Wife's Parents	Husband's Parents Only	Wife's Parents Only	Neither	Total
Upper	3	3	2	1	9
Middle	2	6	4	6	18
Lower[a]	1	3	0	7	11
Total	6	12	6	14	38

[a]Note that in 2 of the 11 lower fraction cases, the founder was a never married male, so there was no possibility of capital coming from a wife's parents.

relatives. It is telling that when they did, the shares were transferred to Lisa Montesi Targetti's daughter, rather than to her son. Just as her parents had endowed her with a share of the patrimony by setting her husband up in a subsidiary firm, she, in turn, endowed her daughter with a portion of the family firm.

The three firms I have just discussed are not alone in having received capital from the parents of founders' wives. Together the data provided by the Camera di Commercio records and by family members reveal that capital investments from wives' parents were common among the firms in my sample, whether or not wives were described as partners. Table 2.2 shows the kin sources of capital for the thirty-eight firms in my sample. In six firms, capital came from both the husband's and wife's parent; in twelve firms it came from the husband's parents only; and in six firms it came from the wife's parents only. Two of the thirty-eight firms were started by single men who never married. Leaving aside these two cases, in which there were no wives to be a conduit for capital, the husband's parents supplied capital in eighteen cases, while wives supplied it in twelve cases. In sum, instances of capital investment by maternal kin were two-thirds of instances of investments by paternal kin — substantial enough to warrant the conclusion that more than the unilineal flow of capital from fathers to sons and grandsons is involved in the reproduction of the Como manufacturing bourgeoisie. Instead, there is a bilateral flow of capital from parents to children of both sexes.[19]

The flow of capital from parents to daughters among the Como bourgeoisie, moreover, goes beyond a strategy of firm and family succession in response to a lack of sons in a particular generation. The latter can be a problem, but not an unsurmountable one, as the histories of several firms I discuss in the next chapter will demonstrate. In three-fourths of the cases (nine out of twelve) in my sample where parents provided capital to a daughter's husband's firm, sons were not lacking. Rather than a substitute for patrifilial succession and inheritance, the financial investments from wives' parents reveal the tip of the iceberg of the complex and, at times, contradictory sentiments and desires that have shaped the flow of capital among the Como bourgeoisie.

Patrifilial Succession and the Children of Daughters

In what is considered a classic kinship study in anthropology, E. E. Evans-Pritchard (1940) called the tracing of agnatic descent through women among the Nuer of the Sudan the "Nuer paradox." The Nuer were, according to Evans-Pritchard, unequivocally committed to determining an individual's political identity—his lineage and clan membership—on the basis of agnatic descent. As the lineage system provided the skeleton for the territorial system of political alliances, agnatic descent constituted the foundational principle of Nuer society. Paradoxically, however, Evans-Pritchard also discovered that a substantial proportion of the Nuer were living in settlements identified with their *mother's* lineage. In addition, there were frequent instances where descendants of the daughters of a lineage had been incorporated into it. These "children of daughters" should rightly have been excluded from membership in their maternal lineage. In her brilliant reanalysis of her former mentor's own data, Kathleen Gough (1971) argued that the Nuer history of expansion and conquest had created a hierarchy of aristocratic lineages, commoner lineages, and slaves, which was conducive to the tracing of agnatic descent through women. The children of daughters of aristocratic lineages who had commoner fathers found it advantageous to align themselves with their mother's lineage—even though they might be treated as marginal members of the group. Marginal membership in an aristocratic lineage was preferred over full membership in a commoner lineage. Over time, moreover, the descendants of these "children of daughters" were sometimes fully incorporated into the lineage as a postmortem process of gender change transformed the "daughters" into "sons" in genealogical memory.[20]

Among the Nuer, daughters could be the conduit for the transmission of agnatic descent. Among the Como bourgeoisie, daughters can be the conduit for the transmission of capital in spite of firm origin narratives that celebrate patrifilial succession. Unlike the Nuer, however, where a form of *gender amnesia* enables a daughter to become a son in genealogical narratives, in Como genealogies and family histories gender is fixed and unchangeable. Consequently, the children of daughters cannot be incorporated into their maternal family firm, except in cases where there are no sons. Instead, through a form of *capital amnesia*, the flow of capital from maternal kin is simply forgotten. In both cases, what is reproduced is not agnatic succession but ideologies of the male generation and reproduction of firms.

Kinship theory in anthropology has come a long way since Evans-Pritchard and subsequent British "descent theorists" claimed to have discovered the jural principles structuring the stateless societies of Africa. In the aftermath of the debate between "descent theorists" and "alliance theorists" as to whether descent or marriage was primary in structuring relations between corporate kin groups—a debate that Schneider (1965) showed was less about kinship than about competing models of culture and social structure—anthropologists abandoned the search for foundational principles and elementary structures of kinship. For a while, some (Ortner 1986) were persuaded of the usefulness of Bourdieu's (1977) distinction between "official kinship" and "practical kinship"—that is, between dominant public commitments and the unofficial strategies of individuals. But this has its own limitations for explaining the heterogeneous kinship practices and discourses in communities.

In his analysis of matrimonial strategies and social reproduction in Kabylia, Bourdieu contrasted official kinship to practical kinship "in terms of the official as opposed to the non-official . . . , the collective as opposed to the individual; the public . . . as opposed to the private . . . ; and collective ritual . . . as opposed to strategy" (1977, 35). Not all the members of the lineage, according to Bourdieu, identify their own interests with the collective interests of the lineage. Women, in particular, do not share men's commitment to the "symbolic and political interests" of lineage unity. Instead, economic calculation, which is repressed in men, "finds more overt expression in women, who are structurally predisposed to be less concerned with the symbolic profits accruing from political unity, and to devote themselves more readily to strictly economic practices" (62). Because they are excluded from "representational kinship," women are "thrown back on to . . . practical uses of kinship, investing more economic realism (in the narrow sense) than the men in the search for a partner for their sons or daughters" (66). Like the poor (213), women are "less sensitive to symbolic profits and freer to pursue material profits" (62).

Bourdieu's analysis is flawed by its characterization of women's interests as oriented toward "strictly economic practices" that are fashioned outside systems of representation—in other words, outside culture. In setting up a dichotomy between "symbolic profits" and "material profits," Bourdieu fashioned a version of Weber's opposition between "economic action" and other actions. Like Parsons's distinction between "instrumental" and "affective" behavior (Parsons and Bales 1955), these dichotomies are grounded in a theory of social action in which some, but not other, interests and strategies are shaped by symbolic representations. "Economic" interests and calculations, above all, are defined as acultural. Among the Kabyle, however, women's attempts to disrupt lineage unity by dividing the patrimony are motivated by "symbolic and political interests" that are no less informed by cultural representations than those of men. Where male descent bonds and male authority are the normative ideal, women's actions may appear to be the "private" strategies of individuals pursuing their own "practical" self-interest. But this is merely because they do not conform to publicly celebrated ideals. Whether pursued by women or by men, whether they are characterized by those studied by anthropologists, or by anthropologists themselves, as "practical" or "meaningful," these "other" goals are no less shaped by culturally meaningful sentiments and commitments.

The flow of capital from parents to daughters among the Como bourgeoisie likewise cannot be reduced to "private strategies" and "practical self-interest" in opposition to the "symbolic profits" of male succession. Rather, it suggests that more complex sentiments and commitments are involved in shaping capital and kinship investments in Como than official firm histories admit. Nor should the "silence" in these official histories about capital investments by the parents of the wives of putative founders lead us to conclude that a patriarchal conspiracy operates among Como capitalists to suppress the role of maternal contributions. This silence, I suggest, is more usefully viewed as a narrative convention that molds complex histories into tidier tales that conform to dominant ideals of male succession. The adage "The grandfather founds the firm, the son develops it, and the grandchildren destroy it" assumes a patrifilial line of male succession in which sons and grandsons carry on their paternal male predecessors' business projects. The flow of capital from maternal kin complicates this story by signaling the existence of other families and other projects. In doing so, it challenges the discursive claims made in official narratives about the unity of family and firm ties.

The Generation of Firms

A convincing origin story effectively suppresses the question of what happened before the beginning. By sweeping us up in the drama of the moment in which the putative founder marshals his personal, familial, and financial resources to create a new enterprise, a compelling firm origin narrative invests our concern in his subsequent history of success. Having been caught up in the narrative movement from the moment of creation to the future of the firm, we do not pause to ask what preceded the beginning. What histories of families, industries, and firms brought the founder to the beginning with the financial and cultural capital he put to use in founding the firm? The official narrative in the Barbieri eightieth anniversary volume, with which I began this chapter, is exceptional in even mentioning a time before the beginning of the firm. Yet the antecedents on which it focuses are not the Barbieri family's history in the textile industry, nor their mobilization of their Milanese bourgeois network to establish them in a newly developing sector of that industry, but the preindustrial, agricultural community of Lomazzo that would be transformed by the arrival of Renzo Barbieri.

Even the most compelling origin narrative, however, cannot obliterate the traces of histories before the beginning. From scientific theories of the origins of the universe to the Christian myth of genesis, all origin stories contain within them the makings of their own critique. If God created the world, then who created God? If the universe was created by the big bang, what created the big bang? Likewise, firm origin narratives contain traces of a past that can lead a critical listener to ask about the time before the beginning. Other individuals, other families, other firms, and other capital leak across the narrative borders of official firm histories, calling into question their definition of the beginning. If the Barbieri firm was the product of a capital diversification strategy of a well-established Milanese industrial family, which became the exclusive property of the putative founder and his descendants only after more than fifty years, then what marks its beginning? All histories flow into earlier histories, making it seemingly impossible to identify a definitive moment of origin. Firm origin narratives meet this challenge by defining the beginning according to the end. What the firm has become—the property and project of Renzo Barbieri's descendants—defines its moment of origin: the date that the founder arrived at its original site.

Whether the firm was founded by an individual or a couple, by a man or a woman, by the son of a bourgeois family or the son of a working-class family, all official firm origin narratives identify a beginning and a founder. The ideal founder is one who, through optimal use of his own personal resources, generates his own firm, his own family, and their own place in society. In doing so, he creates his own destiny. Fathering a family and fathering a business are mutually interdependent projects of creation in this cosmology of kinship and business, family and capitalism.[21] Indeed, as I show in the next chapter, they are integral achievements of male adulthood among the Como bourgeoisie. For the sons of founding fathers who cannot claim to have created their own businesses and, thereby, their own destinies, this cosmology creates both a discursive and material challenge. As we shall see in the next chapter, it is not an unsurmountable one.

❦

CHAPTER THREE

PATRIARCHAL DESIRE

Any social system, to survive, must conform to certain conditions. If we can define adequately one of these universal conditions we have a sociological law. (One of these sociological laws is) the necessity for continuity.

— Radcliffe-Brown, *Structure and Function in Primitive Society*

After [Paolo's] death, there were changes in that Stefano and I took over his duties. But there was no one brought in from the outside. The family character of the firm was assured. The basic idea has been that family members who have a role in the firm are interdependent. Although each has his own specialization, he knows what the others' jobs are so that in the case of one person being lost, as in Paolo's case, any trauma to the firm is avoided. With this kind of collective management, we did not need to make any changes even when Paolo died. Continuity was assured.

— Mario Barbieri, one of the three cousins managing the firm founded by their grandfather

Of Fathers and Sons

The weaving firm of Camisasca Tessitura Serica lay about two hundred yards down a side road in Appiano Gentile, one of the many small townships outside the city of Como. I could see on my map that Appiano was only eight kilometers from the bar at the Agip gas station, where Simona and I usually met before our appointments to interview people at firms or homes on the southwestern outskirts of the city. Over the course of my first year of research in Como, I continually increased the amount of time I allowed for finding firms, especially those located outside the city limits of Como. Most of them, like Camisasca Tessitura Serica, were so unobtrusively tucked away among the homes, maize fields, gardens, gas stations, café-bars, and stores scattered along the unmarked roads on the outskirts of Como that even local residents were sometimes unsure of where they were located. As punctuality is the temporal analog of the precision highly valued by firm owners and frequently cited as a reason for their success, I was concerned about arriving on time lest I be viewed as insufficiently attuned to industrial time — a failing firm owners attribute to all employees of the Italian state, including academics. Simona's obvious amusement at this reversal of the conventional difference between anthropologist and "native" as regards time discipline added to my determination. On this particular crisp December day, however, I was not quite attuned to these "disciplinary" anxieties. As a consequence, we had lingered perhaps too long over cappuccino at the Agip bar where we had been reviewing Phil Ansell's notes from a preliminary interview with the founder and his sons two years earlier. After stopping for directions and retracing our route at least three times, we arrived at the front gate of the factory ten minutes late for our appointment with Signor Borsani.

Signs for two firms were posted on the gate. We rang the one on top, were buzzed in, and motioned to a small front room that appeared to serve as both a reception room and a workspace. A woman who had been marking fabric on a drafting board paused to ring for Signor Borsani, who appeared almost immediately to greet us. Carlo Borsani had the robust, rough-hewn look one might expect of a man in his seventies who had grown up in a farming family; indeed, he fit the image of the worker-turned-owner so perfectly that I began to wonder how I had acquired these stereotypical images. His son Ettore, whom we encountered when Signor Borsani led us to an upstairs office, was considerably taller and had the look of an urbane middle-aged businessman. He left the room without a word, explaining later that he wanted to permit us to interview his father undisturbed. About an hour into the interview, he returned and was introduced by his father. Ettore was very cordial and seemed pleased that his father was getting an opportunity to recount the firm's history. He remembered being interviewed by Phil and asked whether he could see the book that I would write about the industry. I replied that he certainly could, but that it would be written in English. English was fine, he explained, because his daughter was planning to become an English teacher.

Seeing his son reach for his coat, Carlo asked whether he was coming to have lunch "at home." When Ettore responded that he was not, Carlo chided him, "You should tell your mother if you aren't coming to lunch." Simona and I exchanged smiles, both of us amused and touched by this privileged moment of observing a middle-aged man being admonished by his father. Ettore smiled too — more like an indulgent parent than a sheepish son — and went off to his engagement. As we later learned, Ettore, like many firm owners whose family homes are attached to or nearby the factory, was generally expected on weekdays for lunch at his parents' home, which was a stone's throw from the factory (see chapter 5 for a discussion of residence patterns among the Como bourgeoisie). Later, Carlo invited us to lunch, but we declined, intuiting that it would be a bit much to barge in on his wife, who was expecting her son rather than two inquisitive researchers she had never met before. We did, however, accept his invitation to tour the factory with him.

As he led us through the different sections of the factory, Carlo explained when they had been added on and how they fit into the production sequence. Unfortunately, the noise from the automatic looms and other machinery made it very difficult to hear what he was saying. We passed through rooms in which the thread was prepared for weaving, a couple of large weaving rooms jammed full of high-speed automatic looms, and a storeroom. The machinery was impressive — a far cry from the images of an artisanal cottage industry my research among family firms in the Italian silk industry commonly conjures up among friends and colleagues. I was struck by how few workers there were. The *tessitrici* (weavers), all of whom were women, were scattered few and far between the machines, each attending to a large number of them. Toward the end of our tour we bumped into Carlo's older son, Mario, who left quickly after being introduced. Just as we were leaving, we saw the meeting room that Phil had described; on its walls were photographs of Carlo mountain climbing as a young man, along with his diploma from the Setificio (silk manufacturing technical school), and a certificate of recognition from the Unione Industriali for fifty years in the industry. I wondered why our interview had not taken place there instead of in Ettore's office. Whatever the reason, it was apparent that in spite of his enshrinement as the founder of the firm, Signor Borsani no longer had an office of his own.

Camisasca Tessitura Serica exemplifies a firm that has undergone the successful transmission of management and ownership from father to sons. The father, who once firmly controlled the management of the firm, had assumed the status of director emeritus, greeting old clients and granting interviews to researchers. For their part, the sons had fulfilled the second phase of the adage and had "developed the firm." The sons, along with two minor partners, had in 1974 opened a converter firm, which by 1982 was purchasing one-third of their silk for clothing manufacturing. In doing so, they had both diversified their investments and gained a toehold in an expanding sector of the industry that was becoming increasingly crucial for successful marketing.

The transition of management from father to sons in this firm had been hastened by the father's heart attack in 1962, only a few years after his sons had begun working in the firm. During their father's six months of recuperation, Ettore and Guido, who were in their late twenties, had been forced to assume a great deal of the responsibility for the firm's management. On paper they created a *consiglio di amministrazione* (administrative council), with Carlo as president and the two of them as members, but in fact the two sons managed the firm. When Carlo had fully recovered, he changed the legal structure of the firm back so that he was the single administrator. By then, however, the de facto transmission of management was already well underway. Even later, when the firm's legal status was changed again for tax purposes and their father had retired, the sons placed him in the position of *amministratore delegato* (director) so he would not become "psychologically depressed," explained Ettore.

Whereas Camisasca Tessitura Serica in 1988 represented the desired outcome of the transition from father to sons, the firm Seregni illustrated the tensions lurking ominously as the process was about to get underway. Seregni was a large, vertically integrated firm with 250 workers, which encompassed all phases in the manufacturing of a number of synthetic textiles. It had been founded in 1936 and had thrived and grown during the early years of World War II, when it had produced, among other items, fabric for parachutes.

Simona and I arrived at noon (on time!) for our first interview with the current owner-manager, Signor Verderio, who took us up to his office, which was located toward the back of the building. This gave us a better look at the layout of the factory and a greater appreciation of its size. We could see several buildings located on the site, behind the outer automobile gate, through which employees drove and punched their time cards. Signor Verderio had expected only Simona, as she had come alone a month earlier to interview the technical director, Signor Pezzini. He graciously invited us both to lunch and arranged for another place setting in the private dining room, which was just off the cafeteria where the workers ate. We began the first hour of the interview in his office and then continued over lunch, where we were later joined for coffee by Signor Verderio's son and Signor Pezzini, who had been dining with the workers in the cafeteria.

Signor Verderio began the interview by grilling us about the research project. I say "grilling" because he pushed to know more about our goals than the other firm owners had. Like many of them, he had difficulty understanding why an anthropologist would be interested in family firms. Unlike most of them, however, he was not content to assume that whatever our reasons, they were harmless; after his suspicions subsided, however, he gave us permission to interview his son and his mother-in-law. He was openly opinionated, but that made him all the more useful an informant because he bluntly stated his views and prejudices. His son, Lorenzo, was equally unreserved about expressing his views and noticeably more sure of himself than other sons in their twenties. When he and Signor Pezzini first joined us at the table, they were both rather quiet, allowing Signor Verderio to dominate the conversation and interrupt, which he did quite often, when they attempted to speak. After a bit, however, Lorenzo became more assertive and began to argue with his father. Signor Pezzini remained silent for the most part, obviously caught in the difficult position of protecting his relations with both his present boss and his future one.

We learned that Lorenzo was writing his *laurea* thesis in economics, specifically on finance, and expected to finish it by the summer, after which he planned to spend a year in New York, working with one of the firm's two U.S. distributors. When the conversation lagged at one point, I asked who had made the decisions about Lorenzo's education and career. Signor Verderio started to say that he and his wife had never dictated these decisions to their son and had left it entirely up to him, but Lorenzo interrupted. "Do you want to know who made that decision?" he inserted. "My grandfather." He then went on to say that his grandfather had not dictated his career decision, but had brought it about through subtler "psychological means," by continually urging Lorenzo to "help your father." When I asked Lorenzo what aspect of the firm he was most interested in, he initially responded that he was interested in the firm as a whole. He then went on to explain that the part he knew the least about and was least interested in was the technical direction. Lorenzo glanced toward Signor Pezzini when he said this, appearing to reassure Pezzini that he deferred to the latter's expertise in this domain. At this point, Signor Verderio jumped in and began arguing with Lorenzo, declaring that the head of the firm had to know everything about the firm in order to direct it. Verderio recalled that when he had started out he had not known a thing about the industry, but had eventually learned all its aspects. Meanwhile, Pezzini studiously avoided taking either side in this heated discussion.

The lunchtime display of contentiousness and rivalry between father and son at Seregni illustrates tensions common in the early stages of succession. As we shall see shortly, fathers who head firms are frequently described by other family members as *accentratori*—strong-minded autocrats who hold tight control over all decisions in the firm and the family. Lorenzo and his father were unusual only in their open display of the tensions that accompany a son's succession to his father's position as head of the firm. Other successor sons were much less willing to openly challenge their fathers. Lorenzo's assertiveness at such an early age and stage of succession, I surmised, stemmed from his father's more tenuous status as a son-in-law successor. The grandfather of whom Lorenzo had spoken, who had urged him to help his father, was his *maternal* grandfather. In other words, Lorenzo's succession to the headship of the firm rested on his status as grandson to a founder who had only daughters. Signor Verderio, who had been a teacher of literature, had stepped in to manage his wife's father's firm — an arrangement that he, like his son, knew was merely a way of filling in until the founder's grandson stepped into his rightful place as heir and successor. If Lorenzo felt less compelled to show his father the deference displayed by other sons, it was likely because he was well aware that he and his mother owned three times as many shares in the firm as his father did.

Discourses of Reproduction: Unity and Stability

The survival of a family firm beyond the death of its owner-manager depends on the successful transmission of capital and transition of management. In an industry where social networks are dense and word of family conflict gets around quickly, a relatively smooth process is crucial for a firm's reputation. Intergenerational succession is thus both a challenging social process and a challenging discursive process of managing the appearance of firm stability and family unity. While origin narratives bear the burden of establishing firms and families with clear beginnings, succession narratives bear the burden of demonstrating that firms have a clear future. To overcome doubts arising during the transition of management from father to son or sons, family members take great pains to emphasize the harmony and unity of the family.

When, for example, I asked Signora Molteni, a widow whose sons had taken over the management of her deceased husband's firm, whether having five sons had a significant impact on relations within the family, she replied,

> Yes. We are very united and we are very envied and resented by other people. There's another family in Como that wanted to be like us, but they didn't succeed because the children went their own ways.

Signora Molteni went on to discuss how fortunate she and her husband had been in having good relations with their sons' wives — clearly an important factor in keeping the family together. In response to my question as to how she and her husband had been able to maintain good relations with their sons and daughters-in-law, she explained that their sons admired her husband and held him in good esteem. They were, she claimed, devoted disciples of her husband.

In speaking of his married sister, his widowed mother, and himself — who together managed the family's photoengraving firm — Angelo Cadirola offered, "We are three families but we are united." The three families to which he referred were his immediate family (wife and children), his sister's immediate family (her husband and children), and his mother. His sister, Annalisa, echoed these sentiments in explaining why they had been able to kept the firm together:

> Certainly, problems emerge when there are children who eat up the capital of the others, but when a family is united like ours and when they get along, there is no difficulty. We are very fortunate.

In the case of the Barbieri firm, now managed by the third generation, the strong bond among the cousins who directed the firm was likened to the bond between siblings. When I asked the wife of one of these cousins if there was a difference between cousins managing a firm and brothers managing a firm, she responded:

> In this case, the three cousins are like brothers since [the father of the first two] died when he was very young, so the three cousins were raised together and have always been very close.

Mario explained that shortly after Paolo, the eldest of these three cousins, died unexpectedly, the continuity of the firm was assured by the way in which they handled its management.

> After [Paolo's] death, there were changes in that Stefano and I took over his duties. But there was no one brought in from the outside. The family character of the firm was assured. The basic idea has been that family members who have a role in the firm are interdependent. Although each has own specialization, he knows what the others' jobs are so that in the case of one person being lost, as in Paolo's case, any trauma to the firm is avoided. With this kind of collective management, we did not need to make any changes even when Paolo died. Continuity was assured.

As we shall see in chapter 5, the ability of brothers and other family members filling management roles to substitute for one another is touted as a sign of both the collective character of firm management and family unity.

The loyalty of sons to the father, their admiration of him, the close emotional bond between cousins, and the unity of collective management are discursively marshaled to attest to the continuity and stability of the firm. Firm owners and their family members are eager to present a public face of unity that is rooted in sentiments of loyalty. Contractual agreements — both informal and legally binding — also bolster the stability of firms. But people are well aware that these cannot in themselves guarantee continuity. What, for them, is even more crucial is the strength and character of the emotional bonds within the family.

Family unity does not preclude the highly valued "independence" of individuals, especially men, that I discuss later in this chapter. Firm owners do not view these as incompatible or contradictory commitments. As one firm owner put it,

> First my children [a son and a daughter] worked in the firm; then they worked on their own [managing different divisions of the firm]. But that does not mean they were separated because we are always together, but independent. Each of them has to work with their own head, with their own problems, with their own sales. It is right that when your children reach a certain age, even if they are still young, that they are independent; they have to be responsible.

The complementarity of independence, which is viewed as a necessary ingredient of entrepreneurial creativity and responsibility, and family unity, which is viewed as crucial to family and firm continuity, is captured in this statement. Although people are well aware that independence and family unity can come into conflict, ideally the two are in balance, with each enabling the other.

In this chapter, as well as throughout the book, I am concerned with the ways in which kinship sentiments operate both as forces for the continuity of family firms and forces for their demise. In focusing on sentiments, I go against the grain of kinship theory in anthropology, which has conventionally characterized emotion and affect as too unstable to be a productive focus for understanding the structure and dynamics of kinship groups. Indeed, for over fifty years, kinship theory in anthropology has treated law as the basis of the reproduction of social groups and structural continuity and emotions as a destabilizing force.

Kinship Theory and Corporate Continuity

The continuity of the social order was a primary concern of the kinship theorists who studied *acephalous*, or "stateless," societies lacking formal jural institutions. Radcliffe-Brown and other British structural-functional theorists were unequivocal in their view that continuity was a functional prerequisite of all societies: "We must appeal to another sociological law, the necessity not merely for stability, definiteness and consistency in the social structure, but also for continuity. To provide continuity of social structure is essentially a function of corporations" (Radcliffe-Brown 1952, 45–46). Continuity meant more than the stability of the social relations among individuals. In order to transcend the destabilizing effects of human mortality, social systems required the transgenerational continuity of relations between aggregates of individuals organized into social groups. The enduring relations between these social groups over time constituted social structure. In the case of the classic descent-based corporate group, the lineage, this entailed "perpetual structural existence in a stable and homogeneous society," which preserves the "existing scheme of social relations as far as possible" (Fortes [1963] 1970, 79–80).

The extent to which kinship groups such as lineages play a part in the social, political, or religious life of the tribe depends, according to Radcliffe-Brown, on the degree to which they are corporate groups.

> A group may be spoken as "corporate" when it possesses any one of a number of characters: a. if its members, or its adult members, or a considerable proportion of them, come together occasionally to carry out some collective action — for example, the performance of rites; if it has a chief or council who are regarded as acting as the representatives of the group as a whole; if it possesses or controls property which is collective, as when a clan or lineage is a land-owning group. (1950, 41)

Continuity depends, moreover, on shared understandings about rights and duties between persons.

> The sociological laws, i.e., the necessary conditions of existence of a society, that underlie the customs of unilineal succession are: 1. the need for a formulation of rights over persons and things sufficiently precise in their general recognition as to avoid as far as possible unresolved conflicts. 2. the need for continuity of the social structure as a system of relations between persons, such relations being defined in terms of rights and duties. (47)

In attempting to illuminate the social order of societies that they perceived to be most lacking in it, British social anthropologists fashioned a universalistic, jural model of society that granted structural primacy to those normative "principles" and "rules" which most closely resembled the state-enforced laws of Western European nations.

Fortes, who was from the next generation of British descent theorists, argued that true corporate descent groups can exist only in more or less homogeneous societies — in particular those of central Africa. Yet his invocation of Sir Henry Maine's (1931) usage of "corporation" in the analysis of testamentary succession and Weber's analysis of the "corporate group" suggests that Africa served for Fortes as a "simple society" upon which theories of European kinship and law could be mapped.

The most important feature of unilineal descent groups in Africa . . . is their corporate organization. When we speak of these groups as corporate units we do so in the sense given to the term 'corporation' long ago by Maine [1861] in his classical analysis of testamentary succession in early law. . . . We are reminded also of Max Weber's sociological analysis of the corporate group as a general type of social formation . . . , for in many important particulars these African descent groups conform to Weber's definition. ([1963] 1970, 77–78)

Where the lineage concept is highly developed, the lineage is thought to exist as a perpetual corporation as long as any of its members survive. This means, of course, not merely perpetual physical existence ensured by the replacement of departed members. It means perpetual structural existence, in a stable and homogeneous society; that is, the perpetual exercise of defined rights, duties, office and social tasks vested in the lineage as a corporate unit. (79–80)

Fortes's characterization of the central African lineage in these terms seems a clear example of the projection of a core legal structure of European capitalist society — the corporate firm — on to other societies. The idea that the structural continuity of the social groups constituting the social structure is rooted in a system of rights and duties that is the functional equivalent of the formal laws of state society, rather than in the more diffuse moral commitments and emotional attachments between people, had been a fundamental assumption of anthropological kinship theory for most of the twentieth century. This, in turn, assumes that the jural principles defining the "rights and duties" of kinship relations can be readily distinguished from the diffuse moral commitments and emotional attachments between kin. The kinship theorists who proposed this analytical distinction recognized, of course, that sentiments themselves are governed, or at least constrained, by "rules" and are normatively prescribed. Indeed, they admitted that kinship relations were structured not only by precise jural rules of rights and duties but by more amorphous norms such as "prescriptive altruism" (Fortes 1969). Normative sentiments could, however, be the basis of structural continuity. The lack of confidence British descent theorists held in emotions as a force for a stability and continuity — indeed, their distrust of sentiment — was exacerbated by their disciplinary battle against the "psychologizing" of Bronislaw Malinowski, who was Radcliffe-Brown's strongest rival for theoretical hegemony in British social anthropology. As Radcliffe-Brown's brand of functionalism gained ascendance in post–World War II British social anthropology, Malinowski's brand of functionalism was increasingly discredited. The critique of Malinowskian functionalism focused in good part on his ideas about the universal physiological and psychological needs of individuals, which Malinowski viewed as the fundamental requirements of all human societies. In elevating the focus of anthropological theory from the individual to society — itself viewed as a functioning organic system — Radcliffe-Brown and his followers eschewed Malinowski's concern with the organic needs of individuals. Any interest social anthropology might have had in the survival and reproduction of the human organism was displaced on to society through an organic metaphor. The continuity of the *social body* — construed as social structure — by means of its stable equilibrium, rather than the continuity of human organisms, became the proper object of theory in social anthropology.

The survival of the social structure, moreover, was viewed by Radcliffe-Brown and his successors as dependent on structures of law rather than structures of sentiment. Malinowski's fatal error was, for them, the attention he had paid to the latter rather than the former.

> In sum, what is inadequately stressed by Malinowski is that kinship relations have to be seen as a system, within the framework of the total social structure. Their *fundamental juridical nature* then emerges, as Rivers appreciated. (Fortes 1960, 164, my emphasis)

> Questions of right and duty are, however, secondary to emotion and sentiment in Malinowski's analysis of these [Trobriand] data. (164)

Seen from the perspective of Radcliffe-Brown's model of society, the attention that Malinowski paid to the power of sentiment — for example, a father's affection for his son — rather than to structure-affirming law, constituted a prima facia case of psychological reductionism.

> Malinowski had no sense for social organization . . . Kinship is to him primarily a tissue of culturally conditioned emotional attitudes. (Fortes [1963] 1970, 71)

> As I have said, a psychological framework was essential to Malinowski's functionalism. Everything he wrote was riddled with psychological explanation partly because his functionalism meant seeing custom as motive, partly because its instrumental and utilitarian form led back to physiological needs, and the simplest way in which these can be visualized as emerging in action is as the driving forces behind instincts, sentiments and emotions. (Fortes 1957, 170)

Rooted as it was in his theory of the universal physiological and psychological needs of individuals, Malinowski's focus on the psychological forces behind social institutions warranted this critique. In purging "psychology" from the study of kinship, however, Malinowski's critics threw emotion and sentiment out with it. Having concluded that "kinship behavior and not kinship sentiment is the study of the anthropologist" (Firth 1960, 576), they relegated emotion and sentiment to the analytic province of psychology. They declined the challenge of understanding how emotion and sentiment shape kinship and other social relations. Ironically, by failing to explicate the cultural specificity of emotions and sentiments, they lumped them with instincts, thus universalizing them, naturalizing them, and disqualifying them from cultural analysis.

In spite of their inability to set forth clear criteria for differentiating "rights and duties" from normatively prescribed sentiments, kinship theorists had an abiding faith in the ability of the former to ensure the continuity of the social order and a lack of faith in the latter. This confidence appears to have stemmed from their perception that these informal rights and duties were, in both content and function, the closest parallel they could find in stateless societies to the jural institutions of their own society — in whose ability to ensure continuity they appear to have had considerable faith.

Subsequent contributions to kinship theory have reinforced this distrust of emotion and sentiment. In spite of his disagreement with British descent theorists as to whether descent or alliance lay at the core of kinship, Lévi-Strauss concurred with his British colleagues' distinction between "moral norms" (the bonds in the restricted family, such as the value on conjugal faithfulness and parental attachment) and the legal rules governing broader kinship structures (Lévi-Strauss 1969). "Affect" was, for Lévi-Strauss, an epiphenomenon of social structure rather than a constitutive force. Laws and rules, in contrast, were the basis of the elementary structures of kinship and society.

Rule-based models of kinship and social structure have since been eclipsed in anthropology by interactionist (Barth 1966), symbolic (Schneider 1964, 1968, 1972), and practice-oriented approaches (Bourdieu 1977). Feminist kinship theory (Reiter 1975; Strathern 1980, 1988, 1992; Yanagisako 1979; Yanagisako and Collier 1987; Wolf 1972) has challenged the assumption that members of kinship groups share the same commitments and goals by demonstrating that they are not bound by the same "rules." Yet despite these effective challenges to rule-based models of kinship, current kinship studies continue to cast law as a more powerful social force than sentiment.

Legal Surrogates and the Return of the Jural

The privileging of law over sentiment has not been limited to the study of kinship in stateless societies. It has also shaped anthropologists' analysis of kinship in industrial-capitalist society. Marcus (1992), for one, has proposed a historic model of American family-business formations which emphasizes how legal rules and instruments become an integral dimension of family relationships themselves, even as they are being used to adapt family-owned concentrations of capital to the socio-economic environment. His model is based on formations founded by entrepreneurs in commerce and industry during the later-nineteenth-century era of economic expansion in the United States, particularly those on which he has conducted research in Galveston, Texas. In charting the role of law in these kinship formations, Marcus writes:

> It is important to know at the outset that the role of law in these formations has in no way replaced or negated the flexible normative content of middle-class kinship which characterizes American family life. Rather, law overlays, and to a degree complicates kin relations by giving a more formal organization to the extended family than that of most middle-class families. As will be seen from the Galveston case, formations are set on a structured course by their internal administration of patrimonial capital and businesses, but final outcomes of this process still depend very much upon the long-term emotional atmosphere of a dynastic family. Popular interest in formations has focused on their "human drama" aspect to the exclusion of their legal dimension. I argue that without consideration of this dimension, their distinctive nature as groups in modern societies cannot be fully understood. (1992, 16)

While Marcus's model is fashioned from research on family formations in the United States that have endured from the late-nineteenth century to the present as both extended family and business organizations, he has proposed that

> the basic model [of this chapter] also applies with some adjustments to contemporaneous formations in European societies (particularly Great Britain and Ireland), but the pursuit of this suggestion is beyond my scope here. In the broadest terms, what I am describing is a major structural manifestation of the interrelationships between law, wealth-holding, and elite family organization over the past century in Western capitalist societies. (29)

In this chapter I suggest ways in which Marcus's model must be adjusted to fit the processes of succession in industrial-capitalist families in northern Italy. I argue that we need to go beyond the idea that law "overlays" and "complicates" kin relations. Law is undoubtedly a crucial force in the constitution of kin relations, and the "emotional atmosphere" of families is an aspect of the "structured course" on which they are set by legal arrangements. At the same time, however, my analysis of processes of succession differs from Marcus's twist on Bohannan's view that law is "doubly institutionalized custom" (1967, 47). Marcus suggests that the double institutionalization of law might be viewed as working in the opposite direction. In order to control its patrimonial capital through the instruments and expertise of the legal system, a family of wealth reinstitutionalizes its internal relations in a form that permits it to operate in a rationalized social order. (1992, 17)

For Marcus, families of wealth make law their custom, incorporating "legal rules" as a "routine part of the group's structure, concerns, and practices" (18). As I will show, legal rules do indeed influence the routine structure, concerns, and practices of Italian industrial-capitalist families. But these families do not make law their custom. Rather, law is only one of the complex and sometimes contradictory forces of kinship that shape the reformulation and renegotiation of the sentiments, interests, and strategies of family members.

The formula that law "doubles kinship" overlooks the contested character of what Marcus calls the "normative content" of kinship. Among industrial-capitalist families in northern Italy and, I suspect, among most industrial-capitalist families, which norms should be followed, which kinship sentiments should have priority, how precisely legal rules should be obeyed, and what is considered fair and just, as well as practical and efficient, are constantly being rethought and renegotiated. These processes in families are mirrored at the national level in legislative struggles over "family law" — including laws of property and inheritance. Law "doubles" kinship to the extent that struggles over it replicate the tensions and conflicts that occur in families. But political battles at the national level do not necessarily result in laws that duplicate the range and complexity of norms and sentiments in families.

Marcus contrasts his focus on the legal and fiduciary arrangements that shape dynastic families in Western industrial-capitalist societies with the conventional focus of anthropological studies of lineages, descent groups, and "the community of kin focused on reverence for ancestors in small-scale, tribal societies" (1992, 4). Anthropological common sense, he writes, has been to focus on the anthropological staples of "the politics of kinship, family rituals, and reverence toward ancestors," whose role he views as less important in the reproduction of dynastic motivation and ideology after a certain point in the history of a dynastic family.

I agree with Marcus that the politics of kinship, family rituals, and reverence for ancestors have been anthropological staples. As my discussion of British kinship theory has demonstrated, however, at the core of their analysis of lineage-based tribal societies was precisely the focus Marcus chose: law and corporate continuity. Sentiment, emotion, and the symbolic realm of ritual were deemed secondary to the "jural principles" viewed as crucial to the continuity of the social order. Indeed, the legal institutions that Marcus contends are crucial in shaping dynastic families' "distinctive nature as groups in modern societies" (1992, 16) are precisely those from which descent theorists derived their model of the function of jural principles in the structure of tribal society. Rather than rethinking anthropological categories, Marcus's model of the role of law repatriates a core analytic category of descent theory: the politico-jural domain. We might say that his model "doubly institutionalizes" the customs of anthropological kinship studies by granting primacy to the role of law in ensuring and structuring the continuity of kinship corporations.

After the poststructuralist critique of anthropological theory, it is easy to see how the idea that law and its functional equivalent in stateless societies ensure the continuity and stability of the social order became a sine qua non of descent theory. What is less obvious is that the ideal-type on which this model of corporate continuity appears to have been based is the legally incorporated capitalist firm. As a structure of contractual relations backed up by the coercive power of the state, the corporate firm constituted the ideal-type for a theory of continuity in which contractual agreements enable social groups to transcend the ephemerality of its members' lives. In capitalist society, the reification of these contractual agreements endows a configuration of contingent social relations with a fictive stability. In "descent-based" societies, the reification of norms as "jural principles" does the same. Entailed in this reification is a faith in the jural; indeed, a kind of jural transcendentalism that mistakes a legal fiction for a social guarantee pervades much of early kinship theory.

In this chapter, I lay the groundwork for my attempt to show that this faith in the jural is unwarranted when one examines the very institutions that provided the models for kinship theories of corporate continuity. As I will show in this chapter and in chapter 5, among industrial-capitalist family firms in northern Italy, law constitutes neither the basis of the continuity of corporate kin groups nor a force for their reproduction. Although law provides legal instruments that can help bourgeois families adjust to changing political-legal contexts, in the balance, Italian law works more to undermine family corporate continuity.

Legal incorporation of the firm makes it possible for, among other things, a firm to continue as a legal entity beyond the death of its individual owners. It makes it possible for collectivities of individuals to act as if they are the same entity over time despite the change in their membership. But it cannot guarantee their continued existence or their fulfillment of contractual relations. Firms face daunting challenges to continuity that cannot be ensured by legal agreements. These include not only productive challenges, but ideological and emotional challenges. As structures of sentiment and production as well as legal entities, family firms are undermined by kinship sentiments as well as enabled by them.

In taking for granted the functional utility of kinship structures such as lineages, kinship theorists did not adequately study them as complex structures of sentiment and power. They did not ask why (and which) members of lineages care about the continuity of these social collectivities or how their goals are shaped by their location in these collectivities. Instead they projected onto society *writ large* the desires and goals of specifically situated actors. Evans-Pritchard (1940), for example, never asked why Nuer senior men were motivated to reproduce lineages. Having identified the Nuer lineage as the basis of Nuer social structure, he did not think it necessary to ask Nuer men themselves why they wanted lineages to continue. Had he done so, he might have appreciated the role of sentiment in what he called Nuer "social structure."

Just as Marxist theory assumes that all capitalists are motivated to accumulate capital and expand the capitalist firm, so descent theory assumes that all men, or at least all fathers, want to reproduce their lineages, families, or other corporate kinship groups. Both engage in a teleological functionalism of confusing effect with cause. "Capitalists" and "fathers" are treated as universal agents rather than as social actors who have been constituted by specific historical and cultural forces. This blinds us to the processes through which sentiments and desires are constituted along with the actors that are motivated by them. Whether the desire is for lineage continuity or firm continuity, continuity is treated as a goal motivated by a system rather than the emotionally constituted desire of specific actors.

In the following discussion, I show how a kinship sentiment — the patriarchal desire to transmit the firm to sons — operates as a force of production and reproduction in family firms (see chapter 1 for a discussion of my conception of sentiments as forces of production). Rather than assume why capitalists strive to continue their firms in the next generation, I ask what sentiments motivate particular members of capitalist families to work for particular kinds of continuities. In doing so, I pay heed to a finding of which kinship theorists have long been well aware: that the continuity of some kinship relations and groups entails the demise of others.

Patriarchal Desire

In the official origins narratives of firms discussed in chapter 2, the ideal founder is a man who has the generative power to create his own firm, his own family, and his own destiny. Fathering a family and fathering a business are interdependent projects of creation in the cosmology of kinship and business, family and capitalism, which are conveyed in firm origin stories. To head a family is to provide for it, including to provide the productive means of the independence of the family and the means to reproduce that independence in the next generation. All men who head family firms and who have sons want to be succeeded by them. Indeed, many men say that the only reason they have worked so hard to build a successful firm is so that they can hand it on to their son or sons.

Fathers' commitments to passing their firms on to their sons has to be understood in relation to a dense system of meanings about the male self, its actualization through men's projects, its relation to the projects of other men, and its perpetuation through the lives of sons. *Independence* is a key symbol in this ideology of masculinity, and a close examination of its multiple meanings reveals a complex and contradictory set of desires among men. Independence is something fathers say they want both for themselves and for their sons. In the realm of work, being independent means being your own boss, being an employer rather than an employee (which, in Italian, is to be literally a *dipendente*). As many heads of firm put it, the problem with being an employee is not only that you cannot advance after a certain point, but that you never achieve the satisfaction of being independent. In the realm of the family, being independent means being the head of your own family (*il capo della famiglia*). In bestowing upon their sons the means of production, fathers give them the means of their economic independence. As one successor son reported, "My father always said to us [his sons]: 'I will not leave you money, but the means to make a living.'"

Given men's desires to be independent from the authority of other men and their disdain for any man who is not, it is not surprising that many men also say they do not trust anyone but their own sons to take over the firm. It is not only hired managers who cannot be trusted to put the firm before other interests, but even other kin. This includes brothers' sons and sons-in-law. The problem with these junior male relatives is not their lack of a biogenetic connection, but their lack of a moral commitment. Only a son who has been raised from childhood by his father is viewed as having a sufficiently deep emotional attachment to his father and his father's lifelong project—the firm—to throw all his energy and talent into it. One father explained that it is precisely to ensure the continuity of the firm that it is necessary to keep sons-in-law from entering the firm:

> Sons follow their father's training, but sons-in-law don't. Sons-in-law could have other ideas, and they could bring the wrong innovations

for the firm. Sons care about the family's name. If you put the same soup in the same bowl, you can be sure that the soup will continue to be good. This has to do with assuring continuity of idea and education — something which can only be done by sons.

Fathers without sons and men without children say they are inclined to sell their firms when they retire, and many are critical of the prevalent practice of filial succession in the industry, claiming that it often leads to disaster. Giorgio Galbiati, one of three sons who had successfully expanded their father's weaving firm, but who had married late and had no children, claimed:

> Today family firms don't work if there isn't someone who can lead them. You need someone who can do this, whether he's a family member or not. Perhaps in the past it was different, but now, unfortunately, there is no choice. Profit margins are much more reduced today, so the firm will survive only if it is competitive, if it is up-to-date, if it functions well. Once upon a time, things were slower and changes were slower and so you could get away with making mistakes. Today the possibility of getting away with mistakes is much smaller.

When he was asked how he felt about his brothers' sons taking over the management of the firm, he responded:

> The only condition is the capacity of the person — whether he's a son or not. My brother's son started working in the firm unexpectedly because he had some time while he was waiting to do his military service. I would have preferred that he come in some other way; I would have preferred that he had some experience in another firm first. It's better to have a nonfamily partner who earns profits for the firm than a family member who doesn't. If a family member doesn't have the ability to direct the firm, he can just be the owner and leave the management to someone else. If he is capable, good — he should enter the firm, but if he doesn't, forget it!

Similar sentiments were voiced by Gianni Todeschini, who was unmarried with no children:

> I don't have any children, but I have two nephews who are thinking of working in the firm. But if they aren't up to it, they shouldn't come into the firm because I don't want to make the same mistake that a lot of firm owners have of bringing in a son who doesn't have the capability and who doesn't have a feel for the work.

Whether these men would have been ardent supporters of filial succession had they had sons, their criticisms of filial succession are interpreted as envious resentment by firm owners who do. For the latter, transmitting the firm to sons is the whole point of family business.

The meaning of "independence" has become even more complicated as a result of social transformations in Italian society over the past three decades. For men who came of age before the 1960s and the "economic miracle" that transformed Italy from an agrarian society into an industrial one, independence drew its meaning from an agrarian model of society in which the struggle of families to free themselves from the paternalism of landowners made sense of the paternalism in their families. More recently, a concept of personal independence more familiar to North Americans has encroached upon the old one, peppering the speech of entrepreneurs and their children with English phrases such as "self-made man." The bourgeois liberal celebration of the freedom of individuals from even parental authority has brought new power to the contradiction already lurking in the older commitment to the emancipation and actualization of the self.[1]

By the 1980s, moreover, not only sons desired the freedom to make choices about their educations, careers, marriage partners, and lifestyles, but many daughters did as well. The few daughters who had begun to take management positions in their father's firm were just as articulate spokespersons for this idea of personal autonomy as were their brothers. They spoke of the importance of learning how to use your own head and make your own decisions, even if you are working in your father's firm. They were avid supporters of personal initiative in their own children, and they viewed Italian parent-child relations as having improved as parents had become less authoritarian, allowing their children to follow their own predispositions and encouraging them to pursue their own interests. As we shall see in chapter 5, changing gender ideas and practices in Italy, modifications in family law, and demographic shifts were all involved in shaping these emerging attitudes among daughters.

Personal independence is not easy to attain, however, when one is the successor to a father who not only controls the means of one's financial independence but the managerial and technical knowledge one needs to take over those means. Fathers also control the social capital — the relations of trust and good faith with clients, other firms in the industry, and financial institutions — that are crucial to a successor's ability to continue the firm. Not surprisingly, fathers who head firms were described as *accentratori* who made all the decisions in the firm and the family. A successor son told me that "in general, the decisions in my family were all made by my father. My mother was subordinate to him. She was freed only after he died; my father was very authoritarian." When I asked the daughter of a firm owner how decisions were made in her family, she replied, "By my father naturally. He was a patriarch; he made all the decisions."

The characterization of many heads of firms as authoritarian fathers reveals a key contradiction in the patriarchal desire to transmit the means of independence to sons and thereby save them from the disdained position of coming under the authority of another man: What seems attainable in an ideological model of male parity is not when it comes to relationships on the ground — or, rather, in families. Instead, as it turns out, one man's independence entails another man's dependence; to retain his position as head of a family, a man must have a family to head. Once his children grow up, his daughters are lost to him through marriage, for married women are said to come under the authority of their husbands, not their fathers. Fathers are also in danger of losing their authority over their sons, not through marriage but through the latter's employment. A son who works for someone else not only comes under another man's authority, but he also has the financial means to be independent of his father. In contrast, a father whose sons take over his firm has given them the resources to remain independent of employers at the same time that he has strengthened his continuing authority over them. Such a father has the good fortune of having both ensured his authority over an enduring family that includes his sons and, at the same time, provided for their financial and career independence. Such a father, it could be said, has mediated the contradiction embodied in a male ideal of independence that requires the dependence of other men.

While the paternal gift of succession may have its dark side of patriarchal control, a father's desire to be succeeded by his sons cannot be reduced to an instrumental strategy for holding on to power or, worse, an expression of a universal will to power. Neither a crude economic determinism that reduces a bourgeois father's actions to the pursuit of profit or a crude political determinism that reduces his actions to the pursuit of power can adequately encompass the complex sentiments that incite patriarchal desires for succession. One of the limitations of some discussions of power in anthropology and related fields has been the failure to appreciate adequately the altruistic sentiments entailed in both the constitution and deployment of power. Fathers do not necessarily seek to control sons and keep them in a position of dependence for as long as possible. To the contrary, they seek to endow sons with the means of independence. If this necessitates a period of patriarchal control, it is only temporary. At the same time, fathers desire the continuing respect and attention of sons. Patriarchal desires of succession are constituted by a complex array of altruistic and self-serving sentiments of love, attention, respect, and esteem.

The Conundrum of the Second-Generation Self-Made Man

Successor sons would appear, at first glance, to be automatically disqualified from inclusion in the category of self-made men. Having inherited the family business from their fathers, they cannot claim to have generated their own firms and, thereby, their own destinies. In locating themselves in the drama of the generational succession of the firm, these men face the formidable discursive challenge of transforming themselves from sons created by the father to generative fathers who create firms and families. On the one hand, they recognize and laud the advantage of having "grown up in the business." Many of them talked about learning much of what they knew at their father's side, explaining that by the time they began working in the firm full-time they had considerable knowledge of the production process, technology, management, marketing, and finance. They also claimed a deep familiarity with the attitudes and values of capitalist entrepreneurship—a kind of second nature that comes only from early childhood acquisition. On the other hand, they are aware that the infusion of cultural capital from early childhood is not without its disadvantages. Given the importance placed on innovation and entrepreneurial agility in a constantly changing market, those who come by their knowledge through socialization in their father's firm bear the burden of demonstrating that they have not been constrained by this process. Having been stamped by their father's mold, they must demonstrate that they have the energy, drive, and talent to break out of it—to lead the firm successfully into another generation of industrial competition. In short, they must prove that they are second-generation self-made men.

The conundrum of how the son of a self-made man can himself be a self-made man would seem to be unsolvable. But the solution, at least according to the second- and third-generation self-made men I interviewed, is actually quite simple: Because founding fathers reportedly require their sons to learn everything from the most menial, unskilled tasks to the technical and managerial, their sons are required to work their way up the occupational ladder in the firm. Once having provided their sons with this practical education, the founding fathers leave them free to manage the firm. Given the rapidly changing nature of the industry and the market, these sons inevitably find themselves on terrain unfamiliar to their fathers. They must make their own decisions and, thereby, make themselves.

Franco Scotti, who succeeded his father in the management of the family's tinting firm, described how he was initially sent out for a two-year apprenticeship in another firm, then returned to work in all the departments of his father's firm. He began in the provisioning department for six years, then went into client relations, and finally into acquisitions. By the time he took over the direction of the firm, he said, he "had everything in hand." His son, Andrea, who had just started working in the firm, would have to do the same thing.

> I explained to him, Andrea, look you have to work your way *dalla gavetta* [from washing the mess tins]. If you want to be in charge, you have to know everything, otherwise you will be left in the dark. He has to know everything like I do of what goes on in the printing, the finishing, the dyeing processes. And, I'll tell you something, everyone from the department head to the workers will do what you say without arguing because they know it's the right thing.

Other successor sons used the same expression as Franco Scotti, describing working their way up the ladder in their father's firms as having begun *dalla gavetta* — literally, by washing the mess tins. In Antonio Galbusera's case, this initial stage took place in his father's brother's firm.

> I began working in my uncle's firm as an employee. I began really "dalla gavetta," as we say — that is, from the lowest manual work there is. I mopped the floors, cleaned the looms. At the same time, I attended night classes at the Setificio to become a textile technician.

Even Signor Verderio, whose son Lorenzo was getting a degree in economics and finance from a prestigious private university and who already owned more shares in the firm than his father, insisted that his son would have to begin *dalla gavetta*.

Whereas having worked one's way up from the bottom of the firm's occupational hierarchy is offered as proof of a successor's qualifications to head the firm, the claim that he was given the freedom to make his own decisions about his education and career is offered as evidence of his entrepreneurial independence. Considerable inconsistency emerges from parents' and children's discussions of the latter's education and career decisions. This is particularly the case with accounts about how sons came to have particular educational and career paths. On the one hand, sons claim they were left free to make their own choices; on the other, that their *accentratori* fathers decided everything. Whatever the actual processes by which these decisions were made, what people have to say about them reveals the tensions between the bourgeois values of "independence" and "family unity" that suffuse much of the discourse about family relations.

The very fact that successors had to deal with autocratic fathers, however, can be added to their credentials. Having had to wrest control of the firm from such a powerful father can itself be treated as evidence that a son was up to such a challenge. A successor son notes,

My father never gave in; we argued over everything. With my father it was a battle for fifteen years. He was an autocrat who wanted to control everything and he didn't leave anything to me. . . . I had more battles with my father that with anyone else. The only thing we had in common perhaps is that neither of us had an easy life. I had to start from the bottom; I was not treated like my father's heir; I had to earn the position. At the beginning of our careers we both had difficult times.

It seems significant that sons were willing to discuss these struggles only after they were over, whereas daughters were willing to talk about conflicts in which they were currently engaged. I will have more to say about this in chapter 5 when I discuss the experience of daughters who have entered the firm with hopes of succeeding their fathers.

The burden of being a second-generation self-made man is greater for the sons of fathers who moved into the Como industrial bourgeoisie from technical, petty bourgeois, or working-class backgrounds than it is for the sons of fathers who themselves inherited firms. The latter can draw on a family history of entrepreneurship and wealth to legitimate their headship of firms. The former must reconcile following in their father's footsteps with the heroic narrative of their father's self-made success. This leaves them with the daunting task of proving they have themselves demonstrated equal entrepreneurial vigor and talent in re-creating the firm and, thereby, their own success. As we have seen, second-generation self-made sons are not without discursive options for recounting their own ascendance to the headship of firms. Still, no better proof of their worthiness exists than their success in expanding the firm and moving it up the industry hierarchy. The adage "The father founds the firm, the sons develop it . . ." leaves little doubt as to what sons must do to prove their worthiness as successors.

How likely is it that successor sons will achieve this? This opens up an issue that is crucial both for Como capitalist families and for my analysis of the reproduction of firms and class—that of social mobility among the Italian bourgeoisie.

Reproducing the Firm and Social Mobility

Research on social class mobility in Italy reveals that the percentage of self-made men among the business elite is small (Chiesi 1986; Martinelli, Chiesi, and Dalla Chiesa 1981). The slight chance that the son of a small entrepreneur will become a big business leader is cited by Martinelli and Chiesi (1989, 121) as evidence of the sharp break between the worlds of small and big business. As in other leading industrial-capitalist nations like the United States and Japan, there is a relatively stable hereditary business elite that has been successful in reproducing its class status. In Italy, small business owners, blue-collar workers, and landowners have played a less important role in the formation of the business elite than they have in the United States, although there has been greater mobility from the ranks of clerks and middle management. At the same time, however, Martinelli and Chiesi (1989, 121) point out that a number of studies have discovered a high degree of upward mobility in local systems of firms, particularly in central and southern Italy, but also in the north.

However small their chances of joining the ranks of the business elite, almost all family firm owners aspire to move up the Como industrial hierarchy. This is because, for one, the survival of the firm and its transmission to the next generation depends on the accumulation and reinvestment of capital to make the firm competitive in a field in which technological innovation is constant and marketing strategies continually change. For another, if more than one child is to succeed to the management and ownership of the firm and is going to be able to maintain his or her family's class standing, the firm must expand and, most likely, diversify. The wealthiest families among Como's industrial bourgeoisie—the ones who comprise Como's business elite—have considerably more financial resources to divide among their children. But even they must successfully expand and diversify, if only to maintain their standing in the industry and with the local business elite. Reproduction of the firm and movement up the firm and family hierarchy, therefore, are not separate goals pursued by entrepreneurs with different ambitions.

Whether any particular firm retains its standing in the next generation or moves up the industrial hierarchy is the result of multiple factors. Outcomes are very difficult to predict, and these are questions discussed and debated constantly by firm owners and industry analysts. The family strategies of class mobility pursued by the Como bourgeoisie are more predictable, because they are shaped by their location in the bourgeois class and their past trajectory. In order to understand class location and strategies of firm reproduction and mobility among the Como bourgeoisie, we need to first consider what they share as a class and what differentiates them internally.

Who Are the Como Bourgeoisie?

What differentiates the bourgeoisie from the working class in industrial-capitalist society, according to Marxists such as Poulantzas (1975), is the former's ownership of the means of production. No matter how small the scale of their enterprise, anyone who owns and controls capital assets and employs the labor of others is considered a member of the bourgeoisie. These two criteria appear, at first glance, straightforward and unambiguous. All thirty-eight families in this study would appear to fulfill them. All own firms with capital assets and employ the labor of others. Yet, closer scrutiny reveals that the wide variation in the amount of capital assets owned by these families and their degree of control over these assets place them in significantly different relation to the means of production, as well as to the means of reproduction of social class.

Among the capital assets a family may own are the factory, its equipment, the land on which it is situated, the firm's unique technological developments and techniques of production, its designs, and its name. But not all families have exclusive ownership and control over these assets; in fact, only the wealthiest among them do. These wealthy families have substantial net capital assets remaining after bank loans and other debts have been subtracted, and they undoubtedly qualify as owning and controlling what Marx meant by the means of production. But others have little in the way of assets or have negative balances after bank loans and the credit they have been granted by other firms are subtracted. This is especially true of the families who own and manage the smaller firms at the bottom end of the industry hierarchy. A family operating a weaving firm that does subcontracting work for a small number of clients usually rents the land on which the factory is situated, leases looms from a textile machinery company, and, in addition, shoulders bank loans. Classifying such a family as bourgeois stretches the meaning of "ownership" and "control" of capital assets. Firms that perform subcontracting work for a small number of clients are not free to develop their productive capacities in ways that could be perceived as competing with their own clients. In other words, subcontracting firms are constrained in the ways in which they can deploy their capital assets and reinvest their profits. For example, a printing firm that prints fabric for three weaving firms cannot expand into either photoengraving or weaving, because either move could be viewed as competing with their own clients. Vulnerable as they are to both their creditors and their "clients" — the latter of which might just as accurately be called their employers in some cases — a family that owns a small subcontracting firm has only nominal control of the means of production.

In his analysis of property relations, Hegedus distinguishes between juridical ownership and effective "possession." The latter includes "the capacity to direct people's activities as the executors of productive labour," the capacity for disposition over the means of production and the structure of production," and "the capacity to use, appropriate or at least distribute the surplus product" (1976, 94–95). This is useful for distinguishing the owners of small subcontracting firms who do not have effective possession of productive resources, even though they may legally own the firm, from the owners of larger firms who control both their productive resources and the distribution of their products. It is also useful for differentiating family members who have effective control of the productive resources of the firm from family members who do not, even though they may own equal shares in the firm.

Along the same lines, employing workers does not give all firm owners the same control over labor power. Poulantzas's definition of the bourgeoisie assumes a capitalist-worker relation structured by a labor market in which capitalists are free to purchase the most productive labor they can find at the lowest price and, conversely, in which workers are free to sell their labor to the highest bidder. The employment of family members and relatives, however, is constrained by cultural meanings, sentiments, and modes of exchange more complicated than such a model admits. We shall see in chapter 4 that the deployment of labor power and the relations of production in firms are significantly affected by these meanings and modes of kinship.

When we add to these considerations the significant differences in capital assets that families own in addition to those of the firm — in the form of real estate, investments in other firms in the industry, and investments outside the industry — it becomes even more difficult to construe the Como manufacturing bourgeoisie as a homogenous social class who share a structural location. Most families have the majority of their capital assets bound up in a single firm. Only a few are engaged in investment diversification strategies that link their financial fortunes to industries and markets beyond the scope of the silk industry and the region. Indeed, the extent of capital assets controlled by these elite families is very difficult to assess because their holdings and investments are diversified in ways that make them difficult to track down.

A different model of the bourgeoisie has been proposed by Bottomore (1989) who follows Marx in placing small producers along with white-collar workers in the "middle strata" rather than in the bourgeoisie.[2]

> The capitalist class (or bourgeoisie) can be defined, in Marxist terms, as a constituent element in the class structure of a society based upon the capitalist mode of production. This distinctive class structure comprises the owners of the major productive resources (or as Marx expressed it, "the owners of the system of production"), the industrial workers who sell their labour power to these owners, and diverse "middle strata" (including small producers and white-collar workers of varying levels of skill). (1989, 4)

According to this scheme, the families in my study that own less-capitalized subcontracting firms would be in the middle strata and not members of the capitalist class. I agree with Bottomore that these families should not be lumped into an undifferentiated bourgeoisie and that in many ways they are closer to the petty bourgeoisie than they are to the upper bourgeoisie. This raises the question of whether there is a significant difference between the lower end of the bourgeoisie — which includes both petty bourgeoisie and small manufacturers — and white-collar workers. Unlike the latter, the petty bourgeoisie and small producers have access to and partial ownership of the means of production, which makes it possible for them to acquire full ownership and control of the means of production. Some of them succeed in doing so. In Como, as will be seen shortly, a significant portion of the Como industrial bourgeoisie have spent a period of time as small producers on their way to becoming full members of the bourgeoisie, and a significant portion came from the petty bourgeoisie.[3]

A consideration of the class biographies of individuals and families and the trajectories that have brought them into the bourgeoisie raises questions about the limitations of static approaches to social class. A static definition of social class may be useful for some descriptive purposes, as, for example, when we want to know what percentage of a population owns sufficient capital assets to control the means of production. As the basis for understanding the relation between class location and subjectivity, however, static approaches are inadequate. They rest shakily on a crude interest theory in which people who at a particular point in time share similar economic resources share the same "objective interests." This assumes both that "interests" are the logical outcome of an objective, material reality and that they are forged on the spot. They overlook the diverse historical trajectories of the people who constitute a class at a particular point in time, failing to consider how these have shaped their perspectives and modes of action. In other words, characterizing individuals and families exclusively in terms of their current class location obscures the diachronic heterogeneity of class and class subjectivity.

The diachronic heterogeneity of the Como bourgeoisie calls for a fluid model of social class. Figure 3.1 and table 3.1 chart the intergenerational class mobility of thirty-five families in my sample. While I cannot claim that these thirty-five capitalist families constitute a representative sample of the entire Como manufacturing bourgeoisie, they offer useful insights into the heterogeneity of their class trajectories. In figure 3.1 I have traced each family from the class location of the firm founder's parents to the family's class location in 1989. In all but a couple of cases, this spans a period of three generations. I have distinguished the petty bourgeoisie, among whom I include retail store owners

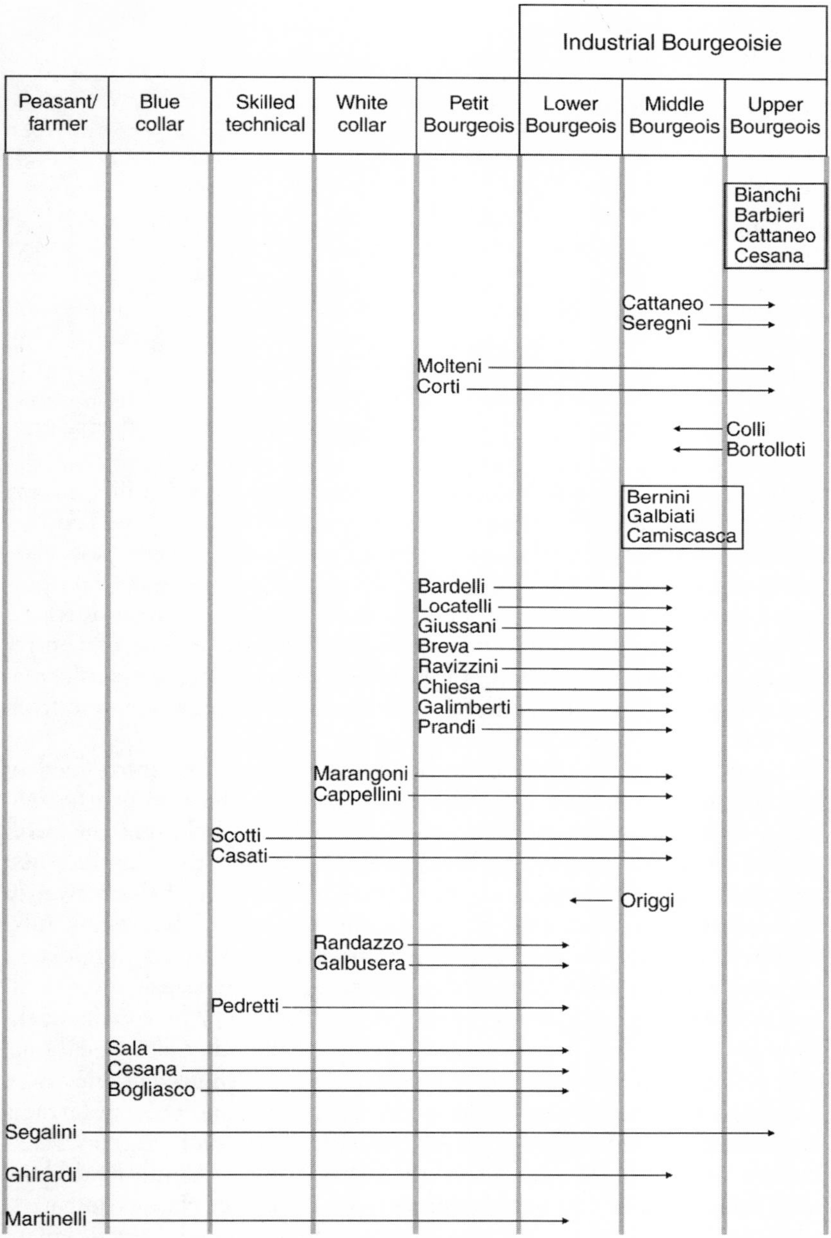

Industrial Bourgeoisie

Peasant/ farmer	Blue collar	Skilled technical	White collar	Petit Bourgeois	Lower Bourgeois	Middle Bourgeois	Upper Bourgeois

Upper Bourgeois (boxed): Bianchi, Barbieri, Cattaneo, Cesana

Cattaneo ⟶ (Middle Bourgeois to Upper)
Seregni ⟶ (Middle Bourgeois to Upper)

Molteni ———————⟶ (Petit Bourgeois to Upper Bourgeois)
Corti ———————⟶ (Petit Bourgeois to Upper Bourgeois)

Colli ⟵——— (Upper to Middle Bourgeois)
Bortolloti ⟵——— (Upper to Middle Bourgeois)

Middle Bourgeois (boxed): Bernini, Galbiati, Camiscasca

Bardelli ———⟶
Locatelli ———⟶
Giussani ———⟶
Breva ———⟶
Ravizzini ———⟶
Chiesa ———⟶
Galimberti ———⟶
Prandi ———⟶ (Petit Bourgeois to Middle Bourgeois)

Marangoni ———⟶
Cappellini ———⟶ (White collar to Middle Bourgeois)

Scotti ———⟶
Casati ———⟶ (Skilled technical to Middle Bourgeois)

Origgi ⟵——— (Middle Bourgeois to Lower Bourgeois)

Randazzo ———⟶
Galbusera ———⟶ (White collar to Lower Bourgeois)

Pedretti ———⟶ (Skilled technical to Lower Bourgeois)

Sala ———⟶
Cesana ———⟶
Bogliasco ———⟶ (Blue collar to Lower Bourgeois)

Segalini ———⟶ (Peasant/farmer to Upper Bourgeois)

Ghirardi ———⟶ (Peasant/farmer to Middle Bourgeois)

Martinelli ———⟶ (Peasant/farmer to Lower Bourgeois)

FIG. 3.1. Intergenerational Mobility of Families. Each family is charted from its founder's parents' class location to its location in 1989. Those founders whose class location did not change have no arrows and are boxed. In cases where the founder's parents came from different classes, I have used the higher location. (N = 35)

TABLE 3.1
Intergenerational Mobility of Families (N = 35)

Founder's Parents' Class Location	Upper Bourgeois	Middle Bourgeois	Lower Bourgeois	Total
Upper Bourgeois	4	2	0	6
Middle Bourgeois	2	3	1	6
Lower Bourgeois	0	0	0	0
Petit Bourgeois	2	6	2	10
White Collar	0	2	2	4
Skilled Technical	0	2	1	3
Working Class	0	0	3	3
Peasant/Farmer	1	1	1	3
Total	9	16	10	35

and merchants, from the industrial bourgeoisie — the families in my sample, all of whom are engaged in the industrial production of goods — in order to understand the movement of families between these class locations. For the same reason, I have differentiated the industrial bourgeoisie into three fractions — upper, middle, and lower — which differ according to the amount of capital possessed and the extent of control over the means of production. Table 3.1 summarizes the same information in tabular form, indicating the number of families that came from each class location two generations ago.

It is no surprise that the majority (twenty-two out of thirty-five) of the capitalist families in my sample had roots in the bourgeoisie two generations ago. However, this result depends on including the petty bourgeoisie in the category of bourgeoisie, since ten of the families had petty bourgeois backgrounds. Only a third (twelve out of thirty-five) of the families in the industrial bourgeoisie had industrial bourgeois antecedents. This indicates that the petty bourgeoisie has been an important source of families entering into the industrial bourgeoisie in twentieth-century Como. Indeed, more families came from petty bourgeois backgrounds two generations ago than from any of the other class locations: white-collar employment (four families), skilled-technical employment (three families), blue-collar working (three families), and peasant farmers (three families). On the other hand, together these nonbourgeois backgrounds account for thirteen of the thirty-five families. Como's industrial bourgeoisie is clearly a mix of families with a range of class trajectories, reflecting the possibilities for class mobility that industrial development opened up in the twentieth century.[4]

The breakdown of the industrial bourgeoisie into three fractions affords another view of class mobility. Only a minority (seven out of thirty-five) of the families were in the same fraction of the bourgeoisie two generations earlier, and an equal number (seven) came from an adjacent fraction or class. The majority (twenty-one) came from two or more class locations away. As Martinelli and Chiesi would have predicted, the upper bourgeoisie had the highest proportion of families (four of nine) that were already in that fraction two generations ago. Even among this "business elite," however, more than half came from other class locations, although predominantly from the middle bourgeoisie and the petty bourgeoisie. The middle bourgeois fraction shows even more recruitment from other classes. Although a couple of middle bourgeois families were formerly upper bourgeois families in decline, eleven had moved into this class location from outside the industrial bourgeoisie. The petty bourgeoisie supplied six of these eleven families. Finally, the lower bourgeois fraction was composed entirely of families that had different class locations two generations ago, again coming almost exclusively from outside the manufacturing bourgeoisie (nine of ten). This high level of recruitment into the lowest fraction of the industrial bourgeoisie bears out the claim that the lower bourgeoisie fraction is a product of the development of the industrial hierarchy in the twentieth century. All fractions of the bourgeoisie are made up of a mix of families from a range of class locations, but the lower fraction has the greatest diversity and the highest level of recruitment from outside the bourgeoisie.

The finding that the members of the lower fraction of the industrial bourgeoisie recently came from outside the bourgeois proper might appear to support Bottomore's scheme of lumping small producers in with the middle strata. But this overlooks the fact that those families who two generations ago were petty bourgeois or in other "middle strata" locations (white-collar or skilled-technical employment) passed through a period of membership in the lower bourgeoisie before getting to their present location. Eleven of the 16 middle bourgeois families show this trajectory. They did not jump from white-collar employee or petty bourgeois shopkeeper to middle fraction industrial capitalist, but worked their way to owning the means of production through a period as subcontractors. Indeed, no fraction of the Como industrial bourgeoisie appears to have been impermeable to class mobility.

The diverse class trajectories that the members of the Como bourgeoisie have followed to arrive at their present location challenges static models of the bourgeoisie and its internal differentiation. To conceive of the Como bourgeoisie solely on the basis of their current relation to the means of production obscures the temporal dimension of class. This is a serious failing, as people come to construe their material realities, their interests, and their possibilities — what Bourdieu has called their "habitus" through the course of their individual biographies and family histories. My own approach to social class is both processual and structural. This does not derive from my commitment to a particular model of social class as a reflection of "objective" reality, but from my interest in understanding how people come to see themselves as having particular goals and interests and particular identities—in other words, how they construct a class subjectivity. I do not take for granted that what motivates people is an objective and accurate assessment of their structural location in capitalist society. Rather, I assume that people's ideas about their identities and their interests are formed in relation to both their past social trajectories and their present location. In undertaking an analysis of the historical construction and transformation of interests and strategies, I treat all "interests" as cultural representations. I assume that people constantly reformulate their interests and that as circumstances change, they reformulate the projects they pursue.

Adopting a processual view of the Como industrial bourgeoisie enables us to appreciate its heterogeneity, both its current diversity and the diverse trajectories of social mobility of its members. In the following section, I describe three fractions of the Como bourgeoisie in terms of their effective control of the means of production, their past class trajectories, and their strategies of class reproduction and social mobility. This discussion lays the basis for my analysis in chapters 4 and 5 of the different dynamic configurations of capital and kinship that shape the development and demise of firms in different fractions of the Como bourgeoisie.

Fractions of the Como Manufacturing Bourgeoisie

I have divided Como bourgeois families in the silk-industry firms into three fractions—upper, middle, and lower—based on a combination of firm and family characteristics that indicate the extent of their control of the means of production, their past social trajectories, and their strategies for reproduction and mobility. Firm characteristics include annual gross revenue, number of employees, the extent to which they sell their own products or work as subcontractors for other firms, and their ownership of other firms. Family characteristics include indicators of past and present social class, including the education and occupation of the founder's parents, the founder's spouse and parents, the founder's children and their spouses and children. Table 3.2 summarizes the firm characteristics of the three fractions, while Table 3.3 summarizes their family characteristics.

The Upper Bourgeois Fraction (Nine Families)

The nine families in my sample that I have included in this fraction all owned firms that in 1985 earned an annual gross revenue of between $5 million to $28 million, with most of them clustering around $10 million. The number of the workers employed in their firms ranged from 50 to 850. This wide range is due to the fact that some firms send work out to a number of subcontracting firms as well as to individual workers (*lavoro a domicilio*), who are not formally classified as employees of the firm. The size of a firm's registered workforce, consequently, is not always a useful indicator of its productive capacity. Neither are the earnings of a single firm a good indicator of an upper bourgeois family's wealth, as these families own (either entirely or have the majority of shares in) more than one firm.[5] Indeed, all nine upper bourgeois families owned two or more firms in the industry, in addition to their primary firm. All of them also had extensive real estate holdings and a range of other investments outside the industry about which I was not able to obtain precise information.[6]

More indicative of this fraction's effective control of the means of production is the fact that none of their primary firms were subcontractors. They all worked for *conto proprio*, meaning that they controlled both the production and distribution of their products. Six of these nine firms, moreover, incorporated all the phases of production required to transform raw silk into fabric ready for sale. Along with their ownership of firms that specialized in other phases of silk production and firms in allied marketing and retailing sectors, this gave them a great degree of control over the deployment of capital and other productive resources.[7]

The family characteristics of this fraction reveal more about its social character. The class backgrounds of the founders of these firms are varied; four of their fathers had themselves been members of the upper bourgeoisie and four were divided between the middle bourgeoisie and the petty bourgeoisie. Only one founder, whose father was a sharecropper, came from a nonbourgeois background. Six of the nine founders, moreover, had fathers who were already firm owners in the silk industry or an allied manufacturing sector. The class backgrounds of the founders' mothers appear to be similar, although here the data are spottier, as this information was commonly not known, or at least not willingly provided, by informants. Finally, the educations of the founders and their children say a good deal about strategies for the reproduction of social class. The founders' highest level of education range from a German degree in textile engineering to a degree from the Setificio, the high

TABLE 3.2
Firm Characteristics of Fractions

Name of Firm	Annual Gross Revenues in US dollars (Millions)	No. of Employees	Type of Production	Proprio or Terzo or Both	Own Other Firms?		
					None	One	2+
Upper (9)							
Bianchi	5.5–11	350	ciclo completo	P			Y
Barbieri	5.5–11	200	ciclo completo	P			Y
Cattaneo	12–27	185	ciclo completo	P			Y
Cesana	5.5–11	370	weaving, dyeing	P			Y
Molteni	12–27	800	ciclo completo	P			Y
Corti	28+	850	ciclo completo	P			Y
Seregni	12–27	250	ciclo completo	P			Y
Segalini	12–27	50	weaving	P			Y
Pezzi	2.5–5.5	80	converter, printing	P			Y
Middle (18)							
Galbiati	2.5–5.5	85	weaving, printing	B		Y	
Cappellini	1.5–2.5	60	weaving	P			Y
Colli	2.5–5.5	80	printing, dyeing	T			Y
Ravizzini	5.5–11	34	converter, printing	P		Y	
Giussani	2.5–5.5	35	converter	P		Y	
Bortolotti	1–2.5	37	weaving	B		?	
Locatelli	2.5–5.5	120	weaving, dyeing, printing	P			Y

Name	Range	No.	Activity		Type			
Camisasca	2.5–5.5	70	weaving		P	Y		
Scotti	2.5–5.5	110	weaving, printing		T	Y	Y	Y
Casati	1.5–2.5	69	printing		T		Y	Y
Fumagalli	0.5–1.5	7	converter		P			
Rossetti	1.5–2.5	37	twisting	Y	T			
Breva	1.5–2.5	95	printing		T	Y		
Chiesa	?	40	twisting		T	Y		
Marangoni	1.5–2.5	100	weaving		P	Y		
Bardelli	up to 0.5	8	converter		P	Y		
Ghirardi	1.5–2.5	73	weaving		B	Y		
Bernini	1.5–2.5	82	printing		T	Y		
Lower (11)								
Randazzo	under 0.3	60	weaving	Y	T			
Sala	0.3 to 0.5	80	photoengraving	Y	T			
Cesana	0.3 to 0.5	25	printing	Y	T			
Bogliasco	under 0.3	10	weaving	Y	B			
Galimberti	0.3 to 0.5	22	dyeing, weaving, converter, printing	Y	B			
Origgi	0.6 to 1.5	60	weaving	Y	B			
Prandi	0.3 to 0.5	23	twisting	Y	T			
Galbusera	0.3 to 0.5	14	weaving	Y	T			
Martinelli	under 0.3	35	photoengraving	Y	T			
Santi	0.6 to 1.5	37	photoengraving	Y	T			
Pedretti	0.6 to 1.5	30	dyeing	Y	T			

TABLE 3.3
Family and Class Characteristics of Fractions

Name of Firm	Founder's Father's Class	Founder's Mother's Class	Founder's Father in Industry	Founder's Spouse's Class	Education of Founder	Education of Son	Education of Daughter
Upper (9)							
Bianchi	upper b.	upper b.	yes, owner	upper b.	Se	SW.Te.	Liceo
Barbieri	upper b.	?	yes, owner	landowners	Ge. Te.	U + Ge	La. (abroad)
Cattaneo	middle b.	?	yes, owner	upper b.	U. Law	some U.	some U.
Cesana	upper b.	upper b.	yes, owner	?	HS	U. Phar.	n.a.
Molteni	petit b.	?	no	?	?	Bus. S.	study abroad
Corti	petit b.	petit b.	no	upper b.	Se	n.a.	U. Psych.
Seregni	middle b.	?	yes, owner	technical	Liceo	n.a.	U. Lit.
Segalini	share cropper	share cropper	no	?	Se	Se	U. La.
Pezzi	upper b.	upper b.	yes	upper b.	HS	U. Law	Liceo: La.
Middle (18)							
Galbiati	middle b.	working class	yes, owner	petit b.	Se	U. Ec. Law	U. La.
Cappellini	white collar	?	no	petit b.	Liceo	Liceo	n.a.
Colli	upper b.	?	yes, owner	naval officer	SW. Te.	?	Liceo: La.
Ravizzini	petit b.	petit b.	no	petit b.	Se	n.a.	HS
Giussani	petit b.	petit b.	no	technical	HS	U.Ec. + ?	Liceo: La.
Bortolotti	upper b.	prof	no	?	SWTe.En	Liceo, Se.	Liceo: La.
Locatelli	petit b.	?	no	?	Se	Se	Liceo: La.
Camisasca	middle b.	middle b.	yes, owner	middle b.	U.Ec.	Se	U.La.
Scotti	technical	?	yes, empl.	work. class	elem.sch.	Se	n.a.
Casati	technical	technical	yes, empl.	white coller	U.	Se	Se
Fumagalli	?	?	?	middle b.	Se	n.a.	U.Ec.
Rossetti	?	?	no	?	Se	?	?
Breva	technical	petit b.	no	petit b.	U.Che.	U.	Liceo: La.
Chiesa	petit b.	?	no	?	HS	Se	?
Marangoni	white collar	?	no	decl. nob.	HS	U.	U.

	Founder's Father's Class	Founder's Mother's Class		Founder's Spouse's Class	Education of Founder	Education of Son	Education of Daughter
Bardelli	petit b.	?	no	petit b.	U.Ec.	Se	Se
Ghirardi	farmer	work. class	no	farmer	Se	U.Ec.	U.La.
Bernini	middle b.	?	no	petit b.	U.Ec.	U.Ec.	n.a.
Lower (11)							
Randazzo[b]	white collar	?	no	white collar	Se	HS	n.a.
Sala	work. class	work. class	no	?	elem.sch.	Middle Sc.	U.Acc.La.
Cesana	work. class	work. class	yes, empl.	technical	Se	n.a.	n.a.
Bogliasco	work. class	farmer	no	work. class	Se	HS	HS
Galimberti	petit b.	petit b.	no	prof.	Se	U.Eng.	n.a.
Origgi	middle b.	?	yes, owner	middle b.	some U.	Se	n.a.
Prandi	petit b.	petit b.	no	work. class	Se	Se	middle sch.
Galbusera	white collar	work. class	yes, owner	work. class	Se	n.a.	HS
Martinelli	farmer	farmer	no	work. class	Se	Se	U.La.
Santi	?	?	no	?	HS	Se	HS
Pedretti[a]	technical	technical	no	n.a.	Se	n.a.	n.a.

Note: The abbreviations used in the columns of this table are as follows:

Founder's Father's Class, Founder's Mother's Class, Founder's Spouse's Class
upper b: upper bourgeoisie
middle b: middle bourgeoisie
petit b: petit bourgeoisie
prof: professional
decl. nob: declining nobility
work. class: working class

Education of Founder, Education of Son, Education of Daughter
elem sch: elementary school
HS: high school (non-college preparatory)
Liceo: college preparatory high school
Liceo La: college preparatory high school focused on languages
Bus. S: Business school (nonuniversity)
Ge. Te: German textile school
SW. Te: Swiss textile school

Se: Setificio (textile high school)
U: university degree
U. Acc: university degree in accounting
U. Che: university degree in chemistry
U. Ec: university degree in economics
U. Eng: university degree in engineering
U. La: university degree in languages
U. Law: university degree in law
U. Lit: university degree in literature
U. Phar: university degree in pharmacology
U. Psych: university degree in psychology
n.a: not applicable
?: unknown

[b] In these two cases, since the founder was not a relative of the current owners, I have used the family characteristics of the current owners.

school in Como specializing in textile production. Their sons tend toward the upper end of their fathers' educational attainment, with more pursuing university degrees than technical diplomas from the Setificio.[8]

The daughters in upper bourgeois families, on the other hand, until recently have had characteristically female bourgeois educations. The majority specialized in the study of European languages, either at the high school or university levels. Language study was often supplemented by periods of residence and study abroad in France, Germany, Switzerland and, more recently, the United States. This gendered division of education, with sons specializing in business or technical educations and daughters specializing in language and culture, provided each with the means of reproducing social class. While sons were provided with training that would enable them to manage the means of production, daughters were given cultural capital to enable them to reproduce their class status through marriage. The study of languages by daughters also served inadvertently to set up a managerial division of labor among siblings once daughters began working in firms in the 1960s. By giving daughters the linguistic and cultural competence to display their proper bourgeois credentials in the marriage market, parents endowed them with skills to communicate with the firm's foreign clients. As we shall see in later chapters, the increasing importance of marketing for the Como silk industry has had unintended consequences for the balance of managerial power among siblings in some firms.

According to Martinelli and Chiesi (1989, 116), there are a number of entrepreneurial types in the history of the Italian business elite, whose characteristics vary with respect to the phase of economic development and the nature of the political regime in which they emerged. In economic terms, the major divide is the period of rapid economic growth in the 1950s and 1960s. In political terms, the major divide is the formation of the democratic regime after the Second World War. Based on their study of entrepreneurial biographies (Chiesi 1977), Martinelli and Chiesi distinguish four entrepreneurial types. The upper fraction of the Como bourgeoisie that had grandparental roots in the bourgeoisie appear to correspond to the main capitalist type that Martinelli and Chiesi conclude emerged during the second half of the nineteenth century — the "traditional entrepreneur," whose cultural and economic roots lay in the precapitalist economy of craft production. These entrepreneurs represent the second generation of wealthy artisans, middle landowners and provincial merchants, and, in some cases, sons of professionals.[9]

The Middle Bourgeois Fraction (Eighteen Families)

The annual gross revenues among firms owned by these families ranged from $500,000 to $5.5 million, with most clustering around $2 million. The workforce in these firms ranged from 7 to 120. With the exception of the three converter firms that did not engage in manufacturing and so had few employees (7–35), the primary firms of middle bourgeois families had a median of 70 employees. Unlike the primary firms owned by the upper bourgeoisie, those of the middle bourgeois fraction were not vertically integrated. With one exception, they encompassed, at most, two phases of production. Thirteen of them were limited to only one phase of production or were a converter firm that did no manufacturing itself. The firms were a mix of those that sold their own products, those that engaged solely in subcontracting work, and those that combined the two. Like the upper bourgeoisie, all these families also owned a majority share of at least one other firm in the industry, but only five of eighteen owned two or more. The rest were limited to majority holdings in one additional firm.

The family origins of the founders' in this fraction tended toward the petty bourgeoisie, with only two of the eighteen founders having fathers who owned firms in the Como silk industry. Unlike the upper bourgeois founders who tended to marry women from upper bourgeois backgrounds, the founders in this fraction had wives from petty bourgeois backgrounds. Yet the educations of founders were very much like those of the upper bourgeoisie: almost half did post secondary study at a university or engineering college. The rest either studied at the Setificio (silk technical high school) or graduated from the high school specializing in accounting. Their children's educations also resembled those of the upper bourgeoisie, with the same gendered specialization into technical/productive (male) or cultural (female) fields, albeit at less ambitious level—more finishing with high school than university diplomas.

Martinelli and Chiesi (1989, 121) argue that because of the impermeability of the Italian business elite, the entrepreneur's education does not work as a mobility channel, but rather as a certification mechanism and a means of role socialization. As in France and other countries, the length of education and especially the elitist content of education are correlated with membership in entrepreneurial dynasties and higher social origin. In Italy, the enterpreneurs coming from the petty bourgeoisie manifest a higher proportion of lower quality educational backgrounds than their colleagues of higher social origin (Martinelli, Chiesi, and Dalla Chiesa 1981). But the lower level of internal stratification of the Italian academic system does not give rise to situations like that in

France, where the mechanism of elite socialization in the Grandes Ecóles and the esprit de corps among schoolmates play for the future managers the role that parenthood, relatives, and marriage alliances play for the heirs of entrepreneurial dynasties.

Middle bourgeois families in Italy place sons in one of the small number of Italian universities that have been, and continue to be, centers for students interested in being certified for managerial jobs. Since the end of the last century Milan and Turin polytechnics have trained entrepreneurs and managers with technical backgrounds, while Bocconi University in Milan provides mainly economic and financial training. The latter also serves as a channel of upward mobility for students coming from the petty bourgeoisie, fostering their acquaintance with the heirs of big capitalist families and entry into their firms. The ties among Bocconi alumni strengthen relations firms, banks, other financial institutions and the professions (Martinelli and Chiesi 1989: 122).

The Lower Bourgeois Fraction (Eleven Families)

The firms owned by these eleven families in my sample had annual gross revenues ranging from $300,000 to $1.5 million and employed between 10 and 80 workers. Again, these figures are less revealing than are the location of the firms in the manufacturing hierarchy and their owners' limited ownership and control of productive resources. Eight of the eleven firms engaged in only subcontracting work, while the remaining three were primarily subcontractors that did a small amount of production for their own sales. All the firms except one were limited to one phase of production, and five of the eleven engaged in the least profitable phases of silk manufacturing: the twisting of thread, photoengraving (to prepare screens for printing designs on fabric), and dyeing. None of the families owned or had substantial investments in other firms.

The founders of these firms had fathers whose occupations had placed them among the petty bourgeoisie, the white-collar/technical class, or the working class; only one had a middle bourgeois background where there might have been some access to capital. The spouses of the founders, likewise, had working-class or skilled-technical fathers. Unlike the other two fractions, these founders were educated primarily at the Setificio or other technical schools. A few had only elementary school educations. Their children's education also diverged from the gendered division of education seen in the upper fractions. Although sons, like their fathers, pursued technical educations at the Setificio or other technical schools, daughters tended to have attained comparatively higher educational levels and to range over a number of fields — including accounting and teacher's education, as well as languages. Instead of acquiring credentials for the marriage market, these daughters appeared to have been pursuing credentials for employment. In light of the limited capital and productive resources their families possessed, it is not surprising that daughters would have been oriented toward education that would prepare them to support themselves while their brothers were being trained to take over the firm. In the next chapter, the limited productive resources of these lower fraction firms will be shown to be a crucial factor in processes of inclusion and exclusion in the family that shape the relations of brothers and sisters, as well as other family members.

Beyond Patriarchal Desire

Fathers and sons occupy center stage in the discourses of succession, continuity, and unity of the Como bourgeoisie. As in the adage "The grandfather founds the firm, the sons develop it, the grandsons destroy it," male succession is the key to corporate continuity. These discourses both reflect and incite patriarchal desires of succession. As a dominant ideal that men strive to attain, patriarchal desire operates as a force of production—a sentiment that drives production and capital accumulation. Production, accumulation, and succession, however, are shaped by more complex processes of capital and kinship than dominant bourgeois discourses of succession convey. The continuity of firms and families are not just a matter of fathers and sons but, as we shall see in the next two chapters, of mothers and daughters, husbands and wives, brothers and sisters, and uncles and nephews.

CHAPTER FOUR

BETRAYAL AS A FORCE OF PRODUCTION

Antonio Galbusera peppered his rendition of his firm's history with frank commentaries on the problems of the industry and the challenges facing small subcontracting firms like his. Among the firm owners we interviewed, he was perhaps the most candid, if not the most polished, spokesman for the *conto terzo* (subcontracting) firms that comprise Como's manufacturing service sector and that fill the production needs of larger firms and converters. When we asked Signor Galbusera where the initial capital invested in his firm had come from, he explained that he had combined savings from his earnings as the technical director of another firm with loans from his maternal aunt and uncle. Signor Galbusera had already told us that he had started his firm with the equipment from his paternal uncle's firm, where he had also worked for a period of time. When I asked how this paternal uncle had helped him, there was an awkward moment as he paused in his otherwise fluid narrative before replying. Then he said,

> We have a proverb here in Italy that says *parenti, serpenti* [relatives are snakes]. I would say that only 50 percent of relatives are snakes. Those on my mother's side helped me; those on my father's did not.

The proverb cited by Signor Galbusera is widely known throughout Italy and hardly confined to capitalist families. Yet, its invocation by firm owners — some of whom also cited its variation, *fratelli, coltelli* (siblings are knives) — alluded to meanings particular to the experiences of capitalist families. Among the Como bourgeoisie, the familiar theme of the betrayal of trust by those from whom one expects unconditional loyalty is associated with the demise of firms as well as the destruction of families. Surprisingly, the proverb was cited more frequently by the owners of small firms — especially those like Signor Galbusera, who were small subcontractors struggling to survive in a highly competitive sector of the industry.

Betrayal was closely tied to another common response from Como firm owners to our questions about their relatives — that is, they commonly had little to say about them. Firm owners frequently claimed to have little knowledge of collateral relatives, including kin as genealogically close as aunts, uncles, and first cousins. In some cases, it was unclear whether they lacked information about these kin or simply did not want to talk about them; in others, it was clearly the latter. When, for example, Luca Castiglioni told us that all he knew about his father's brothers was that they were involved in the industry, we could not help but suspect that this was less than the whole truth. Luca's father, after all, had been a partner in his brothers' firm when Luca was an adolescent. We had little hope of finding out more, however, as Luca put an end to this discussion by stating flatly, "Anyway, they are all dead." As we had just interviewed his cousins, who had taken over the management of their father's firm, we could only assume that Luca meant that the relationship was dead. Later in the interview, Luca told us that his family never had any shares or financial interest in any other firms. Here again, however, we knew from his cousins and from Camera di Commercio records that his father had owned shares in his uncles' firm.

Most firm owners made it clear that they did not want to delve into the specific reasons for the distance between themselves and particular relatives, brushing off our questions with answers such as "We don't have much in common" or "We have gone our separate ways." Some, however, admitted that the distance was the result of a disagreement or an acrimonious family conflict. A few admitted the damage was so great that they were no longer on speaking terms with these relatives. Franco Scotti revealed that he often encountered a paternal cousin at his tennis club but had not spoken to him for over twenty years. The last time he did was just before his cousin stopped working at Signor Scotti's father's firm.

Attitudes ranging from ambivalent to stridently negative surfaced when firm owners talked about the desirability of involving relatives outside the immediate family in the firm, whether as partners or as employees. As we shall see later in this chapter, some owners cited a number of advantages of working with relatives in a firm. But more of them appeared to agree with Signor Scotti when he claimed that the many relatives his father had employed in the firm had created a terrible mess. His father, who had naïvely trusted them, was blind to what had really been going on. It was only after these relatives left the firm, Signor Scotti confided, placing his hands two feet apart, that "you find out they have a knife this long."

Cultural Resource Models of Italian Family Capitalism

The distrust of kin voiced by the Como industrial bourgeoisie contrasts markedly with what economic historians and sociologists claim about the key role that collectivity and commitment to strong extended family ties have played in the success of Italian capitalism. Collective family values have been represented as crucial to the formation of the innovative small firms that have enabled Italian manufacturers to compete successfully in increasingly global markets since the 1970s. According to Piore and Sabel, the "tradition of familialism," which they define as "the use of kinship relations as the structuring principles of industrial organization," facilitated the accumulation of capital and the formation of small firms in Italy (1984, 228).

In the post–World War II revival of a craft-industrial sector in Italy, Piore and Sabel discern the echoes of the familialism that facilitated the flexible use of resources by craft economies that had successfully survived an earlier period of industrial capitalism. They cite as a prime example of such a craft economy the silk industry in nineteenth-century Lyon. In that case, family ties were used to create an alliance of medium- and small-sized firms specializing in one of the component phases of production. The cotton-textile manufacturer Alfred Motte had conceived of this system as a confederation of firms, each owned by a family member, after other strategies had failed in competition with more established mass producers. In the *système Motte* each family member who had come of age was paired with an experienced technician from one of the family's firms. The pair was provided with startup capital — most of which was owned by the family member — to initiate a firm that specialized in one of the phases of production needed by the confederation (1984, 34).

> The new firms often found markets outside, as well as inside, the family, but their financial and emotional ties to the lineage made them dependable partners, even in difficult times. This common loyalty to

the family freed the companies to make the realignments dictated by changing fashions, while ensuring against extreme fluctuations in the demand for particular processes, and providing the necessary trust to maintain a system of common financial reserves, marketing, and purchasing. (35)

A kin-based confederation of firms on the order of the *système Motte* system is not unfamiliar to Como industrial entrepreneurs. Indeed, it represents an ideal to which many strive. But such confederations are limited to a small number of the wealthiest industrial families, all of whom trace their entrepreneurial roots to the nineteenth century. The vast majority of families in the industry — especially those who own the subcontracting firms to which Piore and Sabel attribute the dynamism and flexible specialization of the industrial network — have no such roots, nor much hope of building such a confederation.

Piore and Sabel are not alone in pointing to "family tradition" as a key factor in the success of small firms in Italy. Paci (1982) has traced the roots of small firms in central Italy to the rural family structure of the *mezzadria* system, which required extended families to pool their labor in order to fulfill the terms of their tenancy. Frigeni and Tousjin (1976) contend that the diversification of production and the organizational integration of small business are particularly suited to the traditional large family of Italy. In the case of the artisanal fraction of the new middle class that developed out of peasant families in the Marche region of central Italy, Blim (1990) concludes that the prewar extended-household form of family organization enabled some families to accumulate patrimonial wealth rapidly and ensure its efficient distribution. Others created new extended family ties to this end.

These scholars portray the strong extended-family bonds of prewar rural Italy as a cultural resource that fueled the rapid economic development of postwar Italy. A number of the strengths of postwar Italian capitalism are claimed to have grown out of, or at the very least have been enabled by, extended family ties. These include rapid capital accumulation, "self-exploitation" of family labor, labor flexibility, firm diversification, and the organization of reliable firm networks. Were we to accept uncritically these characterizations of the cozy functional fit between strong extended-family bonds and innovative small manufacturing firms, we might be persuaded to attribute the rapid and successful capitalist development of northern and central Italy to their prewar rural kinship structure. This could easily lead, in turn, to our accepting a corollary to this hypothesis — the attribution of the failure of capitalist development in southern Italy to what Banfield called its "amoral familism." In his much-criticized book, Banfield (1958) argued that southern

Italian's distrust of anyone outside the restricted nuclear family impeded the formation of a public sphere (i.e., "civil society"), thereby contributing to the economic and political backwardness of the south.

This tempting binary of north versus south, strong extended family versus restricted nuclear family, trust versus distrust, industrial network versus weak extrafamilial social network, civil society versus amoral familism overlooks some untidy ethnographic details that are revealed by a close encounter with the workings of family capitalism in Italy. In particular, it overlooks the suspicions, distrust, and feelings of betrayal among kin that are part and parcel of the "familialism" that characterizes family capitalism.

Betrayal as a Force of Production

Among those writing about the relation of family organization to the development of small firm industries in Italy, Blim is the exception. He points out that tensions and conflicts are not unknown to those families in the Marche region who have moved rapidly into the artisanal-entrepreneurial middle class. Perhaps it is because Blim — in contrast to the others — conducted ethnographic research among entrepreneurial households that he recognizes the darker side of extended-family relations:

> Even the solidarity among brothers — the source of many a firm's success — has occasionally turned into a casualty of business fortunes. The stories of brotherly betrayal related by informants are told in a manner shorn of the Biblical — Jacob and Esau — dramatic tone that one might expect to hear. Instead, it is that the gullible one should have known better, the culpable one was cunning, and the wives were the source of all of the trouble. But one is told confidentially, given the cutthroat nature of the business, these things can be expected to happen. (1990, 139)

In this chapter, I extend Blim's sobering remarks about the "occasional" casualty resulting from brotherly betrayal in entrepreneurial families to show that betrayal and estrangement are as much a regular part of the organizational dynamics of the Como family capitalism as are trust and kinship solidarity. As sentiments at play at different moments in the developmental histories of family firms, trust and betrayal are integral to processes of firm expansion, technological diffusion, capital accumulation, the division of firms, and the creation of new firms. They are among the forces of production that incite, enable, constrain, and shape production among Como entrepreneurs (see chapter 1 for a fuller discussion of my definition of forces of production).

In the early years of firm development, sentiments of trust and solidarity among family and kin make possible the pooling of labor, greater flexibility in the organization of labor, and the deferral of compensation, thereby enhancing the firm's competitiveness. In later years, as the firm matures and begins to bring in members of the second generation, limitations to firm growth and expansion fuel sentiments of distrust and suspicion, which operate as forces for the division of the firm, the diffusion of technology, and the destruction of families. Out of these processes emerge new firms, new families, and new solidarities. Together these sentiments operate as forces of production and reproduction in Italian family capitalism.

My argument that betrayal, as well as trust, operates as a force of production and reproduction in Italian family capitalism is intended to counterbalance the Durkheimian tendencies of scholars such as Piore and Sabel and Paci, who focus exclusively on those family sentiments that facilitate the accumulation of capital, the pooling of labor, and the deferral of compensation for the good of the collectivity. My attention to distrust and betrayal, however, does not reflect a vision of capitalist families as peopled by sinister, disloyal, or selfish individuals. It is not my intention to replace a Durkheimian model of collectivity with a utilitarian model of rational actors pursuing acultural, selfish interests. Rather, my goal is to deepen our understanding of the complex ways in which kinship sentiments shape the workings of capitalist family firms in Italy. This requires paying attention to a wider range of sentiments and their more complex interplay than has been done by scholars who have treated family and kinship in Italy as a cultural resource. Before I attempt to do just that, however, a discussion of diversity among the Como bourgeoisie is in order.

Firms and families in all fractions of the Como industrial bourgeoisie undergo processes of division, but the timing and emotional intensity of these splits and the form they take differ. In chapter 3 we saw that the owners of firms in different fractions pursue different strategies of firm and family reproduction. My focus in this chapter and the next illuminate those reproductive processes from another angle. Chapter 5 is devoted to the upper and middle fractions and the challenges they face as strains on capital accumulation and investment emerge in later phrases of firm development. Upper bourgeois families with the greatest capital resources are able to postpone division longest, commonly until the third or even fourth generation. The greater capital of these families enables them to diversify in the second generation, whether by expanding into new areas of production in the parent firm or by creating allied firms headed by children. At the same time, they are able to settle the claims of "outside" children who do not fill management positions in the firm, thus decreasing pressures for the division of the firm. When cousins or second cousins divide the firm in the third or fourth generation, feelings of betrayal are mitigated by the definition of cousins not as members of the same "family" but as "relatives" who are not as tightly bound by sentiments of collectivity.

Families in the middle bourgeois fraction generally are on the borderline of having sufficient capital to diversify and create other firms. In most cases, adult children must remain in the same firm with the hope of expanding them sufficiently to support their families. While they may be able to hold the firm together until the third generation comes of age, tensions commonly begin to mount before this happens as their attempts to invest in their children's futures become forces for division of the patrimony and, therefore, the firm. The resulting conflicts among siblings produce feelings of betrayal stronger than those in the upper bourgeois fraction.

This chapter focuses on the fifteen family firms in the lower and middle fractions of the Como industrial bourgeoisie that are limited to subcontracting and on the processes of division they undergo in the second generation. It is among these families that feelings of betrayal are the most intense and the most frequently encountered. While in the wealthiest fraction of the Como industrial bourgeoisie, flows of capital follow lines of consanguinity and marriage, in the least-capitalized fraction *labor* and *technical knowledge* flow through these networks. Among firms that have relied on relatives for technical labor rather than financial capital, division occurs sooner and is accompanied by greater acrimony. It is among these families that the aphorism *fratelli, coltelli* cuts most deeply, transforming brothers and other kin into strangers who refuse to acknowledge each other even when they pass on the narrow streets of central Como.

In order to understand the implications of my analysis of firm division and the sentiments of distrust and betrayal for the dynamics of the Como silk industry, we need to review first how the industry has been characterized by others.

Decentralization and Flexible Specialization

Piore and Sable argue that since the early 1970s, central and northwestern Italy have been the sites for the emergence of a new type of innovative industrial economy consisting of networks of technologically sophisticated, highly flexible manufacturing firms that have revived craft forms of production (1984, 17). The firms in these networks are said to be engaged in a strategy of constant innovation based on flexible, multiuse equipment, skilled workers, and an innovative industrial community. While economic downturns have periodically led to the revival of craft forms of production that were marginalized with the advent of industrial mass production in the nineteenth century, Piore and Sable contend that the shift that occurred after 1970 in Italy has provoked technological advances instead of a return to simple techniques. Attempts by these small firms to meet the challenge of rising costs and growing competition from abroad have narrowed the gap in cost between mass and craft production, thus effectively challenging mass production as a paradigm (206).

These developments, according to Piore and Sabel, have occurred in two very different sectors of production in Italy: in the machine-tool industry, "which seemed frozen by definition in the perpetual adolescence of craft inefficiency," and among "mature mass producers" in such industries as steel, chemicals, and textiles (206). Of all these industries, the most mature is textiles. A prime example is the textile district of Prato, situated in the provinces of Florence and Pistoia in central Italy, which Piore and Sabel view as competing successfully in global markets. Although they trace the history of Prato's industry from its beginnings, their primary focus is on its reorientation in the 1950s, in response to the stiff competion from wool producers in Japan and Eastern Europe, when local manufacturers created innovative fabrics. They describe how large integrated firms that had previously dominated production reacted to the crisis of the 1950s much as they had done in the 1930s, by laying off workers and selling or renting them equipment for subcontracting work. In doing so, these large firms converted fixed to variable costs — passing on the risks of market fluctuations to their former employees. The result was the creation of a "vast network of small shops employing one to twenty workers (often members of a single extended family) who possessed an intimate knowledge of materials and machines" (214–15).

To combine these small firms into a flexible production system and reduce their dependence on large firms required that they coordinate their diverse skills in "autonomous federations" that were responsive to fashion trends. This role was taken up by the *impannatore*, the twentieth-century descendant of the medieval merchant and the early-modern Verleger (putter-outer), who had survived the period of mass production, remaining "an important, though secondary figure on the edge of the integrated mills" (215). As a consequence, by the mid-1980s the integrated firm was all but extinct in the Prato textile industry.

[The *impannatore*] purchased raw materials, organized a network of small shops to produce cloth according to well-known specifications, and then brought the product to market or sold it to a merchant. But as markets for standardized products became inaccessible, the impannatore became more important: he or she became a designer, responsible for shaping and responding to fashion, as well as for organizing production. The impannatore urged the firms to experiment with materials and processes; and the firms' successes, in turn, fanned the creativity of the *impannatore*, making him or her still more demanding. In this way, the small firms coalesced into a network, and this network expanded — at the expense of the integrated firms. (215)

Piore and Sable bring their history of the Prato textile industry to a close by commenting,

A system that had begun as an expedient — accidentally discovered — gave birth to a distinctive technology — and vital economy. (216)

This "accidental" discovery was, for Piore and Sabel, more than an expedient response to changing markets and competition but also a response to political events of the late 1960s and early 1970s in Italy. In the late 1960s, Italy's "economic miracle" faced the challenge of increasing demands by organized labor, which culminated in the strikes of the *autunno caldo* (hot autumn) of 1969. The alliance forged between southern migrants and northern workers during a period of tight labor markets increased Italian workers' bargaining power and threatened the postwar economic growth that had relied on cheap labor (154). In other words, the emergence of innovative, craft-based industrial networks grew out of the convergence of several political struggles: the struggle among businesses and among nations for a share of global markets, the struggle between capital and labor, and the struggle by southern Italian workers to gain a foothold in the central and northern industrial centers to which they had migrated.

The story of the Prato textile industry can be retold for many other Italian industries, according to Piore and Sabel (221), among them the high-fashion silk industry of Como. The same developments that led to Prato's success — the introduction of new technologies, the decomposition of large firms, and the switch to specialized products — are, for them, "typical of changes in the Italian textile industry as a whole" (332). There is indeed much in Como's postwar industrial history that resembles the Prato textile industry. In crucial ways, however, the history of Como's silk industry history is at odds with Piore and Sabel's account of the postwar "accidental discovery" of the advantages of a decentralized network of firms in Prato.

The Como Silk Industry in the Postwar Years

In the late 1950s and early 1960s — the period considered the "miracle years" of rapid economic development and growth in Italy — Como's silk industry experienced a dramatic rise in production. Firms owners recall with nostalgia the expansive growth and pervasive sense of promise and excitement of this era. New technology, new markets and, above all, new products stimulated the industry. In the 1950s, nylon, polyester, and dacron began to be produced in addition to silk. The industry's looms could be adapted to these artificial fibers because, like silk, they were a continuous thread. By the late 1950s, however, the drop in demand for inexpensive artificial fabrics by developing nations (e.g., Pakistan, India, Yugoslavia), who were increasingly able to produce such textiles themselves, brought a downturn and the closing of some factories. Firm owners responded by shifting their investments to dyeing and printing firms whose technology was still beyond the reach of textile manufacturers in developing nations. The expansion into dyeing and printing led to the increasing vertical integration of the larger firms.[1]

This period of rapid growth was accompanied by a relative calm between labor and management. This was due — both here and in other industrial districts of Italy — to the increased availability of labor,[2] the fragmentation of organized labor due to ideological divisions among trade unions, and productivity increases that enabled managers to pay wages higher than the minimums required by the centralized collective-bargaining system (154).[3]

By the late 1960s, technological developments had reached a high pitch as increasing demand spurred on investments of new equipment in all sectors of the industry. In printing firms, for example, the introduction of mechanized printing enabled one worker to do the work of two.[4] In weaving firms, the first high-speed looms that wove without the use of shuttles were introduced in 1964, and the initial problems of adapting these looms to the production of high-quality silk were overcome.[5] The mean number of employees per firm continued to decrease, as it had steadily done in the postwar years, and the productive output per worker continued to rise as the technology modernized. At the same time, investments in state-of-the-art technology increased firm owners' reliance on external financing. As a consequence, firms were carrying more debt than ever before.

In the midst of this intensification of reinvestment and firm expansion, conflict with organized labor increased. The technological advances enabling owners to decrease the size of the workforce and speed up the production process fanned the flames of labor-management conflict. The early 1970s brought frequent industry-wide strikes, factory shutdowns, and the closing of several firms, including a few of the oldest and largest in the industry. One firm owner described the period in these terms:

We decided to sell our dyeing factory because it had been taken over by the union. For those two or three years, I called our factory the Stalingrad of Como, because there was a very red climate. Things had really grown out of control after we hired a large number of unskilled workers from the south. It just got too turbulent, and one of the reasons we sold the factory was because we just couldn't manage it.

The counterstrategy adopted by firm owners was clear: decentralize production, thereby undercutting the unions' ability to organize workers, and regain management's control of the factory floor.

One of the reasons we founded the new firm was because of the situation with the union, because only in this way were we able to reduce the number of employees. The union was against this — during the years of union contestation it was not easy to manage the firm. The unions were at war with us.

During the 1970s the unions pushed forward the social struggle sometimes rightly, but they made it impossible to manage the firm. Now the decentralization of firms makes the industry more dynamic.

After undergoing six months of having our factory occupied by the workers, we decided to divide the work into a commercial firm and a separate production unit. This way the workers couldn't shut down the factory altogether. Since then we have divided the production into a number of smaller firms. You can have many firms under a single management.

We decided to stay small in our main plant and to give the bulk of our work to outside subcontractors, because we wanted to avoid union conflicts. When there are forty people who work for you it's like a big family, and eventually problems get resolved between us. On the other hand, when there are three hundred, people don't know each other and problems are more difficult to resolve.

These remarks by Como firm owners jibe with Piore and Sabel's account of management's reaction throughout Italy to the increasing political and legislative clout of labor in the early 1970s. In addition to freezing hiring and allowing the workforce to decline by attrition, firms decentralized work, sometimes setting up subcontracting firms that took over a phase of production or duplicated one or more phases done in the main firm. As a consequence, in Como as well as in other industrial regions, workers flowed steadily from large factories to smaller ones.

Decentralization had an additional advantage. It enabled owners to avoid the full brunt of national labor regulations that were passed to appease organized labor. The "disaster" that the labor movement brought to the industry was exacerbated, in the eyes of Como's firm owners, by the new labor regulations put in place after 1968. Owners viewed these regulations as placing unreasonable burdens and constraints on them. Decentralization brought some relief from these regulations. For example, in 1956 the Artisan Statute passed by the Christian Democratic government defined artisan enterprises on the basis of the numbers of employees rather than on type of activity (Weiss 1984; Blim 1990). An artisan firm needed to have a maximum of ten employees and ten apprentices. Artisan firms were granted tax concessions and lighter contributions for worker social insurance and family allowances.[6] As new labor regulations were passed in the 1970s, artisan firms were declared exempt from many of their provisions. This enabled them to avoid the higher payments of social-welfare benefits, to fire workers more easily, and to schedule work hours more flexibly (Piore and Sabel 1984, 228). Artisan firms paid only 80 percent of industrial employers' contributions to the state for the total worker compensation package, including pension, disability, and medical insurance (Blim 1990, 16).[7] In short, the increased power of organized labor, in particular its ability to enact national legislation favorable to workers, was a critical factor in firm owners' move to decentralize production in the 1970s.

Many small firms in Como have their origins in the larger firms' responses to the labor conflicts of the late 1960s and early 1970s — much as Piore and Sabel claim for Italian industrial manufacturing in general (1984, 226). But many others can be traced to earlier periods of the silk industry. All eight of the lower fraction firms in my sample who were solely subcontractors were founded before 1968, as were six out of seven of the subcontracting firms in the middle fraction (see table 4.1). While I cannot claim that my subsample of lower-fraction firms is representative of all small, subcontracting firms in the industry, there is ample historical evidence to back up this finding of the existence and viability of small subcontracting firms before the labor contestations of late 1960s and even long before the 1950s.[8]

Textile production in Como, in fact, has been dispersed among networks of small firms since the beginning of industrial manufacturing in the nineteenth century. This decentralized industrial structure was a continuation of silk production in an earlier, preindustrial period of mercantile capitalism, in which merchants coordinated production much as today's converters firms do. While there have been periods in which economies of scale and social and political forces have favored a move toward vertical integration, in other periods these forces have pulled in the opposite direction. Throughout this history, moreover, firms have relied on outworkers, some of whom worked as subcontractors using their own equipment, while others used equipment provided by the firm. In short, the "decentralization" that occurred in Como's silk industry during the 1970s was just the latest adjustment in an industry that has a long history of such flexibility. The national and international forces of political economy in the 1970s merely reinvigorated a decen-

TABLE 4.1
Date of "Founding" of Firm by Fraction ($N = 38$)

	Upper	Middle	Lower
before 1900	Barbieri (1898)	Locatelli (1908)	
1900–16	Molteni (1902)		
1911–20			
1921–30	Segalini (1920)	Bortolotti (1923)	Randazzo (1926)*
	Cesana (1921)	Galbiati (1925)	Prandi (1927)*
		Scotti (1928)*	
1931–40	Seregni (1935)	Marangoni (1930s)	Bogliasco (1931)
	Pezzi (1934)	Ghirardi (1931)	Sala (1935)*
		Colli (1938)*	Origgi (1935)
		Rossetti (1939)*	
1941–50	Bianchi (1945)	Bernini (1947)*	Santi (1950)*
	Corti (1945)		
1951–60		Camisasca (1952)	Cesana (1950s)
		Breva (1952)*	Galimberti (1955)
		Chiesa (1954)*	Martinelli (1959)*
		Bardelli (1957)	
		Giussani (1966)	
		Ravizzini (1966)	
1960–70	Cattaneo (1966)	Cappellini (1962)	Pedretti (1965)*
		Casati (1969)*	Galbusera (1966)*
		Fumagalli (1970)	
Total	9	18	11

*subcontracting firms

tralized system of production that had long been fueled by family capitalism.

The fact that this dispersed system of production has long characterized the industrial manufacturing of silk renders the term *decentralization* misleading in the case of Como, implying as it does that an industry that had once been centralized became dispersed. The same can be said about describing the industry as "fragmented." In addition, both these terms imply that a deviation from some norm has occurred. While it is true that in the 1970s many of the larger firms hived off various phases of production and sent them out to subcontractors, they were able to do this quickly by drawing on the manufacturing services of already existing small specialized firms in the industry. In other words, the 1960s labor conflicts and the more stringent labor regulations that

TABLE 4.2
Previous Work of Founders of Subcontracting Firms (N = 15)

Name of Firm	Employee of Firm in Same Sector	Employee of Firm in Allied Sector	No Prior Work in Industry
Colli		X	
Scotti	X		
Casati	X		
Rossetti	X		
Breva	X		
Chiesa		X	
Bernini			X
Randazzo			X
Sala	X		
Cesana		X	
Prandi	X		
Galbusera	X		
Martinelli	X		
Santi	X		
Pedretti	X		
Total	10	3	2

were enacted in the 1970s strengthened the small firm sector that had long been a vital part of the industry. It did not create it; nor was this sector "accidentally" discovered. As Weiss (1984, 230) concluded in her study of the impact of state assistance on small business in Italy, the greatest upsurge of small entrepreneurship occurred *during* the heyday of Italy's economic miracle rather than after the period of labor conflict.

The existence of these small, specialized firms alongside larger, more vertically integrated firms meant that owners of the latter in Como did not have to set up their factory foremen and managers as subcontractors, as did the larger firms in Prato. Accordingly, the career histories of the owners of subcontracting firms in Como do not reveal the kinds of alliances with former employees that Piore and Sabel describe for Prato. Table 4.2 shows that ten out of fifteen of the founders of subcontracting firms in my sample had worked as an employee of a firm in the same sector before opening their own firms and three more had been employees of firms in another sector of the industry. Although several of these subcontractors had some help from other firms in starting their own businesses, these were not their former employers. Instead, the help came from firms that needed their services or from equipment manufacturers that stood to gain from the purchase or lease of equipment.

The long-standing existence of Como's decentralized industrial structure provided an extensive network of subcontracting firms, as well as

vertically integrated firms, in which ambitious young technicians could
gain entry-level jobs and practical training that would prepare them for
the day when they might open their own firms. The transformation of
some employees into the owners of subcontracting firms was a well-
established pattern of upward mobility in the industry. Indeed, this was
as an integral part of the process of continual reproduction of this industrial service sector. It also resulted in a widely recognized phenomenon: the metamorphosis of employees (*dipendenti*) into competitors (*concorrenti*). This brings me back to the topic of betrayal.

From *Dipendenti* to *Concorrenti*

Many owners of subcontracting firms started their careers working as
skilled technicians or technical directors in other subcontracting firms,
usually with the clear intention of learning the firm's techniques. Giu-
seppe Sala, who owned a very successful photoengraving firm, admitted
that he had worked for six different firms before initiating his own,
precisely so that he could steal their techniques. When he was hired in
his first job, he knew nothing about the photoengraving process, but
shortly after he began attending design school in the evenings. After
four years, he moved to another firm because he wanted to acquire a
wider range of techniques before opening his own firm.

Signor Sala's strategy of on-the-job training enabled him to learn the
production techniques in a newly developing sector of the industry, in
this case photoengraving. Similar strategies were employed by others to
gain practical knowledge of established techniques in older sectors of
the industry. Mauro Prandi, the founder of Torcitura Seta Galli, was an
example of the latter. For eighteen years, Prandi directed the Italian
division of a Lyon textile firm. Having learned what he needed from the
French firm about this early phase of production—the twisting of raw
silk in preparation for weaving—Signor Prandi collaborated with a Milanese silk merchant in 1927 to open a silk thread–twisting firm that
eventually became a competitor of the French firm.

The thin line between on-the-job training and industrial espionage is
widely recognized in the industry. It reinforces an owner's disinclination
to place nonfamily members in upper-level managerial and technical positions. Yet when enterprising employees leave to open a competing
firm, sometimes taking both clients and technical knowledge with them,
their actions are much less likely to be condemned as a form of betrayal
if they are not relatives of the owner. After all, that is what Como entrepreneurs say one should expect of the nonrelatives one employs. Relatives are another matter: they are both more loyal and more disloyal. It

takes an expectation of trust and a history of collaboration of the sort one has with family and kin to lead to true betrayal.

Parenti, Serpenti

Stamperia Scotti and Stamperia Casati were two firms linked by such a history. We stumbled across them by sheer ethnographic serendipity. The discovery of their kinship connection and their linked histories led me to the realization that in Como *parenti, serpenti* (relatives, snakes) was linked to another pair of social identities: *dipendenti, concorrenti* (employees, competitors) In other words, just as relatives can turn into snakes, so employees can turn into competitors.

Stamperia Scotti

In 1928, at the age of twenty-three, Piercarlo Scotti, whose father had himself worked as a skilled technician in the industry, started a printing firm with two partners. The three of them had previously worked together as technicians in a printing firm that had gone bankrupt. Like many such small subcontracting firms, they began with the most meager equipment and workforce: two printing tables and four workers: Piercarlo, his wife-to-be Lucia, and the two partners.

Piercarlo and Lucia married in 1932, and after the births of a daughter and a son in 1934 and 1942, Lucia stopped working in the firm. During World War II, the partnership dissolved, and Piercarlo became the sole owner of the firm. From 1948 to the late 1960s, a large number of relatives worked in the firm (see fig. 4.1). These included: Piercarlo's older brother, who worked in the firm for fifteen years as manager of the warehouse; Piercarlo's younger sister, who worked for twenty years in the shipping department, until 1965; Piercarlo's older brother's two sons (the older one worked in the firm for ten years in a quasi-managerial role; his younger brother worked for six years on the shop floor); Piercarlo's wife's brother, who headed the finishing department; Piercarlo's wife's brother's son, who started as a technician and then became a technical director of one of the departments of the firm before leaving the firm; and Piercarlo's wife's sister's two sons, who likewise started out as technicians and later became technical directors before they left.

Until the mid-1960s, the family managers in the firm included not only the owner and general manager, but the directors of the various departments and the shop foremen. After he left the firm, one of the five nephews who had been such a director started his own printing firm;

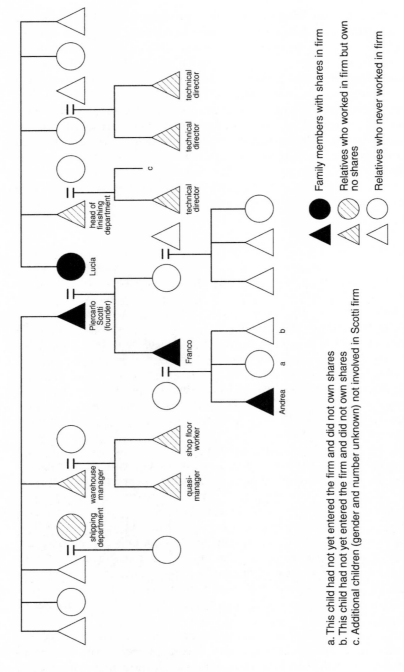

a. This child had not yet entered the firm and did not own shares
b. This child had not yet entered the firm and did not own shares
c. Additional children (gender and number unknown) not involved in Scotti firm

FIG. 4.1. Relatives Involved in the Scotti Firm

three others became directors of other printing firms. The timing of their departure from the firm was clearly tied to the succession of Piercarlo's son Franco to the headship of the firm. Franco began working in the firm in 1960 at age seventeen, while he was studying for his degree in chemical dyeing at the Setificio. As he began to take over the management, his uncles and cousins began leaving. Whether they were pushed out or left of their own accord is unclear, but Franco made it clear that he had been happy to see them go. He was, it will be recalled, the son who felt that his father's trust in their employee-relatives had been ill founded and that their long knives had been revealed only after they left the firm.

Stamperia Casati

The second firm, Stamperia Casati, was founded forty years later, in 1969, by Pietro Casati—a man who, from our first encounter, struck me as the model of an efficient, rational manager. Perhaps it was his careful but straightforward style and his calm openness, which contrasted with the more flamboyant and unpolished style of many of the other owners of subcontracting firms, that led me to identify him as an example of the "new entrepreneur." On the other hand, it might have been his impressive career mobility. As the son of a technical director who himself first worked as a technical director, Signor Casati had rapidly developed a small subcontracting firm into a diversified network of subcontracting firms, in each of which he owned a controlling interest. In addition to his printing firm, he was a partner in a converter firm, a dyeing firm, a second printing firm, and a clothing manufacturing firm.

Signor Casati explained that he had studied at the local silk-industry technical school, and then went on to get his *laurea* at a nearby university. From 1958 to 1969, he worked in the firm of his father's sister's husband, starting as a technician and eventually being promoted to technical director of the firm. In 1969 he started his own firm in a small town just outside Como. The firm was owned entirely by Pietro, his wife, and his younger brother. His father helped out during the firm's earlier years, as he had just retired from his position as head of the finishing department in his sister's husband's firm—the same one in which Pietro had worked.

When I asked Pietro why he had decided to start his own firm, he answered:

> I understood that in the firm I was directing I couldn't go forward. I opened my own firm more for moral satisfaction than for material reward, at the beginning. The owner of the firm where I worked was

my uncle—the husband of my father's sister. In a short time, I had become director of this firm; from 1960 I was director. I left to start my own firm because my uncle and I had different views, although we have retained a good relationship. Now his son manages this firm. It's one of the best printing firms in all of Como, Stamperia Scotti. Just before I decided to start my own firm, my cousin—my uncle's son—had begun to take over the management of the firm and very soon we found ourselves in competition for its direction; and seeing that we both had very strong characters . . .

The revelation that Signor Casati was one of the relatives who had worked with a concealed knife in Stamperia Scotti was a somewhat disorienting experience. I was taken aback at having inadvertently stumbled upon Franco Scotti's cousin, as well as by the dissonance between the image Franco had conjured up of an armed, sinister relative and my impression of his cousin. Despite these contrasting images, the histories recounted by the two men ran closely parallel, the only difference being that Signor Casati claimed that he had risen to the post of general technical director of the firm before leaving it, whereas his cousin described him as director of only one of the departments.

The early years of these subcontracting firms conform, at first glance, to what one would expect of small manufacturers whose survival has been said to rely on "self-exploitation" (Piore and Sabel 1984, 228). But closer scrutiny of their capital, labor, and management histories reveals that the "self" whose long hours and low remuneration were relied upon to survive included more than the firm owner. They usually also included wives and relatives. The labor investments of these workers in the initial period of the firm's development were crucial because of the low level of initial capital investment. Thus, despite firm owners' suspicions and fears of betrayal by relatives, many small firms relied on their labor in their early years.

The capital that former employees had to invest in their firms was very limited. It came, for the most part, from their own savings and from small loans from relatives and business associates. Bank loans were used for later expansion, the acquisition of land, and technological renovation, but rarely for the startup of firms. In a few cases, loans came from clients who were expected to comprise a majority of the subcontracting firm's business. Antonio Galbusera, for example, was able to start his weaving firm with very little capital in 1966 because he rented a large warehouse and leased looms from a textile equipment firm. Fourteen years later, he was approached by a client who needed to be supplied with a particular kind of fabric for five years. Galbusera did not have the capital to invest in a sufficient number of looms to fill the production needs of this client, so the client bought the looms and rented them to him. Over the next two years, by operating the looms day and night, Galbusera gradually was able to pay for them.

Relatives also made up a significant part of the firm's workforce in its early years. As in the case of Stamperia Scotti, it was common for a wide range of relatives—both consanguineal and affinal, both matrilateral and patrilateral—to work in the firm. Nine of the fifteen subcontracting firms in my sample employed relatives, especially during the early years of the firm. For example, in the firm founded by Federico Segalini (see fig. 4.2), his younger sister worked as an *orditrice*—the worker who prepares the warp—in the firm. Five daughters of Federico's brothers were also employed in the firm—four of them as outworkers with looms in their own homes and one as a secretary. Another nephew became a subcontractor for the firm, using looms supplied by the firm, which were placed in a warehouse owned by the nephew. The daughter of a niece was employed as a receptionist. Finally, Federico's wife's sister kept the firm's accounts for over forty years.

Just as the owners of more highly capitalized firms tend to downplay the capital investments of relatives (see chapter 2), so the owners of subcontracting firms tend to downplay the labor investments of relatives. This tendency became apparent to me only over the course of my interviews with other family members, who often mentioned relatives whom owners had failed to tell us about. The owners' forgetfulness appeared to be linked to their preference for a narrative of individual achievement rather than one of collective investment. It also appeared linked to owners' ambivalence about involving relatives outside the immediate family in the firm. In spite of this ambivalence, owners recognized the advantages of employing relatives. Relatives increased the labor flexibility of the firm because they could be asked to work extra hours when needed. One could not ask the same of other employees, especially given the stringent labor laws of the Italian state, without incurring high labor costs. Relatives also made possible a more flexible division of labor and management, because owners felt they could trust them with management and administrative tasks.[9] Finally, relatives who worked on the shop floor were expected to set an example of work discipline and quality standards for other workers. In short, according to some owners of small subcontracting firms, employing relatives increased both labor flexibility and management control.

At the same time, the disadvantages of employing relatives were also clear to firm owners. Every one of the advantages mentioned above had its down side. Relatives might be trusted with more important tasks and be willing to be more flexible in their schedules, but they also had to be paid more. They might be more interested in the success of the firm, but one had to be especially careful to avoid offending them. It was more difficult to criticize their work and very difficult to fire them. Several

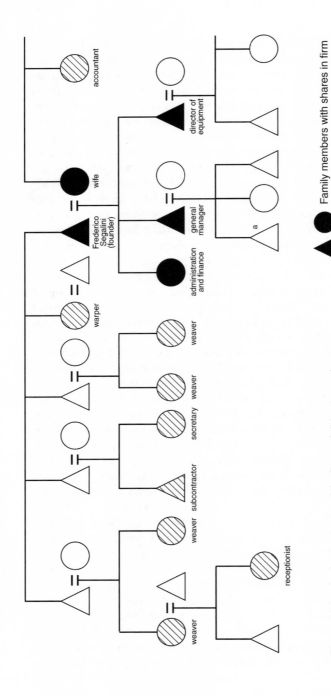

a. These children had not yet entered the firm and did not own shares

FIG. 4.2. Relatives Involved in the Segalini Firm

firm owners claimed that they had been aware of these disadvantages but had hired relatives against their better judgment to please their wives or siblings. They recounted how this had led eventually to problems or disasters. The ultimate disaster entailed relatives leaving to open competing firms, taking substantial numbers of clients with them.

Finally, although owners did not put it in these terms, there was the fraught issue of the ambiguous boundary between family and relatives. As we shall see later in this chapter and in chapter 5, relatives are both in the family and not in the family. Their ambiguous status is mirrored in their ambiguous claims to the firm. Between owners' expectations that relatives will do more for the firm because of the bond of kinship and their statements that relatives working in the firm are "only employees" who are no different from other workers is a gray zone of contested claims and potentially contentious disputes.

Competition and Collaboration

Owners of subcontracting firms frequently complain about the difficulty of surviving in the face of competition from smaller firms who willingly engage in a level of "self-exploitation" that they consider unreasonable and even uncivilized. These complaints are most strongly voiced by entrepreneurs in those sectors in which the least amounts of capital are needed to start up a firm. Signora Viganò, the owner of a photoengraving firm, explained that it is difficult to survive in this sector not only because of the unpredictability of fashion and, therefore, the fluctuating demand for printed fabric, but because there are so many smaller photoengraving firms who will do the work for less money. Her son Angelo chimed in that tiny family firms consisting of just a married couple and their children who are willing to work long hours for small profits are cropping up all the time.

The irony of these complaints is that those who make them are often the very same firm owners who farm work out to small household production units in order to increase their flexibility of response to fluctuating markets and to minimize their payment of benefits required by the state. The Viganò family firm, for example, had always employed outworkers. In 1988, in addition to the seventeen employees working at their plant, they drew on the services of fifteen to twenty *lucidi esterni* — design tracers who worked at home. In order for the Viganò firm to retain the advantages of being a small artisan firm, these outworkers were registered as subcontracting artisan firms themselves. The majority of these firms consisted of one or two members of a family (mostly women) working at home.

Some subcontracting firms do 75 to 90 percent of their work for a

single client, making them entirely dependent on them. Most have ambitions of freeing themselves from this dependency by broadening their
clientele. It is widely considered "suicidal" to have only one client, both
because this makes one extremely vulnerable to market fluctuations and
because this reduces the bargaining power of the subcontractor in negotiations with the client over the costs of his services. The ideal among
Como subcontractors is to follow the path taken by the Prato subcontracting firms that Piore and Sabel claim were able to break their
dependence on the big firms during the 1970s. In modifying their products to suit the needs of other manufacturers in addition to their main
client, these firms apparently were able to collaborate with other small
firms to make more and more diverse products (Piore and Sabel 1984,
222). A few successful Como subcontractors like Signor Casati have
succeeded in accomplishing this. By expanding the range of services he
offered his clients, Casati had gone from printing fabric according to
the designs they gave him to offering his clients designs for fabrics and
the clothing styles for which they might be useful. Having expanded his
services to include those of a converter firm, Casati had been able to
increase his list of clients to include clothing manufacturers as well as
converters. Consequently, no client made up more than 15 percent of
his firm's sales.

Successful subcontractors like Signor Casati strive to move from providing a service to other firms to controlling the sale of their own products, thereby increasing their profit margin and broadening their clientele. For a weaving firm, this means moving from weaving particular
kinds of fabric ordered by converters or larger firms to selling their
fabric directly to clothing manufacturers and fabric wholesalers. A
firm's ability to do this rests on its success at developing the commercial
arm of the firm in order to deal directly with clients — both domestic
and foreign. Signor Casati's success at this was directly related to his
skill in building partnerships to invest in allied firms, including a converter firm that sold fabric printed by his firm, Stamperia Casati, as well
as fabric printed by other firms. Two young cousins we interviewed who
were taking over their fathers' photoengraving firm had similar hopes of
opening a printing firm and a retail outlet that would produce and sell
their own designs. Whether they had Signor Casati's business acumen
remained to be seen.

Pietro Casati's path of upward mobility in the industry was far from
common. Success stories like his are the exceptions that affirm the possibility of such mobility and, at the same time, warn of its unlikelihood.
Formidable constraints must be overcome for such a transformation to
take place. These include not only limitations of capital and knowledge,
but structural constraints deriving from the very same features of a decentralized industry that make firm mobility possible. For one, expan-

sion into a neighboring sector of production may be blocked because it would bring a firm into direct competition with its own clients. The cousins in the photoengraving firm, for example, were acutely aware that if they began to print their own fabric, they might be accused of stealing the designs of their own clients. Even if they could avoid such suspicions by printing designs that were clearly different from those of their clients, they would potentially be in competition with them for sales to wholesalers, converters, and clothing manufacturers.[10]

These constraints suggest a less rosy picture of mutual collaboration than that painted by Piore and Sabel (1984) and Sabel (1982, 225) of the willingness of firms in Italy's industrial networks to help each other expand their productive capacities.[11] Although he is well aware of the intense competition between the small firms in these industrial networks, Sabel argues that they are overcome by incentives for sharing knowledge.

> Each firm is jealous of its autonomy, overly proud of its capacities, but fully conscious that its success and its very survival are linked to the collective efforts of the community to which it belongs and whose prosperity it must defend. (1982, 225)

> One kind of dependence on related firms is implicit in the firm's innovative activity. At first the firm's comparative advantage derives from intense specialization. The disadvantage of this concentration of attention is that it distracts attention from all the others. The moment the firm begins to expand and move beyond its original specialty it finds itself dependent on the help of neighbors with complementary kinds of specialties; and because the neighbors can never exactly anticipate when they too will need assistance, the help is forthcoming. (225)

The owners of Como's firms had a rather different assessment of the extent of mutual assistance and collaboration among firms in the silk industry. Those who owned large- and middle-sized firms complained about the widespread unwillingness of Como entrepreneurs to share information or collaborate in developing products, innovative techniques, or industry-wide infrastructures. They characterized the local entrepreneurial culture as "closed," attributing this to the "provincialism" of Como itself. Those owners who had been officers in the Italian Silk Manufacturers Association — a national-level organization whose membership was predominantly from Como — decried the "conservative," "provincial" mentality of Como, they claimed impeded the development of effective industry-wide initiatives.

Sebastiani Molteni, one of the brothers managing one of Como's largest firms, complained bitterly of the difficulty of getting other firm owners to collaborate on joint ventures. The first was their failure to support attempts to develop a local business school to teach workers the kinds of skills Signor Molteni felt were needed to keep the industry abreast of the latest developments in marketing and information technology. The second was the difficulty he had confronted trying to convince other firms of the usefulness of sharing credit-rating information on clients. Finally, he complained of the jealousy and resentment his family firm had incurred when they acquired the brand name of a firm that was about to disappear. They had done so because they felt it would be detrimental for the industry as a whole to lose such a famous brand name. As a result, however, they had come under great criticism from others in the industry. Apparently, the latter would have been happy to see a competitor disappear. Only one other family — another of the wealthiest bourgeois families in the industry to whom the Molteni were related by marriage — was supportive; all the others were jealous.

> The mentality of Como is closed. Como is a valley and its mentality is the same. Perhaps it has to do with being in a closed city. The attitude of Comaschi is a passive conservatism. The most reticent are the converters.

Signor Molteni's complaints, like those of other owners of large, vertically integrated firms, were unsurprising, given that converters are their main competitors. Converters rely on and reinforce decentralization of the industry — for without it they would not be able to draw on subcontracting firms that compete to offer the best service at the lowest price. But large and middle-sized firms rely on them as well. Hence, the demand for the services of subcontracting firms by larger firms invigorates the very sector that the owners of the latter criticize for their provincialism.

The large- and middle-sized firm owners' characterization of the small firm sector as "closed" was affirmed by the owners of small firms themselves. Most of them admitted to being very closemouthed — indeed, they prided themselves in this — about their techniques and production process and their dealings with clients, even to the extent of not revealing who their clients were. They claimed a studied indifference to what other firms in their sector were doing, appearing eager to dispel any notion that they were concerned about "other people's business."

Signor Casati, the upwardly mobile owner of Stamperia Casati, echoed the criticisms of the larger firm owners. He too complained of the lack of cooperation among firms, specifically the firms in his sector of printing. Unlike the wealthier firm owners, however, Signor Casati attributed this lack of cooperation to the family character of the firms. Middle-level firm owners like Attilio Bortolotti, on the other hand, conceded that Como entrepreneurs are very "closed," but also argued that because Como is located on the border of the country, its entrepreneurs have always had a knack for dealing with the outside world. Bartolotti's firm was situated in the middle of the hierarchy, and he articulated a middle position: Como's firms may be "closed" but they are not "provincial."

The uneven commitment to collaboration and sharing of technical knowledge among firms in Como is paralleled by an uneven commitment to innovation. Firm owners specializing in the twisting of fibers (*torcitura*) were the least interested in innovation. Owners of these firms claimed that the standard production process left little room for innovation or creativity.

> There is nothing new to invent in our sector. We have to stay abreast of the times to be competitive and we have to do a good job, not just have good ideas. Our products are not in the camp of technological innovation. Our sector has tradition. (Virgilio Prandi, the owner of a twisting firm)

Similarly, some subcontracting weaving firms filled orders for standard types of fabric that did not allow much room for innovation. Indeed, their clients wanted fabric produced precisely as they had ordered it, without variation. Dependent as they were on their clients, these subcontractors were apprehensive about effecting any changes other than those that decreased production time or increased efficiency and reliability. Cristina Galbusera, the daughter of one such subcontractor, who had hopes of one day taking over her father's firm, complained about her father's unwillingness to innovate and take risks:

> I would be more open to innovation than my father; I would change what we produce even though it isn't easy. I would move toward other fabrics that are used in high fashion. Of course you have to have good collaborators and financial investors. . . . I have had some offers to form a partnership with a firm that would help us do this, but my father said no, so I had to abandon this idea completely. . . . My father is apprehensive; he worries a lot. He has always resisted any changes that bring risk. Once he gets going with a type of production that he knows will do well in the current market, he won't change anything. He is afraid of any risk and wants security.

At the same time, she admitted that their position as a subcontracting weaving firm made innovation quite difficult.

> We produce a very standard type of fabric, so we can't really be very innovative because the equipment is pretty set. There really isn't much margin for change.

Cristina's father, in contrast, was the consummate spokesman for the values assigned the highest priority by subcontractors: precision, quality, and timeliness. Responding to our question about the reasons for the success of his firm, Signor Galbusera explained,

> The two most important things are to be precise and to deliver your orders on time. Our clients call me "the only German in Como," because I am so precise and punctual.

Specialization and small size, according to these subcontractors, enhance the control of labor, which in turn assures quality. Piercarlo Venturini, owner of one of the smallest firms in my sample, explained in response to the same question about the reasons for the success of his firm:

> I work exclusively with silk and I don't have any interest in any other fabric. I became convinced of this when the industry went through its crisis. Those who had diversified too much had to close because of the costs of growth and their inexperience. Instead, small size guarantees direct control. From 1965 to the present my firm has grown, self-financed at each step, but I have always had it in mind not to go beyond a certain size — a human size. My success comes from understanding what clients want and assuring them good service. What comes first is quality, then filling orders on time, and then price.

Tight control of the labor process by means of direct surveillance and supervision brings with it the paternalistic management style that Blim describes in his study of small firms in the Marche region. This entails a combination of "authoritarian and personal, informal and intrusive" management in which the employer is "both padre and padrone — both fatherly in the paternalistic sense and commanding in the tradition of the old sharecropping landlord" (1990, 146).

Small subcontracting firm owners like Signor Galbusera affirmed their commitment to this management style:

> In our firm it's not like there is a boss, in some absolute sense. It's not that there is the owner and the workers, but there is the entrepreneur and the collaborators. We don't have any union members, not a single one. I haven't heard a single employee complain about pay or ask for a union vote. . . . That's why I say that the success of a firm is not just a result of the entrepreneur — well, it may be 70 percent that. But the remaining 30 percent is made up of other things: the employees who help, who do good work. If there is some problem, we resolve it together.

According to Signor Galbusera, more important than the amount of pay is treating workers with respect and praising them. He claimed that he did not depersonalize his workers or treat them like numbers, as did other firms. In accordance with his attempts to humanize his relations with workers, he practiced what he called a "personal method" of hiring workers.

> Instead of giving them a test of their intelligence or personality, like many other firms, I see this as treating them like a number. I have a personal method that almost no one else uses — or maybe a lot of them use it, I don't know. I ask the local priest about information on the family of potential employees. If he or she is from a good family, with good moral standards, I don't care if they don't have experience, they will learn. There can be exceptions — a black beast born inside a good family — but these are rare cases.

Such detailed knowledge of workers' families, their political orientations, and their work skills and capacities, as Blim notes, gives employers "a powerful lever for gaining control over their labor forces" (1990, 146).

Small firm owners commonly expressed pride in having excellent relations with their workers and of being free of union conflict or, in the case of Signor Galbusera, free of unions entirely. A couple of them claimed proudly that they had never fired a single worker, even when they could have legally done so. Signor Venturini, from whom we will shortly hear in greater detail, operated a cafeteria (*mensa*) for his workers on the factory premises and ate lunch with them regularly because he felt that eating together promoted a sense of community. He directed the dining hall manager to place wine and water bottles on the table so that each worker could take as much as he or she wanted, rather than being limited to the skimpy glasses served in most company dining halls. Because he also wanted to familiarize the workers with fine dining so they would not feel intimidated if they found themselves at a formal dinner, he insisted that the table be set correctly, with a fruit plate, a second fork, and all the other accouterments of a "proper" table.

One firm "value" that subcontractors did not discuss, not surprisingly, is the evasion of fiscal responsibility through the failure to fully report the work of employees. Given reports of the widespread use in Italy of *lavoro nero* (unreported labor) — itself only a part of the *economia sommersa* (underground economy), which some estimates place at 25 percent of the nation's gross domestic product (Blim 1990, 162) — it seems likely that such practices exist among small subcontracting firms as well as larger firms in Como. To what extent is difficult to know, nor did I ask owners about this sensitive topic. While it may not be as crucial to the profit structure of Como's silk industry as Blim (1990, 162) claims it is to the small-scale producers of San Lorenzo Marche, I suspect that it is widespread.[12]

The perspective of proprietors of small subcontracting firms was colorfully articulated by Piercarlo Venturini, the previously mentioned owner of the dyeing firm Pedretti. Signor Venturini was introduced in chapter 2, where he was cited as an example of an owner whose official firm history overlooked the complex configuration of family collaboration and investment entailed in the creation of the firm. It will be recalled that because Signor Venturini had never married and had no siblings or other kin working in the firm, I had initially mistakenly identified Pedretti as one of the few firms in the industry that could not be considered a family firm. Signor Venturini touted the virtues of small, specialized firms that brought a more human dimension to the production process. Expansion for him risked both losing direct control of production and also losing the "human dimension" of work.

> I believe in choosing a plan and sticking to it. In my case, I chose to dye only silk — no artificial fiber. I believe in specialization. I intend to maintain the same small size and the same emphasis on high-quality silk dyeing. Small firms are more flexible, both in terms of personnel and in terms of adaptation to the market.

His motto of "*piccolo è bello*" (small is beautiful) was part of what he called his "existential philosophy."

> I think it's always important to have one chicken on the table. When I have ten or fifteen or twenty of them, I can't eat them all and I don't know what to do with them.

Signor Venturini's "one chicken on the table" strategy makes sense in light of the constraints faced by most small subcontractors. Not only are they constantly struggling to keep costs down and quality up in the face of intense competition from other small firms, but both their limited capital and their structural location make attempts at expansion into other sectors of the industry very risky. A safer alternative to expansion is to reinvest profits in technological renovation.

Hitting the Kinship Glass Ceiling

Constraints on expansion face the second generation in subcontracting firms from the moment they begin working in their fathers' firms. As they draw close to the end of their schooling, which usually takes the form of a degree from the local technical school specializing in silk production, most sons, and an increasing number of daughters, begin working in the firm. Whereas before the war children started working in the family firm after they had completed middle school at around the age of sixteen, those who did so in the mid-1980s generally waited until they were eighteen. Many worked side by side with employees — filling a role between workers and management — both working in production on the shop floor and overseeing the work of others.

Where brothers are partners in small subcontracting firms, the entry of their sons is constrained by the limited productive resources of the firm. While several sons might work in the firm, each brother can be succeeded as co-owner-manager by only one son. Even this often strains the productive capacity of most firms. The two Martinelli brothers who operated a photoengraving firm were in this precise position. Each had a son who had begun working in the firm, preparing to take over his father's technical specialty. Anxiety over the likely division of the firm, were it unable to survive the transition to the next generation, was evident in the articles of incorporation of the firm. When the firm became a *società in nome collettivo*,[13] the brothers who were partners in the firm stipulated that neither could initiate a business in the same sector that might compete with the firm nor could they participate as a partner in any other competing firm.

The fears embedded in these stipulations do not come out of nowhere. They arise from the predictable, if not inevitable, break between brothers who are partners in a firm. That *fratelli Marazzi* are likely to become ex-*fratelli* is common knowledge. As brothers' sons enter the firm, tensions and conflicts begin to mount. Competition may emerge between the cousins as to which one shows greater promise as director of the firm. The son of one brother who is considerably older than his cousins may consolidate control over management before the latter have even entered the firm. When the younger cousins finally begin working in the firm, their challenge to their older cousin's authority can lead to an intense struggle over management and ownership. It is at this point that family conflict erupts, resulting in either the division of the firm or the departure of relatives who have been working in the firm but do not own a majority of the shares. The sloughing off of relatives is an emotionally wrenching process, especially as during its course men often turn their backs on their brothers in order to endow their sons with the firm. The outcome is the estrangement of brothers.

At times this break occurs even when there are no competing nephews in the second generation. The Galbusera firm is an example of such a case, in which a nephew took over his uncle's firm but only with considerable family bitterness. Antonio's father (Pino) and his father's brother (Ezio) opened this weaving firm together when they were in their twenties. When Pino died suddenly at the age of twenty-nine, Antonio and his mother, who was only twenty-two years old, were living with Pino's parents. Pino and Ezio had also been partners in a fabric store, and upon Pino's death, Ezio bought out the shares Antonio had inherited from Pino.

Ezio eventually passed ownership of the fabric store on to his son, who had no interest in working in the weaving firm. While Antonio was attending the Setificio, Ezio got him a job in one of the larger weaving firms, where Antonio worked until moving to his uncle's firm. It is significant that Antonio made this move in the year that his paternal grandfather died.

In 1963, Antonio married, and shortly after he and his wife had twin daughters. At this point, he decided he was not earning enough in his uncle's firm and began searching for another job. After he left, his uncle could not keep the firm going and closed it. Antonio and his wife, who was working as the head of payroll in a furniture firm, decided to take over the firm. Ezio would not give it to Antonio because he blamed him for the firm's decline. Antonio was able to obtain loans from his mother's sister and his wife's sister to take over the firm. After that, Antonio rarely saw his paternal kin whom, it will be recalled, he likened to snakes.

A variation of the estrangement of uncles and nephews that had emerged more recently is the estrangement of uncles and nieces. With daughters increasingly taking up management roles in firms, fathers were increasingly having to chose between their brothers and their daughters. Signor Casati, for example, who had brought his younger brother into his firm as a manager, found himself with an ambitious daughter who fully expected to take over the firm. The potential for conflict was evident only three years after Elisabetta Casati had started working in the firm. While her father had described his younger brother as a minor partner in the firm, Elisabetta made it clear to us that he did not really count and that the firm belonged to her father. This made her the unambiguous successor to the directorship of the firm. The looming conflict between Elisabetta and her uncle to which this would likely lead was illustrated by what had happened in the firm Bardelli e Fratelli.

The converter firm Bardelli e Fratelli was founded in 1950 by Armando Bardelli as an individually owned firm (*ditta individuale*). The Bardelli family had been bread and pasta makers for seven generations. Signor Bardelli's father made the first mechanical pasta maker and had a factory in which he employed 120 workers. World War II disrupted the business, and in its aftermath the family was left with nothing. As a consequence, Armando had to seek work elsewhere. He took several jobs, including working for a year as the director of personnel in a gambling casino. It was there that he claimed to have earned the money to open his firm. When gambling casinos were outlawed, he staked his claim in a converter firm. Five years after opening the firm, Armando was joined by his two brothers. Once the brothers had begun working in the firm with Armando, the firm's legal status was changed from a *ditta individuale* to a *società in nome collettivo*. The division of management was worked out so that in 1985, Armando was the general manager and his remaining brother was in charge of the dyeing factory and the acquisition and sale of goods. According to the Camera di Commercio file, in 1972 Armando owned 68 percent of the shares and his brothers respectively owned 25 percent (Achille) and 7 percent (Agostino). The distribution of ownership remained constant until Agostino left in 1982 to open a store. At that point, Agostino sold his shares to Armando, leaving the latter with 75 percent and Achille with 25 percent.

All three of Armando's children attended the Setificio, but none of them finished. The eldest, Giulia, started working in the firm as a designer when she was twenty-one years old. The second daughter, Patricia, also entered at the age of twenty-one, and the son entered at the age of twenty. Giulia quickly established herself as the leader among the siblings and the most ambitious. At the age of twenty-five — only four years after she had entered the firm — Giulia opened her own converter firm. She explained to us that she had done so to force her father to chose between her and his brother, whom she considered incompetent and a burden on the firm. She felt that her father was unable to see this because of his affection for his brother. Faced with the prospect of alienating his daughter or alienating his brother, Signor Bardelli chose to do the latter. Within five years, Giulia had succeeded in driving her uncle out of the firm and taking control of management for herself and her siblings. Her uncle left to start a clothing firm with his own daughter. Giulia declared that she had not seen him since he had left the firm and had no interest in doing so.

There are rare exceptions to this process of the sloughing off of relatives and the consolidation of ownership and control by lineal descendants of the owner. The one case in my sample where this had occurred was telling in its kinship idiosyncracies — a cousin who had worked as the technical director of a small subcontracting firm for years was made co-owner with the owner's widow, who had no children. The printing firm of Stamperia Cesana was founded as a dyeing and weaving firm in 1955 by Massimo Cesana and a partner. As the firm grew it divided and the other partner broke off, leaving Cesana as the sole heir in 1960. Cesana's cousins (his mother's sister's son), Angelo Cassina and his sister, who had already been working in the firm before Cesana became the sole owner, continued as a technician and clerk in administration, respectively. In 1966, Signor Cesana married Anna De Michele, who never worked in the firm. The couple had no children, and seven years later Signor Cesana died, leaving behind an ambiguous will. In it, he left half the firm to Cassina and half to his wife. It was not clear, however, whether he intended to distribute the fixed property of the firm, including its machinery and factory, in the same manner.

A copy of the will left by Signor Cesana was included in the firm's

Camera di Commercio file. It was dated four years before Signor Cesana's death and read:

> Being of sound mind, I annul all other wills and in this one name as my heir my wife Signora De Michele Anna in Cesana. As regards the exercise of the printing firm that I own, I leave half to my wife and half to my cousin Signor Cassina Angelo.

For five years, the ownership of the firm remained up in the air until an agreement was reached that Cassina and the widow should be equal partners in the firm. Without the factory, the firm would be unviable, and Cassina convinced them that the factory had been erroneously included among the property transferred solely to Anna De Michele. To rectify this, a new declaration was made in which the factory and the land were included among the property of the firm, which was divided equally between Cassina and the widow. Cassina became the manager of the firm, and the widow's younger brother was brought in to represent her half share in the firm. The younger brother had studied law and had no previous experience in the industry, but he was chosen by his family to help his sister because he was the only one of six siblings who, at the time, did not have a conflicting commitment and was considered the closest to his sister. In return, his sister transferred 20 percent of her share (10 percent of the firm) to him.

A case such as this is the exception that illustrates the rule that relatives do not rise above the kinship glass ceiling to succeed to the headship of firms in Como. What from the perspective of a kinship analysis are predictable outcomes of a system of patrifilial succession and inheritance are experienced by the siblings, uncles, aunts, nephews, and cousins who are sloughed off as a form of betrayal. In the process, the "self-exploitation" of the family is reconceptualized as a form of kin exploitation by those who suddenly find themselves cast outside it. Whether they leave the firm before or after the next generation of their relatives have consolidated their control over it, these ex-employees — many of whom consider themselves ex-relatives — take with them not financial capital, but technical and managerial knowledge. In addition, they take social capital in the form of contacts and collaborative relations with clients. In other words, they leave endowed with the primary means of production of subcontracting firms.

Relatives, of course, are not the only employees who leave firms with crucial means of production in hand. Nonrelatives who have worked for the firm as technical managers do as well. But relatives tend to be identified as members of the owning family and, as such, they absorb the goodwill and trust of clients more than do nonrelatives. This makes them both more valuable and more dangerous.

Independence, Betrayal, and the Generation of Firms

The continual exodus of skilled and industry-wise technical managers, both relatives and nonrelatives, from subcontracting firms generates a constant supply of potential founders of new subcontracting firms in Como. This process is integral to replenishing the pool of start-up firms, only some of which will thrive and survive. Spurring on the continual generation of new firms is both the demand for their services by larger firms and the gendered sentiments and desires that motivate Como entrepreneurs — predominantly men — to be their own bosses. Like the artisans in the Marche region (Blim 1990) who value the freedom of self-employment, these men are strongly committed to reaping the fruits of their own labor. Their drive to open their own firms demonstrates how employees' desires for economic independence — which in the 1960s incited workers' demands and strikes — can lead to the pursuit of projects that are themselves forms of capitalist action. In other words, the same sentiments and desires that incite workers' resistance to capitalist relations of production can, under the right conditions, operate as productive forces for the generation of new capitalist firms. Combined with the larger firms' reliance on subcontracting firms — a reliance itself created in part by workers' resistance to capitalist labor discipline — this pursuit of independence reproduces capitalist relations of production.

The desire to open one's own firm and, in doing so, to be one's own boss does not arise out of a religiously based ethic of ceaseless striving for accumulation. Neither is it the expression of a "rational" economic strategy dictated by Como entrepreneurs' habitus. Rather, it is the activation of a gendered ethic of personhood and family in particular circumstances. Its specifically masculine ethic of capitalism is reflected in the fact that the former employees who start up firms are almost all men. Women, with rare exception, do not initiate firms. Those who head them have succeeded fathers or husbands who founded or themselves inherited firms.

The generation of new firms by former employees who then become the competitors of small- and medium-sized subcontracting firms heightens people's sensitivities to trust and betrayal. Among subcontractors, trust and betrayal in the family and the firm are inextricably tied up with issues of control over technical knowledge and client relations, which constitute their primary means of production. To put it another way, for lower- and lower-middle fraction bourgeois families with limited financial capital, trust and betrayal are inherent aspects of the struggles over relations of production — that is, over people's power to use or exploit a force of production and to exclude others from doing so. These struggles are especially fraught because the owners of subcontracting firms exploit a force of production that challenges the conventional Marxist distinction between two types of forces of production: the means of production and labor power. In a Marxist scheme, the former (means of production) includes raw materials, tools, and technologies, while the latter (labor power) entails the mental and physical capabilities that human beings exercise in transforming raw materials into products through the use of tools, technology, and knowledge. The practical technical knowledge that is crucial to the success of subcontracting firms straddles the boundary between these two forces of production. Practical technical knowledge integrates both labor power (mental and physical capabilities) and means of production (technology). Betrayal occurs when a former employee transforms what his employer treated as the former into the latter.

Rather than characterize trust and betrayal as contrasting moral commitments and forms of social action that lead, in one instance, to continuing family solidarity and, in the other, to the breakdown of this solidarity, I recognize both as integral aspects of the recurring process through which new family firms are generated and the industry regenerated. The notion that trust makes families while betrayal destroys them stems from a moral tale of human social action that obscures the processes through which trust develops over time into betrayal among Italian capitalist families and betrayal, in turn, generates new collectivities of trust.

❦

CHAPTER FIVE

CAPITAL AND GENDERED SENTIMENTS

Andreina Balzaretti leaned out the window of the top floor of the three-story building that housed her family home and motioned for me to come up by way of the stairway on the far right. I was relieved that I had come through the right gate and would be able to park my car inside the courtyard, since the house was on one of the more bustling commercial streets of central Como. As I had entered the narrow driveway, I spoke to a woman with a small child who showed me where to leave the car. I found out later that she was the wife of one of Signora Balzaretti's younger brothers—one of the three of six brothers who had not gone to work in the family firm. I encountered another of these brothers—an attorney—as I was leaving the building, which housed the families of all three younger brothers, who, unlike their three older brothers, did not work in the firm. In addition to their older sister' family, their widowed mother also lived in the building (see fig. 5.1).

Signora Balzaretti was one of the first women I interviewed when, in the ninth month of my first year of research in Como, I finally felt I could ask the firm owners I had been interviewing if I could meet with their mother, sister, or wife. Although I had interviewed women man-

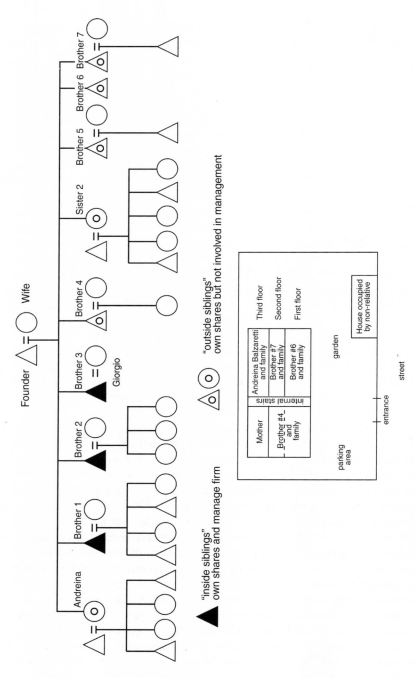

Fig. 5.1. Galbiati Family Residence

agers of firms and others who worked with their fathers and brothers, I had not yet interviewed female family members who were not directly involved in the management of the firm. I had been concerned that male heads of firms would be uneasy and even suspicious of my interest in interviewing the women in their families, and, indeed, many of them responded as expected. Yet for every head of firm who explained that such an interview would not be possible because his mother, sister, or wife was on vacation, too busy taking care of the family, or knew nothing that would be of use for my study, there was another who appeared to have no reservations about my talking to the women in their family. Giorgio Galbiati was among the latter, and, like most of the women we contacted, his sister Andreina Balzaretti readily consented to be interviewed.

As I climbed the stairway of the building, I could not help but notice its contrast to the elegant, smartly decorated small villa that Giorgio Galbiati and his wife occupied on the outskirts of Como. As I was soon to learn from Signora Balzaretti, the rundown condition of the stairway and the exterior of the building was an apt metonym of the state of the family. The apartment itself in which Signora Balzaretti and her husband, a professor of chemistry at a university in Milan, lived with their four children, on the other hand, was very comfortable, though modestly furnished.

Giuliana Balzaretti herself was attired in a manner that declared her lack of fashion pretensions. She had a way of bending forward when she spoke that was at the same time attentive and meek. I began to understand why she had seemed rather abrupt and almost gruff on the telephone, even though she had expressed a willingness to be interviewed. She struck me as someone who felt awkward and ill-confident in social situations and who, consequently, might give the impression of being unfriendly. Once we began talking, beginning with my questions about her parents and family history, she grew increasingly relaxed and expressive. By the end of the interview she was confiding information about the tensions and conflicts in the family that I had suspected but had not expected her to discuss so candidly.

We moved quickly through the standard family information I had been collecting from both firm owners and their family members — dates of births, marriages, and deaths; educational levels and careers — about which the women were much more well informed. (During several interviews, male firm owners had simply phoned their mothers during the interview to ask for this information.) We then moved on to Signora Balzaretti's educational history and her decision to pursue a career as a teacher. Like most women born in Como bourgeois families in the 1930s, Signora Balzaretti had never considered participating in the management of her father's textile firm. Nor did her parents consider this a possibility, even though, she claimed, they left her free to make her own decisions.

Neither she nor her sister, she explained, ever had any interest in the family business, and to this day they knew little about it.

I then asked whether her father's relation with the three older brothers, who worked in the firm, had been different from his relation with the younger three, who did not. Although my intention at the time was to find out about relations in the family when the siblings were children, Signora Balzaretti launched without hesitation into a detailed account of the turmoil that had erupted in the family since her father's death seven years earlier. I already knew from my interviews with Signora Balzaretti's brothers that of the eight siblings in the family, only the three eldest brothers had entered the firm. The three younger brothers had become professionals — one a doctor, the other a lawyer, and the third an engineer. The two sisters, of whom Signora Balzaretti was the eldest, were married to, respectively, a university professor and a businessman who was not in the silk industry.

The eldest brothers had begun working in the firm in the late 1950s, and during the 1960s and 1970s they had expanded tenfold the firm's productive capacity. By the early 1970s their father had handed management of the firm entirely over to them and had assumed a role of symbolic leadership. All this I learned from Giorgio Galbiati, who also told me that around 1965 his father began transferring some of his shares in the firm to the three eldest sons. In 1973, the father worked out a system to give Giorgio and his two brothers control of the entire firm. He had the firm's assets evaluated and divided this amount into eight equal parts, one for each of his children. He then "sold" the shares assigned to the children who had not entered the firm to the three eldest brothers. The "payment" for these shares was deferred, however, and all money remained in the firm, with the agreement that the other brothers and sisters would withdraw their money only after their father had died.

The "agreement," I soon came to realize, had been worked out exclusively between Signor Galbiati and his eldest sons. Signora Balzaretti and the rest of the siblings who did not work in the firm, to whom she referred as the "outside siblings," were not consulted or involved in any way in fashioning its terms. Indeed, they knew nothing about the agreement until shortly before their father died. In 1982, their father had called all of them to a family meeting in which he announced that he had transferred his shares to his eldest sons, and that upon his death these sons were obligated to compensate the other children for the latter's shares. The eldest sons were also to pay their mother a regular stipend. Signor Galbiati ended the meeting by urging the "outside siblings" not to withdraw their shares of the capital from the firm in the near future, because the firm would suffer. He outlined a plan in which his eldest sons would pay their younger siblings a fair interest rate for keeping their capital in the firm.

A year after the meeting, Signor Galbiati died, leaving no will and none of his instructions in writing. Confusion and disagreement as to the nature of the agreement quickly turned into an open breech when the eldest brothers informed their younger siblings that the firm could not afford to pay the promised interest that year. Signora Balzaretti and the other "outside siblings" were especially upset because they and their widowed mother had planned to use the first interest payments to renovate the family home, which, as I noted, was badly in need of repair. After her husband died, Signora Balzaretti began talking about her desire to repair and remodel the building, especially so that the two younger sons could bring their families to live there. One of her older sons had apparently given them the go-ahead since there would be enough money from the interest owed them to pay for the repairs. Later, however, Giorgio told them there was not enough money and that they would have to postpone the repairs.

There could not have been a more poignant sign of Signora Galbiati's desire to keep her family, including the "outside" siblings, together than this plan to renovate the family home. But her desire for family unity after her husband's death was thwarted by her elder sons' decision to use the money to strengthen the firm—a decision they made in the name of their vision of family unity and continuity. Anger turned to outrage when the "outside" siblings discovered that their mother had not been regularly receiving her stipend. This was especially difficult for them to accept in light of the fact that the elder brothers had invested in new equipment and had even bought out another firm—actions that the older brothers perceived to be necessary for the survival of the firm. Giorgio Galbiati, who had borne the onerous duty of conveying the bad news to his siblings, was convinced that his mother had incited some of them to protest, and subsequently refused to speak to her.

Signora Balzaretti explained that she and the other "outside" siblings had no intention of demanding that the firm be divided equally among all of them, and she acknowledged the years of work her older brothers had put into managing the firm. But, she said, as things stood at the moment, they were too unequal. What was especially troubling to her was the obvious inequality in wealth between the elder brothers and the rest of them. The former lived in plush, modern condominiums or small villas in the best residential areas on the outskirts of Como. Those outside the firm could not even afford to renovate their apartments in the old family home.

There was a second dimension to the inequality among siblings about which Signora Balzaretti was even more upset—namely, the increasingly noticeable inequality between the opportunities available to their respective children. In 1985, the children of the eldest brothers and sisters were in their late teens to mid-twenties, and most of them seemed destined for university degrees. But the equality of educational achievement among these cousins was not matched in other aspects of their lives, at least not according to Signora Balzaretti, who pointed out that her brothers' children had been given opportunities to study English in the United States while her children had not. Her sister was doing relatively well because her husband was a businessman, but because Signora Balzaretti's husband was a professor they were not as well off as her other siblings. Signora Balzaretti reported that this inequality among the grandchildren was also upsetting to her mother, who apparently had been the one to urge her husband to call the meeting laying forth the method by which the "outside siblings" would be compensated for keeping their shares in the firm.

Along with her younger brothers, Signora Balzaretti was dismayed by her father's failure to leave a will. She found it difficult to understand how a man as conscientious and scrupulous as her father could have left his affairs in such a mess. She said she had no intention of litigating the matter and was quick to point out that she had not consulted an attorney nor solicited the opinion of a notary public as to her inheritance rights. This disclaimer, of course, glossed over the fact that one of her younger brothers was an attorney. However, she did mention other "good Catholic families" in Como in which an equitable division of the patrimony had been worked out among siblings, only some of whom worked in the family firm.

Less than half a mile away in another neighborhood near Como's center, the family compound of the Barbieri family displayed the signs of the kind of family that Signora Balzaretti had in mind (see fig. 5.2). On the lot behind the original family home, Carlo Barbieri, who had taken over the firm founded by his father, had built a condominium in the 1960s to accommodate his growing family at a time when his children were starting to marry. The long driveway to the condominium was fenced off from the old family home, which had been sold to an unrelated family. In 1985, the condominium and an adjoining house that shared the same garden were home to Carlo Barbieri's widow, his son Mario's family, the families of two of his four daughters, and his never-married sister. It was this sister, Renata Barbieri, who I had come to interview at the suggestion of her nephew Mario, who felt confident that she would be able to fill in the details of the family history that he had been unable to provide.

A quick glance at Renata Barbieri's living room indicated that Mario was right. Prominently displayed throughout the room, on chests and shelves, were at least twenty framed photographs of family members which left little doubt that its occupant lived amidst a rich family life of baptisms, weddings, anniversaries, and birthday celebrations.[1] Combined with the elegant furnishings of what appeared to my untrained eye to be heirloom pieces that she had inherited from the parents she

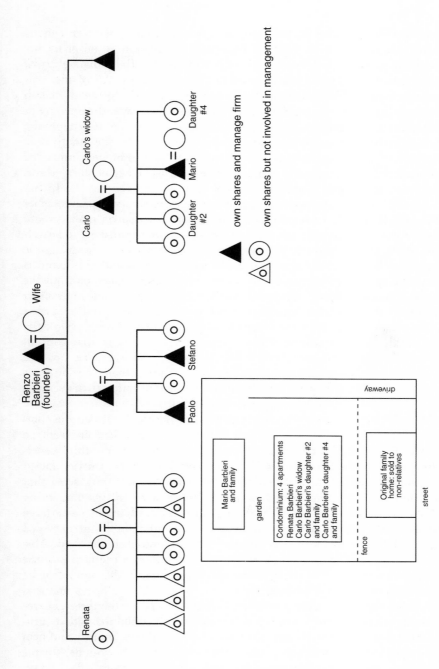

FIG. 5.2. Barbieri Family Residence

had lived with and cared for until their deaths, Renata Barbieri's living room announced her central role in the family. In spite of never having married, or perhaps because of it, she had become the female elder of the Barbieris and the repository of the family history. All of this was affirmed during the course of the interview, not only by what Renata told me but by the constant flow of family members who dropped by or telephoned that afternoon. Among these were the wives of two nephews, her brother's widow, and one of the nephews managing the family firm.

The family history Renata Barbieri provided complemented and added substance and sentiment to what I had gotten from her nephew Mario and the firm's fiftieth anniversary publication (see chapter 2). In her account, the poignant aspects of family events took center stage rather than being offstage incidents in a firm history focused on management succession, technological innovation, reinvestment, expansion, and diversification. Her youngest brother's death at the age of twenty from a fall in the mountains became more than an unpredicted demise that resulted in there being only two brothers to take on the firm management, but the heart-wrenching loss of a beloved brother in his golden youth. Her older brother's death when his eldest child was only six years old became a continued absence that she labored to make up for through her close friendship with his widow and sons rather than an event that concentrated the firm management in the hands of the only surviving brother. Untimely deaths became family tragedies, weddings became celebrations to cherish, and births good fortune to give thanks for rather than events in the anthropologist's developmental cycle of the family.

Reviewing this family history with Renata Barbieri revealed the complex configuration of business and family events that had enabled the Barbieris to beat the odds and survive the succession to the third generation. Without a doubt, having ample capital had been a major factor in the grandfather's ability to launch the firm initially on a scale that gave it a solid foundation and later enabled it to incorporate other phases of production. As we saw in chapter 2, the founder came from an upper bourgeois Milanese industrial capitalist family that provided him with both financial and social capital to establish the firm. This alone, however, could not, guarantee the continuity of the firm into the third, and possibly fourth, generation. The unpredictable unfolding of individual and collective biographies, in addition to the firm's financial success, was also crucial in enabling the family to pass the three-generation threshold. To put it simply, sufficient capital combined with a sufficiently small number of male successors facilitated family unity and firm continuity. The premature death of the youngest of the founder's three sons and the death of the eldest when his own sons were still children left the family with a sole male successor who managed the firm along with his father until the next generation took over. The succession by cousins whose relation was uncomplicated by a competition for leadership between their fathers, in turn, eased the transition to management by the third generation, which has been a stumbling block for many other capitalist families. The incorporation of the deceased brother's widow and family into the Barbieri family core strengthened the sentiments of unity and loyalty to the grandfather and founder, who was still alive when his grandsons began working in the firm. After her husband's death, the eldest son's widow and her two boys lived in a small house nearby the Barbieri family home and every evening came to have dinner with her parents-in-law and the remaining unmarried daughter, Renata. In short, the untimely death of his son placed the founder at the head of the family, with his relationship to a pair of his grandsons unmediated and unfettered by any intermediate filial authority.

The contrasting state of affairs in the families of Andreina Balzaretti and Renata Barbieri serves as a useful introduction to the range of variation in processes of capital and kinship that characterize the upper and middle fractions of Como's industrial families and the key factors and processes behind it. Some of these are more readily apparent than others. For example, Signora Balzaretti's marriage to a professor resulted in an all too common problem among entrepreneurial families in the middle fraction — it produced heirs with little prospect of succeeding to the management of either of their parents' family firms. Such children require the conversion of financial capital into cultural capital in the form of education and other markers of distinction in order to maintain their class status. These conversion strategies compete with those of their mother's brothers' children, who need the financial capital to reinvest in the firm in order to secure their class futures. Family disunity of the sort symbolized by the disrepair of the Galbiati family home is the predictable result. Renata Barbieri, on the other hand, had never left her father's family. She had no children and, consequently, no need to invest in her children's futures; hence, she could nurture both her brothers' children and transmit her shares in the firm to them. Like her brothers' untimely deaths, the fact that Renata's had never married decreased the potential for tensions among competing investments in the next generation. Other variations among the upper and middle fractions call for more sustained scrutiny.

Family/Firm Reproduction and Division among the Middle and Upper Bourgeoisie

This chapter focuses on processes of family and firm reproduction and division among the upper and middle fractions of the Como bourgeoisie. The negotiations and struggles over the concentration and dispersal of capital among these families parallel the negotiations and struggles

over the control and deployment of practical technical knowledge
among the lower and middle fraction subcontractors described in the
previous chapter. Among the upper and middle fractions, firms are generally started with investments from family, relatives, and associates.
This pooling of capital, which is simultaneously a strategy of capital
diversification, parallels the pooling of labor and technical knowledge
among the lower fraction. In the upper and middle fractions, however,
one family generally buys out the other investors over time and con-
solidates its control of the firm in order to develop it for the next
generation.

For families like that of the Barbieri in the upper fraction, processes
of family growth, maturation, and segmentation are at the same time
processes of the concentration and diversification of capital. Family segmentation entails the creation of new firms in allied sectors of the industry as opposed to the creation of competing firms in the same sector, as
it often does in the lower fraction, leading to family conflict and estrangement. The process of family maturation and segmentation among
the upper fraction is anticipated and managed by strategies of capital
diversification. This is not to say that upper fraction families are immune to conflicts and division. Struggles over capital and control of
family and firm management are invariably a part of these processes.
But these struggles are focused on the accumulation and dispersal of
financial capital rather than on the accumulation and control of technical knowledge and labor. Moreover, as we shall see, families with large
amounts of capital are able to postpone division of the patrimonial capital by investing in their heirs' enterprises or by paying sufficient interest
to them. The larger the patrimonial capital, the longer division can be
postponed. Family and firm segmentation is merely the interim step toward eventual division.

Families like the Galbiati in the middle fraction, however, lack sufficient capital to support this interim stage of family and firm segmentation. Not only are they unable to finance the business enterprises or
other money-earning careers of the third generation, but if there are a
large number of siblings in the second generation, the firm usually is
unable to sustain a livelihood for all of them. As a result, some siblings
manage the firm while others must pursue alternate careers or, in the
case of sisters, marriages that will sustain their class status. Over time,
the siblings who leave the firm forge strategies of class reproduction
that conflict with those of the siblings who succeed to the management
of the firm. The resulting clash of strategies between the "inside" siblings and the "outside" siblings becomes a crucial obstacle to both firm
reproduction and family unity. As the siblings who manage the firm
strive to accumulate capital and reinvest it in the firm for the future of

their children, the outside siblings, who wisely anticipate that their children will not succeed to the management of the firm, press for the distribution of capital to invest in their children's educations and careers. It is at this point that the tensions between the different class reproduction strategies of family members build into conflicts that divide the family, some of whom move into other fractions of the bourgeoisie.

The diverging processes of firm and family reproduction among the upper and middle fractions of Como's industrial bourgeoisie emerge out of shared sentiments of capital and kinship—among them, fathers' desires to pass the firm on to their sons. As we saw in chapter 3, fathers strive to endow their sons with the means of production that will be their means of independence from subordination to other men. Where there is more than one son, this process entails a division of labor between them. This division of labor in the management of the firm is both the first step toward the continuation of the firm in the next generation and the first step toward firm and family division.

The Fraternal Division of Management

A common pattern of the division of management labor among siblings—until recently, almost exclusively brothers—can be seen by following the Barbieri firm over two generations. When the elder brother, Bruno, was brought into the family firm in the late 1920s, his father trained him to be the general manager of the firm, introducing him the full range of the firm's operations. His younger brother, who entered the firm about six years later, was assigned the more restricted job of managing the commercial relations of the firm. Although the younger son eventually became the general manager after his older brother died unexpectedly, the father's initial plan was clear and reflected the general expectation of the times. Eldest brothers took over the general management, while younger brothers were set up to direct particular divisions of the firm, such as commercial relations or technical production. In the next generation, the management was shared by three male cousins instead of brothers, but the division of labor was organized along the same lines, with each taking over the respective functions of administrative, commercial, and technical management. The differentiation between their responsibilities became even more clear and formalized after the death of the second generation, but as in most firms, there were no written job descriptions. While each cousin had a distinct set of responsibilities, they all emphasized and lauded their ability to substitute for one another as a sign of the collective unity and integrated management of the firm. As one of the cousins put it,

The fundamental idea is that the members of the family have roles in the firm that are interdependent. Each has his own specialized work, but always knows what the others are doing so that we can avoid any crisis in the firm if one of us leaves, as was the case with Paolo [who died suddenly the year before]. This way the continuity of the firm is ensured.

The same plan was followed in the transition to the second generation of another of Como's largest firms, with the elder son taking over the general direction of the firm while the younger son handled commercial relations. This logic governed succession in the next generation, only in this case the management was divided among six sons of the eldest brother, as the younger brother had none. As each son entered the firm, he was introduced to a number of divisions and management roles and only over time settled into directing a specific area. By the mid-1980s, the six brothers had the following division of labor, starting from the eldest to the youngest:

Luca: general director
Matteo: technical director
Nicolò: director of fabric production for women's clothing
Andrea: director of finances and administration
Sebastiano: director of fabric production for ties
Dario: director of production of finished products (e.g., scarves)

Each brother had authority over his own sector, but major decisions were made by the administrative counsel, which consisted of the six brothers and their father, who was no longer involved in the daily management of the firm. Although the eldest brother was the general director, major decisions were made by majority vote of the administrative counsel, with the father voting only in the case of a tie. As the family owned and controlled several smaller firms in addition to the main one, each had by law its own administrative counsel, headed by one of the brothers. However, the main firm constituted the effective holding company of the smaller firms, and its administrative counsel provided the collective management for all of them. This collective management extended to decisions such as the brothers' salaries, which had been set at the same amount — except that those under forty years of age received a little less.

By the early 1970s, some upper fraction firms began to involve daughters as well as sons in management, especially where there was a shortage of sons. The division of management again followed a similar logic, except that brothers — whether older or younger — were generally designated as the successor to the father and assigned the role of general director, while their sisters were put in charge of specific divisions. In the Cattaneo weaving firm, the only son was put in charge of financing and general management, while each of his three sisters managed one of the following sections of the firm: fabric for women's clothing, fabric for ties, and foreign sales. By assigning his only son the general management of the firm, the father clearly indicated his plan that his son succeed him as the head of the firm. The sisters appeared to have questioned this decision, however; since they had a larger collective share of the firm, by the late 1990s they had taken over the general management. As a result, their brother left to take over another firm.

Although financing, investment, and administration were generally reserved for one of the siblings, any one of these management functions could be delegated to a hired manager in large firms. Indeed, even in firms where there were several siblings heading divisions, there were often hired managers heading others. For example, a vertically integrated firm might have hired a director to manage its printing or weaving division. Technical direction, in particular, tended to be assigned to hired managers, especially because in upper fraction families, the children's university educations had not provided them with technical training. A university degree in economics, business, or languages tended to lead toward general administration, financing, and commercial sales, although sons who had studied engineering could handle the technical direction.

The division of management among brothers and sisters in family firms of the middle fraction were similar, with the only exception being that brothers often took charge of the technical direction rather than leaving it to hired managers. The relative importance of technical expertise to the success of middle fraction firms — positioned as they are between the larger capital resources of the upper fraction and the reliance on technical knowledge of the lower fraction — led fathers to send sons for technical training, whether at the local technical school or at the university, where they majored in engineering or chemistry. In the late 1980s, sons in middle fraction firms were increasingly pursuing training in computers and information science and subsequently being put to work computerizing production and accounts, whereas hired directors were filling these functions in the upper fraction firms. The do-it-yourself ethos of the lower fraction firms, with their emphasis on tight control of technical expertise and the production process, was evident as well in middle fraction firms — which combined this ethos with the value placed on creativity, design, and administrative innovation among the upper fraction.

The importance of technical expertise and innovation in the middle fraction is also reflected in their willingness to include sons-in-law into the firm management — an openness not found among the upper fractions. The strict boundaries between the family as a property owning collectivity and in-laws as excluded from holding shares in the firm are unambiguously clear in the upper fraction. Sons-in-law or daughters-in-law, no matter how accomplished or skilled, are not considered candidates for firm management. Among the middle fraction, however, there were several firms in which daughters' husbands had been given management roles, including that of general manager. In particular, sons-in-law with technical expertise had been made technical directors of middle fraction firms. As one middle fraction firm owner put it, if you have only daughters, the best solution is to have her marry a capable technician.

Daughters: From Dowry to Shares

Although she never married, Renata Barbieri received the kind of education that distinguished the daughters of the upper fraction of Como's bourgeoisie from those of lower fractions and qualified them as suitable marriage partners for men of their class. In 1923, after she graduated from a *liceo classico* — a college preparatory high school — Renata's parents sent her to an exclusive Catholic college in France for a year. She and her sister then went on to finishing school in London for ten months. Fluency in other European languages was to become of practical use for later cohorts of daughters, but Renata's study at colleges in France, Switzerland, or England was not tied to any expectation of work in the family business. Nor were these studies abroad ever intended to lead to a university degree or professional training. Rather, it was to provide her with a "modern" European education — in other words, to equip her with the cultural capital to make her a marriageable young woman of the upper bourgeoisie of Como. According to Renata, her parents were a bit ahead of their time, because sending daughters to study abroad was considered almost too modern in the early 1920s. By the 1930s, however, it was a standard practice among this fraction of the bourgeoisie.

The study of languages and literature continued to be the norm for Renata's brothers' daughters who were born between 1939 and 1947, except that they continued their studies beyond *liceo classico* at Italian universities rather than at finishing schools abroad. While their brothers and male cousins studied economics, business, or engineering in preparation to manage the firm, the women of these cohorts, who came of age in the 1950s and 1960s, majored in languages or literature. Like their father, Renata's brothers strongly encouraged their daughters to study languages and even sent them to spend summers in England and France. As one of the daughters pointed out, being sent off alone to a language program abroad was a striking contrast to their school year in Como, when they were never allowed to go out alone or even with friends. Like their aunt Renata, her nieces did not pursue their language studies with the idea that it would be useful in the firm.

The expectation that a daughter would work in the firm simply did not exist. Renata's nephew, Mario Barbieri, characterized this gender norm as a family tradition:

> The tradition that has continued to the third generation has been that only the men in the family would enter the firm, because in each generation there have been men capable of managing the firm. The women did not work in the firm, and if there had been a shortage of men, we would have hired people outside the family. Today it is different, but still among my generation there is an unwritten preference for males to take over the firm, and the women know that this is our tradition. This isn't to say that women cannot enter the firm, but the tradition still has not been broken. There isn't room for all [in the firm], and we instinctively look to the males.

Mario left little doubt that he would prefer to see the tradition of male succession to management continue in the next generation. Managing the firm, he offered, is a very burdensome job and, consequently, more suitable work for a man. He hoped that his own daughters would pursue work outside the firm. At the same time, he was aware that not all his nieces agreed with him.

The eldest daughter of one of Mario's cousins, who had recently graduated with a degree in economics and was working for a financial firm in Milan, did indeed have different ideas. When asked whether she had thought about working in the family firm, she replied that the firm was not particularly stimulating professionally and that Como was too provincial. But she also made it clear that she resented not having been given the opportunity to enter the family firm.

> It is not that I never thought of it, but that no one ever offered me the opportunity. I didn't choose it; they don't want me to enter the firm. It was a family decision; they have never let anyone who doesn't have the surname enter the firm; for them the surname is important. And only the men have worked in the firm.

She also rejected out of hand the idea of accepting the role that a couple of her aunts had been given, of managing a retail outlet for the firm. Running a store was, for her, a waste of her talents and a matter entirely different from managing a manufacturing firm. As we shall see shortly, this was a widespread sentiment among many of the young women in the upper fraction of the Como bourgeoisie, and some had acted on it and moved into management positions in their fathers' firms.

The educational and career expectations of daughters in the middle fraction of the Como bourgeoisie evolved in parallel during this period, although predictably with slightly lower levels of educational distinction. Whereas Andreina Balzaretti's father's sister had been a housewife who never worked in the family firm or attained more than a middle-school education, Andreina became a teacher—one of the few respectable jobs a bourgeois woman could hold in the late 1950s and early 1960s. Like the daughters of the upper fraction, many of her peers studied languages and felt little inclination, nor were they invited, to enter the family firm. By the late 1960s, however, some daughters of middle fraction families were being urged to study at the local technical high school or even the university to prepare for work in the family firm. In contrast to daughters in the lower fraction families, whose formal education had commonly been cut short after middle school so that they could work in the firm—often on the shop floor with the other employees—until they married and had children, these middle fraction daughters were being brought into management and trained as potential successors to their fathers.

Women's educational histories until the mid-to-late 1960s conformed to the expectation held by all fractions of the Como bourgeoisie that daughters marry and become part of their husbands' families. Given that status, the only way a daughter of the upper fraction could remain a member of her natal family was not to marry. This is precisely what Renata Barbieri did. In middle and lower fraction families, daughters had the additional option of marrying a man with technical skills that could be put to good use in the family firm. By recruiting a husband who was a *bravo tecnico* into the family firm, these daughters strengthened their claims on family membership despite being married (see the case of the Franchini family, discussed in chapter 2). In the upper fraction, however, sharp boundaries drawn around the family as a property owning unit precluded the incorporation of even technically and managerially skilled sons-in-law. Exceptions were made only when there were no sons, but, even then, son-in-law managers were merely an interim strategy toward succession by a grandson (see the case of the Seregni firm in chapter 3).

If bourgeois daughters were expected to, and usually did, leave their natal families upon marriage, how then did families deal with their claims to inheritance? After all, as will be discussed in the section to follow on Italian inheritance law, equal division of the patrimony has been the law, if not the practice, since the imposition of the Napoleonic code on northern Italy in 1808. The answer is that fathers and brothers in propertied families in northern Italy kept, until recently, the patrimony—despite daughters' legal rights to inheritance—by a variety of strategies. In Como, the common practice was for fathers to give daughters their share of the inheritance in the form of a dowry or other pre-mortem payments, including real estate. As was seen in chapter two, upper and middle fraction parents frequently invested in their sons-in-law's firms (see Table 2.2, which shows that this was true of five of nine upper fraction firms and six of eighteen middle fraction firms).

It is highly unlikely that these premortem payments came close to the portion of the patrimony due these daughters. But daughters hardly had the resources, either political or material, to enforce their legal rights. Propertied men, whether landed aristocracy or bourgeoisie, after all, shared an interest in male inheritance and female dowry; and every daughter's husband was also a father's son. Daughters also had some stake in the undivided strength of their natal patrimony, for fathers and brothers were their only refuge from a failed marriage. Moreover, the continuing success of a woman's natal family was a source of symbolic capital that enhanced her position both in relation to her husband and in the community at large. As we shall see in the section to follow, until recently daughters could not count on much help from their mothers in getting their legal share of the patrimony.

Settling daughters' claims to the patrimony with a dowry waned after World War II, and by the 1960s fathers and brothers were instead paying them lump sums or giving them shares in the firm. In the latter case, the sisters often passed these on to their children. If and when sisters or their children cashed in on these shares depended on several factors, including the number of sisters, the earning capacity of the firm, and its capital assets. The earning capacity of upper fraction firms made it attractive for sisters to hold on to their shares rather than sell them to their brothers. At the same time, their brothers often had sufficient liquid capital to buy out their sisters' shares.

What was feasible for upper fraction families was not, however, for those in the middle fraction. Fathers and sons in these families did not have enough liquid capital to buy out their daughters and sisters. All their capital was tied up in the firm. Moreover, daughters' marriages tended to coincide with sons' entrance into the firm. During this period, fathers and sons needed all the firm's capital assets and profits to finance the expansion and technological modernization necessary to develop the firm for the next generation. Hence, the "agreement" Signor Galbiati and his sons had made with the "outside" brothers and sisters to postpone payment of their shares was a common strategy to postpone the division of the firm's capital and finance the transition to the next generation.

At the same time, however, this strategy required giving daughters shares in the family firm. Thus, in their effort to concentrate ownership and control of the firm in the hands of their sons, fathers turned their daughters into shareholders who were not actively involved in the management of the firm but who were actively interested in it as an interest-bearing enterprise. If their brothers were unable to produce sufficient profits to satisfy their income needs, the sisters could sell their shares. Most family firms had set up contractual agreements that gave family members the right of first refusal in the sale of shares. If the brothers did not have sufficient liquid capital to buy out their sisters, however, the latter could insist on liquidating their shares and bankrupt the firm. Thus, what fathers passed on to their sons along with the firm were sisters who were a constant threat to capital accumulation and rein- vestment — in other words to their brothers' means of production and independence.[2]

Daughters: From Shareholders to Managers

By the late 1980s it was evident that the family "tradition" of bringing only sons into the firm, which was articulated by Mario Barbieri and others of his generation, was becoming increasingly difficult to sustain. The strain on bourgeois practices of male succession and inheritance came from changing gender norms that began to affect families in all classes in the 1960s.

This transformation was evident first in the decline in fertility and family size in Italy. By the late 1980s, Italy had a total fertility rate of fewer than 1.2 children per woman, the lowest in the world after Spain (Perez and Livi-Bacci 1992). Lamentations about the decline in fertility were common in the popular media, and it was also a frequent focus of academic investigations (Golini 1994; Palomba 1995). Of course, the birthrate in Italy had already begun declining at the end of the nine- teenth century (Cipolla 1965, 583), a century later than in France but a few decades later than other western European countries, and a few decades earlier than other Mediterranean states (Livi-Bacci 1977, 3). Once it began to decline, it did so quite rapidly. From Unification to the 1890s the rate was constant at about 36 per thousand. After World War I, it fell to 30, then to 20 after World War II, and to 18 in the 1950s (Livi-Bacci 1977, 50–51).[3] In the north, in particular in the region of Lombardy, the birthrate and marital fertility were significantly below the national average and less than half that in the south (see Livi-Bacci 1977, 62–63). In general, the most substantial decline in rates through- out the north took place between 1911 and 1931 (Livi-Bacci 1977, 287). But a sense of crisis and the realization that a significant social transformation was occurring became all the more heightened in the context of the post-1960s labor and women's movements.

By the late 1960s, the Italian women's movement was openly chal- lenging gender inequality and the state policies that codified it (Birn- baum 1986; Bono and Kemp 1991; Kemp and Bono 1993). The revi- sions in family law that accompanied the legalization of divorce in 1975 both reflected and reinforced this shift in family and gender norms and practices in Italy. The causal dynamics among these shifts in gender norms, legal policies, demography, and economy will no doubt continue to be debated for a long time, but their interrelation in this period of intense political conflict seems indisputable. The long and the short of their cumulative impact was that by the 1980s bourgeois daughters were no longer willing to settle for less than their legal share of the patrimony. An increasing number of them expected not only an equal share of the inheritance, but equal control of the family firm. At the same time, many fathers, finding themselves without sons as a result of decreased family size, were becoming less resistant to the thought of being succeeded by a daughter.

The early signs of this transformation in Como's upper fraction bourgeois families were manifest in the mid-to-late 1960s in the form of concessions that fathers made to their daughters. Among these was granting them a management role in some sector of the family business, although not its core manufacturing activity. Often this meant that daughters were brought into the firm to oversee marketing or foreign sales—a task for which their studies of European languages had prepared them. Sometimes daughters were put in charge of the fashion-related aspects of the firm, including preparing fabric designs that would be shown to potential buyers in clothing manufacturing. In a few families, this entailed creating firms to assist in selling the main firm's products.

Carlo Barbieri, for one, set up his two daughters in a business to sell fabric produced by the family's factory along with ready-to-wear clothing and other items. The daughters began managing a small retail outlet while they were completing their university studies, working only on Saturdays and one weekday. Over the next twenty years the business expanded to include four outlets that employed ten clerks. Unlike the allied firms that were often set up for sons as a first step in a process of diversification and eventual division of the family firm, the retail business managed by the sisters was an appendage of the family firm. Although it could conceivably have led to the family's expansion of their business into an adjacent sector or the industry, it did not. Whether this was because it was not successful enough to stand on its own or whether it was never intended to is difficult to ascertain.[4] The fact that the retail firm was owned by the main firm and not by the sisters themselves argues for the latter explanation. Moreover, although the sisters managed the day-to-day operations of the firm, the firm was legally under the direction of their male cousin who headed the main firm. As I discovered in my interview with her, one of the sisters was not even sure who were the legal owners of the firm. I later found out from the Camera di Commercio files that it was the family corporation as a whole.

Inclusion of daughters in the management of the firm's core productive activity was rare. While fathers and brothers were willing to concede that women could manage sectors linked to fashion, design, and
sales, industrial manufacturing was considered a male domain. There
were, however, notable exceptions to this rule. The Cattaneo sisters
were one of these. Like the Barbieri sisters, the three Cattaneo sisters
had begun to work in their father's firm in the 1960s as they were
completing their university educations. But rather than setting them up
in a retail outlet, their father had placed each of them at the head of a
division of the weaving firm, much as other fathers had done with sons.
Although he put his only son in charge of the general direction of the
firm, his daughters were well informed about the firm's finances and
management. The siblings and their father had monthly business meet-
ings at which all important decisions were discussed and made jointly.
During the period in which they were raising young children, the sisters
appeared willing to concede the role of general director to their brother,
although at least one of them hinted that she had misgivings about the
traditional gender hierarchy. As did other women managers of Como
firms, she drew on dominant gender stereotypes to argue for women's
capacity to manage firms, including "natural" female sensibilities and
insights about design, fashion, and human relations. When I asked her
whether she thought there were some areas of management that were
more suited to men or women, she replied:

> I would say that in managing the firm, handling problems with work-
> ers is a task that is well-suited for men, while the development of
> fabric collections, sales, and relations with clients are better handled
> by women.

Combined with her other comments, she appeared to concede a fairly
narrow sphere to male competence. By the late 1990s, the three sisters
had taken over the general management of the firm and, not surprisingly, their brother had left to open a new one. The sisters then
hired a male manager to oversee production.

Demographic shifts worked along with changing gender expectations
to place daughters in management positions previously reserved for
sons or nephews. By the 1980s, the cohort of children that had been
born into the smaller sibships of the 1960s were coming of age and
were ready to be groomed to succeed their fathers. Given a reduced
sibship size, many of them lacked males. This left fathers with the
choices of hiring a nonrelative manager — perceived as the first step toward eventually selling the firm — grooming a nephew as successor, or
turning to their daughters. Faced with these options, an increasing number of firm owners began to revise their gender expectations or at least
to suspend them in an effort to give daughters a chance to prove them-

selves. A significant number of daughters were being trained in their fathers' firms in the 1980s. Not all of them found the work to their liking, and the rate of attrition among daughters appeared to be higher than among sons.[5] But again, there were notable exceptions, and by the 1990s a few of the most successful and visible firms in the industry were headed by daughters.

Succession and inheritance in both the middle and lower fractions of Como's silk-manufacturing families were also affected by these cultural and social shifts. As far as inheritance was concerned, daughters in both the middle and lower fractions were as influenced as those in the upper fraction by the increasing calls for gender equality by the women's movement. But a significant difference emerged between the fractions in the ways in which changing gender ideology shaped management succession. Simply put, the more central that practical technological expertise was to the success of a firm, the less likely it was that a daughter would succeed her father as director. As we saw in the previous chapter, in contrast to the larger upper fractions firms in which design, financing, and marketing as well as industrial manufacturing were crucial to the firm's success, small subcontracting firms in the lower fraction are more specialized in a phase of production. Because they compete with other small firms to provide these services to larger firms, their competitive advantage is based on quality, cost, and reliability. Firms in the middle fraction fall between the upper and middle fractions in requiring technical knowledge for effective firm management. Although gender ideologies and expectations were changing in all fractions, the widespread perception that technical expertise is a male skill made it more difficult for daughters to take over middle and lower fraction firms. In comparison to women's growing insistence on gender equality in inheritance, gender conventions continued to shape educational choices, and few women pursued technical training. Sons in the lower and middle fractions were still much more likely to enroll in the local technical school or to major in engineering or chemistry at the university than were daughters (see table 3.3). Even when daughters attended the technical school they tended to focus on design and other nonindustrial aspects of silk production. Hence, daughters in middle and lower fraction bourgeois families were at a distinct disadvantage in qualifying as successors to their fathers' firms.

A case in point was the Casati printing firm. Starting a small subcontracting firm in the late 1960s, Pietro Casati had successfully combined his technical and marketing skills to become the printer of high-quality fabrics for prestigious designers such as Ferre and Armani. In 1973, about the same time that he constructed a new plant, he brought his younger brother, who had studied at the local technical school, into the firm as a partner. Signor Casati and his wife had three daughters, all

born in the 1960s. By the mid-1980s, when the eldest of these was
twenty years old, he expanded his holdings by becoming a partner in
several firms in allied sectors of the industry. Among these were a second printing firm, a converter firm that sold fabric for women's wear —
80 percent of which was produced by his own printing firm — and a
firm that manufactured clothing. The latter two firms moved him closer
to the market and into a sector where design and marketing skills were
more important than technical expertise in manufacturing.

When we first interviewed Signor Casati's eldest daughter, Elisabetta,
in 1985, she was enthusiastic about working with her father. She made
it clear that she wanted to eventually take over management of his business, including the printing firm, with her younger sisters. Three years
later, however, she was no longer at the printing firm. Instead, she was
working at the clothing firm. She explained,

> I worked there [at the printing firm] for six months, but unfortu-
> nately the work was a job for a man — really technical and also be-
> cause of the relations with the workers. Anyway, it didn't suit my
> character.

At the clothing firm, she worked with a designer her father had hired to
help her put together fashion collections. Rather than dealing with techniques of printing and the management of a mostly male workforce, she
spent most of her time interacting with the firm's clients, who were
clothing wholesalers and retailers. Although this required a great deal of
traveling, since the majority of their sales were to other European countries, she was comfortable doing this. Her younger sister had begun
working in the converter firm, but the youngest sister was studying at
the local technical school. Whether one of these sisters would eventually
manage the family's printing firm or whether their father's younger
brother would direct it while they took over the marketing firm remained to be seen.

Mothers: From *in* the Family to *of* the Family

Like their daughters, mothers in upper and middle bourgeois families
have been, until quite recently, *in* the family but not full members *of* it. I
mean by this that because of their limited ownership of family property,
mothers and daughters had limited control over both the family enterprise and other aspects of family life. In a familiar irony of gender inequality, mothers had less control over the very activities that were defined as "female" domains, because they were excluded from "male"
domains.

The exceptions to this norm of gender hierarchy are telling. They include wives who owned substantial shares of the family business. These shares usually had been inherited from fathers who had made investments in their sons-in-law's firms as a form of premortem settlement with their daughters. In some cases, the shares were purchased in the name of the daughter; in others, they were held by the father and then passed on to the daughter after his death. More than a dowry of real estate, ownership of shares in the family firm gave wives considerable power in upper bourgeois families. In contrast to wives who did not own substantial shares in the firm, those who did were better informed about the business and more frequently consulted about major decisions — not just regarding the firm but all areas of family life. In some cases, they played an active and visible role as comanagers of the family firm.

Elda Pezzi Mascheretti, who comanaged the firm G. Pezzi with her husband until their son took over, was a case in point. I discussed in chapter 2 the origin narrative of this converter and weaving firm. By tracking the firm's records in the Camera di Commercio, I showed that despite the father and son's narrative linking the firm to the Pezzi family's history in silk manufacturing, the mother's family's capital was crucial. It was his wife's parents' capital that enabled the firm's "founder," Guido Pezzi, to buy out his original partners and to transform a partnership into a family firm. In spite of his nominal ownership of the firm, Guido never owned the majority of its shares. Instead, they were held by his wife, Elda, and her family and later by Elda and their children. Elda was much more than a passive shareholder. Although her husband was, on paper, the director of the firm, she shared fully in its management and headed its design department, which is crucial in a converter firm. She withdrew from active participation only after her children took over management of the firm.

Even wives who owned shares and participated in the management of firms, however, assented to the prevailing norm that a mother's first responsibility was the welfare and happiness of her family, especially her children. In short, a mother's primary duty was to manage the family rather than the firm. As the emotional center of the family, mothers were accountable for the strength and character of its personal bonds and, ultimately, for its unity. Before World War II, bourgeois fathers by and large made decisions about their children's educations as well as their career choices, exercising control over both family and firm. After the war, mothers gained increasing authority as well as responsibility over the children. By the 1960s, the management of children and the household had become the domain of mothers. They kept informed about educational options and opportunities, maintained relations with teachers and schools, and organized the day-to-day operation of children's activities and lives. As one wife explained, she did everything to "protect" her husband from having to deal with the children, since he was burdened with managing the firm.

The complementarity of this gender division of labor between husbands and wives meant that there was little conflict between the family and the firm, especially during the early years of marriage and parenthood. The husband's work in the firm was viewed as providing the material resources to sustain the family, while the wife's work in the family provided the emotional resources to keep it together. Each spouse was the managing director of his or her respective domain. After the 1960s, this gender complementarity became increasingly strained as wives' attempts to keep the *family* together after their children had become adults began to conflict with husbands' attempts to keep the *firm* together for their adult sons. The new political and social circumstances in which women found themselves managing their children's lives and planning for their futures generated new tensions even as wives and husbands pursued old gender projects. These new circumstances were the product of significant changes in family law and in the occupational and class structure of Italy.

Italian Inheritance Law and the Agency of Women

Since the imposition of the Napoleonic code on northern Italy in 1808, equal division of the patrimony among all children regardless of gender had been the law, if not the practice. Article 745 of the Napoleonic code required that daughters as well as sons share equally in inheritance. It also abolished primogeniture and made children by second marriages equal inheritors with those of the first (Mengoni 1961, 45). It stipulated that testators with one child had to leave him or her at least half of the estate; if there were two children, at least two-thirds of the estate had to be divided equally among them; if three or more, three-quarters (Davis 1973, 142). When Napoleon's empire collapsed in 1815, Austria took over Venice and Lombardy again. After struggling to suppress Italian resistance, the Austrians, whose inheritance codes struck a compromise between the egalitarian principles of the Enlightenment and the values of a conservative ruling aristocracy, were less respectful than they had previously been of inheritance laws and customs that emphasized male inheritance, entail, and primogeniture (Davis 1973, 142). The Civil Code of unified Italy, which was modeled upon the Napoleonic code, governed Italian inheritance from 1865 until the enactment of the new family laws of 1975.[6]

Italian inheritance law recognizes three basic types of inheritance rights: legitimate (*legitim*), testamentary, and legal. Legitimate inheritance has absolute priority over the others — it represents an "overriding duty" (Davis 1973, 175). What proportion of the estate is reserved for the heirs, who the heirs are, and the proportions they receive are complexly codified.[7] If there are legitimate descendants, then ascendants are excluded. If there are illegitimate descendants, then they inherit with the legitimate descendants or, if there are none, with the ascendants. The proportion of the estate that must be legitimately inherited varies between one-third and two-thirds. It is, for instance, one-third if the heir is a single illegitimate descendant. It is one-half if there is a single legitimate descendant. It is two-thirds with two or more legitimate descendants, and it is divided in equal shares among these descendants, regardless of gender.

Testamentary inheritance applies only to what is left after the *legitim* distribution. The testator's will is restricted by a number of provisions, among them that the inheritor must be eighteen and mentally competent (Lessico Universale 1979, 199) and that illegitimate children may not, if there are legitimate children, receive more than would be their share if legal inheritance were followed (181). Legal inheritance takes effect when there is no will and applies to the part not distributed by *legitim*. Again, there is a complex set of rules governing the proportion received by various kin under different scenarios (summarized in Davis 1973, 181). In general, Davis notes that legal inheritance "places much more emphasis on the nuclear family than does the law of *legitim*, which, by excluding siblings and other collateral kin, emphasizes the direct line of descent and ascent. Even in legal inheritance, however, priority is given to the descendants and then to ascendants over spouse and siblings" (180). If there are no surviving kin, the legal inheritance and the *legitim* go to the state (Mengoni 1961, 5).

Until the revision of the Civil Code in 1975, widows' legal inheritance rights in Italy were limited to usufruct, not actual ownership. This meant that upon her husband's death, a wife had the right only to be supported by a stipend and to manage the patrimony until her sons came of age. After that she was dependent upon her sons to manage the patrimony and to provide her with a stipend. As a consequence, widows shared their sons' interest in keeping the patrimony intact, and they were unlikely to be strong advocates of their daughters' inheritance claims. Even in the 1980s, widows who had been raised in landowning or upper fraction capitalist families tended to emphasize the value of an undivided patrimony and the perpetuation of their husbands' and fathers' projects.

What was true of women from upper bourgeois family backgrounds, however, was not of the wives and mothers in the middle fraction. Most of these women were not daughters of propertied families, and they did not grant priority to the continuity of the family firm. Family unity and continuity was, for them, not necessarily dependent on the continuity of the family business. Instead, these women stressed their commitment to equal inheritance by all children, whether sons or daughters, whether inside the firm or outside the firm. Indeed, their commitment to equality among siblings disposed them to try to help those children they viewed as most in need of it. This commonly meant helping daughters who had fewer financial resources than sons, but it also meant helping "outside" sons.

The revisions to the Civil Code in 1975, referred to as the Nuovo Diritto di Famiglia, went a long way toward strengthening the ability of mothers in these middle fraction families to lobby for a more equitable division of property among their children.[8] Along with legalizing divorce, the new family law also established spousal community property for the first time and strengthened the inheritance rights of wives. Supporters of the reform argued that if divorce was to become possible, women would need financial resources and, therefore, rights to their husbands' property.[9] Their arguments prevailed, and with the passage of the Civil Code, a woman with two or more children became entitled to at least one-third of the patrimony if her husband died intestate (without leaving a will). She became entitled to at least one-fourth if he died leaving a will giving to someone else the proportion of his property that he could freely assign to whomever he wishes (the *quota disponibile*). This one-fourth is considered her *legittima* or *diritti riservati*. A crucial provision in the Civil Code is the inclusion within the community property of spouses of acquisitions made even separately during the marriage, the property assigned for the practice of an enterprise of one of the spouses founded after the marriage, and any increase in the value of the enterprise.

Although these legal reforms were intended primarily to provide financial support for divorced women, their more important impact among the Como bourgeoisie was the strengthening of wives' position in relation to their husbands and their children, in particular their sons. These effects were not immediately apparent to the Como bourgeoisie, but only became so over time as people realized that the property rights of wives and mothers had tipped the balance of power in families. Once they had been endowed with legally enforceable claims to family property, mothers became more than a moral force; they became political and economic actors with considerable financial leverage over their husbands and children.[10]

Whether the legislators who crafted the 1975 reform of family law intended it to or not, the revised Civil Code reformulated the social agency of wives and mothers in such a way as to transform bourgeois women's family strategies. In the 1980s, these emergent strategies were not motivated by a feminist vision of autonomy, but by old gendered ideals of collectivity. The vast majority of wives and mothers in the

upper and middle fractions of Como's bourgeoisie were not proponents
of *la liberazione delle donne*. Most were conservative Christian Democrats steeped in what they viewed as a "traditional" feminine commitment to *la famiglia unita*. What had changed was not their commitment
to keeping the family together, but the kind of family they came to
envision as a possibility. The changes in family law made it possible for
these mothers to champion a new kind of collectivity — namely, their
inclusive family of adult children, their spouses, and grandchildren.
Long before they were widowed, wives could see beyond their husbands' deaths to their futures in these new inclusive families. Keeping
the family together meant for husbands consolidating control over the
patrimony for their sons — the successors of the family firm — for wives
it meant distributing the patrimony more or less equally among all children. In short, what emerged out of these new possibilities was a clash
between the cherished projects of the male self and the female self.[11]

I am not suggesting that in the 1980s bourgeois mothers were about
to take their sons to court over inheritance rights. Quite the contrary;
this was the last thing mothers wanted, because to enter the domain of
the courts was to dissolve the family, which was precisely what mothers
were trying to avoid. *Una famiglia unita* can hardly be preserved
through a court battle. Fathers and sons who had taken over firms, for
their part, had nothing to gain by entering into a legal dispute. As everyone knew, and as financial consultants were quick to point out, firm
owners had everything to lose in a court battle. During litigation, which
is notoriously slow in Italy, the firm's assets are often frozen and management is taken over by the court. Hence, legal battles paralyze firms
and ultimately destroy them. Especially after passage of the new family
law, fathers and their successors had every reason to avoid litigation.
Daughters and nonsuccessor sons, however, were likely to be less re-
strained. After all, they had their own families to build and their own
children to endow. Moreover, now that bourgeois daughters were increasingly marrying men who were professionals (*liberi professionisti*),
they could not rely on their husbands' family businesses for their children's occupational and financial futures.

A father's best strategy, consequently, was to keep negotiations regarding inheritance and succession outside the domain of law and inside
the domain of the family. Only in the latter domain, with its normative
ideals of collectivity and unity, could a father hope that a way could be
found to postpone the division of the patrimony until some time in the
future when the firm could endow the futures of all his children and
grandchildren. If he left a will that endowed *some* of his children and
grandchildren with more than *others* , he would destroy the possibility
of that future and the myth of the collectivity.

Given the portion of the patrimony legally reserved for wives and children, moreover, the portion that a father can distribute by leaving a will—the *quota disponibile* (disposable property)—was and continues to be very restricted in Italy. In contrast to British and U.S. inheritance law, in which individuals have wide-ranging freedom to decide how much, if any, of their property to leave to their children, Italian inheritance law dictates that the majority of an individual's property go to his family members. As I noted above, Italian inheritance law specifies the precise portions that each family member is to receive depending on the configuration of the family at the time of an individual's death.[12] For example, after the revisions to the Civil Code in 1975, the disposable property of a man survived by a wife and more than one child is only one-fourth of his total property. Thus, even if he willed his entire disposable property to a son taking over the firm, the most such a father could hope to give him [and, this is only if there is only one other child] is one-half of his property—hardly enough to keep afloat a middle fraction firm under constant pressure to reinvest its profits. By writing a will that leaves his entire disposable wealth to only *some* of his children, moreover, a father uses the legal resources available to him to advance *his* project and, thereby, risks prodding other family members, including his wife, to do likewise.

It is not surprising, therefore, that in the 1980s and 1990s, many middle fraction firm owners, like Signor Galbiati, were not heeding the advice of financial consultants who were publicly lamenting the fact that many firm owners in Italy were dying without having written wills. In at least two other firms in the middle fraction in which the founding father was still living in 1985, the sons who had taken over the firm reported that they had an "understanding" with their sisters about leaving their shares in the firm for the time being. The precise nature and stability of these agreements were unclear, and in both cases the fathers had not yet gotten around to writing a will. As the financial consultants complained, fathers who had considered ways of bringing about an orderly transmission of the firm patrimony and management often procrastinated and in the end failed to make a decision. The consequences of such indecision, according to these business consultants, were unstable agreements among heirs, untenable forms of shared firm ownership and management, and fights within the family over the value of their shares—all of which would lead to the inevitable paralysis of the firm.

That men whose disciplined ambitions had achieved so much would fail to leave wills that might prove crucial to the future of their firms and families cries out for explanation. The answer to which I have pointed was poignantly illustrated by the stalemate that characterized the Galbiati family in 1985. Although not all families had such a visible, material symbol of the stalemate in the family's projects of capital and kinship as the Galbiati's family home, the strain and disrepair of family relations was common, especially among families in the middle fraction. It was a stalemate that signaled the end of the firm even before the grandsons could even get their hands on it.

The Grandsons Destroy the Firm

At the end of chapter 2, I pointed out that a convincing origin story effectively suppresses the question of what happened before the beginning. Here I note that a compelling narrative of destruction suppresses the question of what happened after the end. Narratives of the breakup and closing of firms sweep us up in the drama and trauma of disagreement, disappointment, and disaffection among family members who had once been intimates and loyal allies. These narratives invite us to scrutinize what had gone on before the firm and family to find an explanation for what happened at the end. In doing so, they discourage us from raising questions about what people did after the closing of the firm. Just as I suggested in chapter 2 that we can profit from knowing what took place before the "beginning," so I suggest that we can profit from knowing what happened after "the end." Particular configurations of family — a specific *famiglia unita* — usually dissolve with the closing of firms, but capitalist family projects do not. One need ask only what happens to the firm's and the family's capital — both financial and social — when the firm dissolves to see beyond the end of the firm. Unless they have entirely depleted their financial and social capital, its owners use their remaining assets to start new firms. Hence, the end of the firm marks the end of a particular collective project and the beginning of new ones.[13] It is as much a beginning as an end.

CHAPTER SIX

❦

CONCLUSION

In the introduction to this book, I proposed that capitalists, like workers, are made, not born. In this concluding chapter, I argue that they are made not only through contingent struggles with other classes and other fractions of the bourgeoisie, but through struggles within their own families. These struggles shape not only family and firm relations and processes; they are also processes of class-making and self-making. All fractions of the Como bourgeoisie participate in these struggles, which take place on the same juro-political field. By this I mean that they are all constrained and enabled by the jural and fiscal policies of the Italian state, including inheritance laws, tax laws, and labor policies. These state laws and policies, I have shown, are constantly changing in relation to cultural and political transformations, thereby rendering all struggles — whether in families or between classes — historically contingent.

The two gaps I identified in Marx's and Weber's theories of capitalism in chapter 1 were: first, their failure to provide an adequate theory of capitalist motivation and, second, their failure to include kinship and gender in their analyses of capitalism. In this chapter, I show these two gaps to be different facets of the same omission. I argue that kinship and gender are crucial in motivating capitalist action and in processes of class-making and self-making among the Como bourgeoisie.

Before I address this issue, however, I need to first take stock of what the preceding chapters have revealed about what the Como bourgeoisie do and do not share.

Unity and Diversity among the Como Bourgeoisie

The preceding chapters have shown that the capitalist ethics and practices of Como family firm owners vary even though they share the same core sentiments, desires, and meanings of kinship and gender. The adage introduced in the first chapter, "The grandfather founds the firm, the sons develop it, the grandsons destroy it" reflects the hopes and anxieties of the patriarchal desire for succession by sons that prevail in all fractions of the Como bourgeoisie. Encapsulated in this adage and in the origin narratives scrutinized in chapter 2 are masculine sentiments of kinship, gender, and personhood that incite fathers in all fractions to endow their sons with the means of production that are their means of independence from the authority of other men. Yet, the differences in productive resources — capital, technical knowledge, and labor — that families in different fractions of the Como bourgeoisie control make for processes of family and firm reproduction and division that are too diverse to be encompassed in a single model of bourgeois class reproduction.

Among the upper and middle fractions, firms are usually initiated with capital investments from family, kin, and associates. This pooling of capital, which is simultaneously a strategy of capital diversification, parallels the pooling of labor and technical knowledge among the lower fraction. But the pooling of labor and technical knowledge creates different challenges to family and firm continuity than does the pooling of capital. As we saw in chapter 4, the subcontracting firms owned by families in the lower and middle fractions of the Como bourgeoisie, which relied on relatives for technical knowledge and labor, experienced tensions and strains earlier than those owned by families in the upper fraction. This led them to break apart sooner — generally, early in the second generation — than firms in the middle and upper fractions. Among these families, moreover, feelings of betrayal were the most intense, leading frequently to the severing of ties with kin who formerly had collaborated in a firm.

The upper bourgeois families with the greatest capital assets, in contrast, commonly were able to postpone division of the firm until later in the second generation or the third or even fourth generation. For these families, processes of family growth, maturation, and segmentation were simultaneously processes of the concentration and diversification of capital. The division of management responsibilities among siblings or cousins was both the first step toward the continuation of the firm in the next generation and the first step toward eventual firm and family division. The greater capital of these families enabled them to diversify in the second generation, whether by expanding into new areas of production in the parent firm or by creating allied firms headed by children. Hence, family segmentation entailed the creation of new firms in allied sectors of the industry, rather than competing firms in the same sector, as it often did in the lower fraction. At the same time, upper bourgeois families were able to settle the claims of "outside" children who were not actively engaged in firm management, thus mitigating pressures for the division of the firm. All of this decreased the likelihood of severe family conflict and estrangement.

This is not to say that upper fraction families were immune to conflicts and division. Struggles over capital and control of family and firm management were invariably a part of these maturation and segmentation processes. But these struggles were focused on the accumulation and dispersion of financial capital rather than on the accumulation and control of technical knowledge and labor. As the former is a quantifiable and more easily divisible resource, struggles among the upper bourgeoisie tended to be less acrimonious than struggles among the lower bourgeoisie.

Families in the middle fraction of the Como bourgeoisie also lacked sufficient capital to support an interim stage of family and firm segmentation. Not only were they unable to both reinvest in the firm and finance the enterprises or careers of the third generation: if there were many siblings in the second generation, the firm could not incorporate all of them. As the siblings who managed the firm strove to reinvest in the firm to strengthen it for their children, the "outside" siblings pressed for the distribution of capital to invest in their children's educations and careers. The resulting clash between the class reproduction strategies of the "inside" siblings and the "outside" siblings became a crucial obstacle to both firm reproduction and family unity.

These variations in family and firm processes are linked to differences in the flexibility of boundaries around the family. The importance of technical expertise and innovation in the middle fraction leads to more flexible boundaries, including the inclusion of sons-in-law in the firm and the family. This openness is not found in upper fraction, where strict boundaries are drawn between the family and in-laws, who are sometimes even excluded from holding shares in the firm. Among the latter, sons-in-law and daughters-in-law, no matter how accomplished or skilled, are not considered viable candidates for firm management. Exceptions are made only when there are no sons, but even then a son-in-law manager is merely an interim strategy leading toward succession by a grandson. In the middle fraction, however, there were several firms in which daughters' husbands had been given leading management positions, including that of general director of the firm.

The diverse class trajectories of Como entrepreneurial families, moreover, challenge static models of class. To define Como entrepreneurs merely on the basis of their current relation to the means of production is to assume that people's outlook and "interests" are the logical outcome of an objective material reality at a particular point in time. This fails to consider — among other things — how people's particular historical trajectories have shaped their orientations and goals. In chapter 3, I traced the varied sociohistorical circumstances surrounding the entry of families from different fractions into the bourgeoisie. One of the important consequences of these varied histories is that families are not committed to the same bourgeois strategies of class reproduction, especially as regards inheritance and the concentration of the patrimony.

Added to these differences in past trajectories of Como bourgeois families are differences in the way they have been transforming in response to legal and political changes. As I noted in chapter 5, all fractions are being affected by the cultural and legal shifts stemming from the women's movement and the push for gender equality, including the 1975 revisions to family law. Strains and conflicts regarding inheritance and succession, which formerly took place between brothers, have increasingly involved brothers and sisters as daughters have become less willing to settle for less than their legal share of the patrimony. Yet while daughters in the middle and lower fractions are as committed to gender equality as those in the upper fraction, they have not been as successful in taking over management. The widespread perception that technical knowledge, especially when it comes to industrial machinery and chemicals, is a male domain has made it more difficult for daughters to take over middle and lower fraction firms in which management is closely tied to technological expertise. Because these gender conceptions continue to shape educational choices, few daughters have had the technical training to qualify as successors to these firms. Hence, some daughters in the middle fraction have been passed over for their husbands, who might otherwise be considered unqualified in kinship terms, when the latter have technical expertise. Daughters have been more successful in taking leading roles in management — in some notable cases succeeding their fathers — in upper fractions firms in which design, financing, and marketing are more crucial to the firm's success.

These variations in class trajectories; in the timing and forms of family and firm segmentation, division, and reproduction; in succession practices; and in capitalist ethics raise the question of whether the Como bourgeoisie can be said to constitute a class that shares anything on the order of a collective outlook — in other words, a class subjectivity. The answer, I suggest, lies in the very tensions and struggles out of which emerge different family and firm processes and entrepreneurial ethics.

Kinship and the Making of the Bourgeoisie

A processual approach to class offers a promising alternative to a static, functionalist Marxist theory of class (Poulantzas 1975) in which people are construed as standing in definitive relation to the means of production. Viewing classes as arising over time through an open-ended process of struggle with other classes enables us to understand how the members of these classes come to view themselves and others in class-specific ways (Thompson 1968; Hall 1988). In other words, it enables us to conceptualize the process of class formation as simultaneously a process of self-making.

Struggles *within* classes as well as struggles *between* them can be incorporated into an analysis of the processes entailed in the formation of class and class subjectivity. Building on Gramsci (1971), Hall (1988) has argued that ideas have to win ascendancy through a specific and contingent process of ideological struggle in order to become the dominant ideas of dominant classes. For Hall, class interests are not "objective features(s) of a structure of positions in a social system . . . from which dangle the appropriate forms of consciousness"; instead, they change historically (1988, 45). As class is not the sole determinant of people's interests, the members of a class can have conflicting and contradictory interests. Hence, the dominant ideologies and interests of a class must be constituted through contingent processes of ideological struggle (45). This struggle takes place not only *between* the fractions of the bourgeoisie but *within* fractions as well (42).

This processual approach to class formation and class subjectivity can be extended, I suggest, to include the contingent processes of ideological struggle *within* families, thus enabling us to incorporate kinship and gender into an analysis of class-making and self-making. As we have seen in the previous chapters, in spite of variations in the timing and character of intrafamilial struggles among the fractions of the Como bourgeoisie, these struggles are shaped by the sentiments, desires, and meanings of kinship and gender, as well as the disagreements over these, that are found in all fractions of the bourgeoisie. The struggles within families are simultaneously struggles over ownership and control of tangible resources (capital, property) and struggles over intangible forces of production—including discourses, norms, and practices of kinship and gender. These struggles over the material and immaterial are intertwined; they shape each other's forms and outcomes. Through these struggles, some discourses, norms, and practices gain ascendance to become the dominant ideology of families, fractions, and the Como bourgeoisie as a whole. In other words, intrafamilial struggles are part of the contingent process through which dominant bourgeois ideology and subjectivity are formed. They alone do not determine bourgeois ideology and subjectivity, of course, because other struggles, including those between fractions and classes for control over production and political hegemony, are also crucial to this process. But they are a crucial part of the historically contingent process of class-making and self-making among the Como bourgeoisie.

A case in point is the historically contingent struggle in families over inheritance and succession. The patriarchal desire to transmit the firm to sons, which has driven and shaped capital accumulation and firm development in all bourgeois fractions in Como, is rooted in ideas about the masculine self, independence, and authority. The analysis of origin narratives in chapter 2 revealed that fathering a family and fathering a business are mutually interdependent achievements of male adulthood among the Como bourgeoisie. In chapter 3 we saw that fathers' desires to hand the firm on to their adult sons has been both a goal and a strategy of firm and family continuity. The tension between male succession and laws requiring the equal division of the patrimony among all siblings was kept in check, with male succession clearly maintaining its dominance, until the 1970s. In that decade, as we saw in chapter 5, the balance was tipped by cultural movements and changing state policy, so that by the 1980s, patriarchal desire was no longer clearly dominant. As interrelated changes in family law, decrease in family size, and cultural shifts in gender norms eroded male succession, patriarchal desire has given way to what has become increasingly viewed as the higher goal of family continuity. In other words, male succession was downgraded from a goal to a strategy. It was reconceptualized as a means toward the end of keeping the family and the firm together.[1] These shifts in succession and inheritance have affected processes of firm and family reproduction along with gendered notions of selfhood and the "interests" of families.

Another site of contention among family members that has been crucial in processes of class-making and self-making among the Como bourgeoisie is the struggle over the boundary between *the family* and *the firm*. The struggle for ownership and control of productive resources is linked to the struggle over competing ideas about the boundary between the firm and the family. Family members do not all share the same view of where one begins and the other ends, or even if the two are separate entities. Instead, the boundary between them is continually contested, reformulated, and asserted. Where the boundary lies at any point in time both reflects and affects processes of family and firm reproduction.

The Family and the Firm: Reification and the Consciousness of the Bourgeoisie

The idea of the family and the firm as distinct social entities, each governed by its own distinctive logic, was dominant in Como bourgeois discourse during the 1980s and 1990s. The official ideology of firm owners in all fractions was that the firm must have a life apart from the family. At the same time, they claimed, the family would continue whatever happened to the firm. Above all, decisions about one should not affect decisions about the other. If family goals, such as assisting members of the family, become the priority in the firm, one was likely to make decisions that were bad for the firm. Even where the two entities were composed of the same individuals, they were claimed to be distinct. For example, both Annalisa Cadirola and her brother Angelo explained that their mother, who had not worked previously in their father's firm, had taken over its management after his death to keep it going for them. Not surprisingly, they felt strongly committed to continuing the firm and hoped to eventually hand it on to their children. Yet, both brother and sister emphasized that they do not mix *family issues* with *firm issues*.

The only individuals in my study who openly expressed disagreement with this distinction, interestingly, were two firm owners who managed firms in collaboration with their spouses. Carla Mainini, who comanaged the firm she had founded with her husband, declared that for her there had never been a distinction between the family and the firm. She described how her children had been brought up in the firm, spending innumerable hours there, and she emphasized the absence of any spatial distinction between the family and the firm. Guido Pezzi, who with his wife comanaged a firm that had been heavily financed by his wife's parents, expressed similar views. In asserting that working with his wife brought them closer together and that having his son enter the firm made the family more close-knit, he articulated a view of the tight integration of family relations and firm relations. His daughter, who had left the firm after working in it for several years, echoed these views, although in a somewhat less positive light. She reported that when she had left the firm, it was viewed as tantamount to leaving the family. The Pezzi family's perspective, however, was in the clear minority. Although many felt that working together in a firm kept them in closer contact as a family on a day-to-day basis, they were quick to emphasize that their solidarity as a family would not be diminished if they did not work together.

In drawing this distinction between the family and the firm, people do not deny that the two are interconnected and that labor and money flow between them. Rather, what they claim is that they are distinct, meaningful social realms. In explaining how family members did not draw salaries from the firm in its early years, for example, Signor Segalini reported that the family had "one common pot" from which everyone took only what they needed to live so that they could invest as much as possible in the firm. Similarly, Pietro Targetti reported that when he was growing up there was little distinction between the finances of the firm and the finances of the family. When his mother went to buy groceries, she wrote checks drawn upon the firm. Yet just because money flowed freely between the firm and the family did not mean they were considered the same thing. Signor Targetti's father was so committed to the view of the two as separate entities that he never talked about the business at home.

Discussions of family unity reveal an intriguing complexity in the relationship between family and firm. As we saw in chapter 3 (see the section "Discourses of Reproduction: Unity and Stability"), the claim of family unity is simultaneously a claim about the solidarity of the family and a claim about the strength of the family firm: its viability, its ability to accumulate capital, manage production, and handle the transition of management from one generation to the next. Family unity is an ideal, a commitment, a discursive strategy, an intentional misrepresentation, an illusion, and a hope. Behind the claim of family unity is the assertion that the family both ensures the continuity of the firm and transcends it. Not only does the family hold the firm together, but it will endure even if the firm dies. In fact, as we have seen, families commonly break apart and relations outside the nuclear family are often severed or at least greatly weakened after firms dissolve.

The boundaries of the family differentiate it from a realm of social action that is governed by a cultural logic — a business ethic — that is viewed as a potential threat to the unity of the family. These boundaries also distinguish the family from kinship relations that are considered external to it. The dominant definition of *the family* among the Como bourgeoisie includes only members of a nuclear family: a married couple and their children. Older couples with married children sometimes include their children's spouses and their grandchildren in their families, but there is a general hesitancy to include more than one conjugal pair in *the family*. All other kin who fall outside this boundary are relatives (*parenti*), who are not viewed as committed to an enduring solidarity. Indeed, as we saw in chapter 4, there is a steep drop-off in commitment and loyalty outside the family. While an individual may have strong ties with other individuals in other families — as in the case of adult married sisters — the restricted definition of *the family* excludes these individual bonds and sets the boundaries around the group in which solidarity can be expected.

The distinction between *the family* and *the firm* is rooted in a normative gender division of labor in which women take care of the family while men take care of business. Indeed, this gender division of labor is integral to the constitution of the family and the firm as distinct social domains. The family as a zone of nurturing emotional support, as distinct from the competitive zone of business, is both made by women and where they belong. As one widow put it, her husband's philosophy was "wife in the house, husband in the firm." Other women, even those who married in the 1970s, reported that as soon as they were married, their husbands made it clear that wife and work were two spheres that should be kept separate. As noted earlier, some husbands, especially those in the upper fraction, even made it a point not to discuss business at home. The fact that the few individuals who did not concur with the distinction between the family and the firm were those from families in which husband and wife comanaged the firm is telling; for them, the gender basis of the distinction made no sense.

For the majority of families, however, the gendered distinction between the family and the firm makes sense of fathers' and sons' management of the firm, while conceding the management of the family to wives and daughters. This is not a parallel gender division of labor and power, because while the firm is, in a sense, the family minus women, the family is not the firm minus men. Men are still expected to be the heads of families — and, as we saw in chapter 2, the founders of firms — even though women are responsible for its emotional character, its day-to-day functioning, and, ultimately, its unity. On the other hand, by making women responsible for the family, this gender ideology appoints them guardians of its continuity and solidarity. As a result, as we saw in chapter 5, mothers' attempts to keep the family together can conflict with fathers' attempts to continue the firm. Thus, a discursive formation that legitimizes the exclusion of women from the firm invites them to challenge it.

Reification casts the family and the firm as social entities that are more stable and less complex than the transitory relations of kinship and capital that actually constitute them. In representing the family and the firm in these terms, people do not deny that firms are affected by family relations and that families are affected by what happens in firms. Rather, they claim that in spite of this, the family and the firm are, and should be, constituted by distinctive cultural logics. What is denied is that the relations in both family and firm are a complex, compromised mix of sentiments, desires, and meanings that cannot be contained within the discursive boundaries defining them. This denial is crucial to the process of reification through which two distinct social entities are discursively carved out of an integrated field of practice.[2] Reification naturalizes the boundary between the family and the firm, making sense of the exclusion of some family members from owning and managing the firm in spite of their legal rights to them, thereby facilitating capital accumulation, firm expansion, and reproduction, and the "independence" of bourgeois sons.[3] At the same time, by identifying the goals that are appropriately pursued in each domain, it differentiates the "interests" of the family from the "interests" of the firm.

As is the case in many contingent struggles through which dominant ideologies emerge, the family and the firm are not merely discursively constituted. They are also institutionally affirmed by state policies, including regulations governing the incorporation of firms and their legal responsibilities. The limits on the fiscal liability of firms incorporated as *società di capitale* (joint-stock companies) lead the owners of all but the smallest of firms to register them as such.[4] This, in turn, affirms the existence of the firm as an entity distinct from the family, even when family members are the sole owners of its shares. Because incorporation makes it possible for a firm to continue as a legal entity beyond the death of its shareholders, it endows the firm with a social agency that appears to transcend the lives of any group of individuals. Family members are drawn into and constrained by this legal fiction, even while they benefit from it. Here again (see the discussion of inheritance law in chapter 3), law influences the ideas and practices of Como bourgeois families. It does not, however, determine them. Law is only one of the complex, and sometimes contradictory, forces that shape concepts of the family and the firm. Like the discourses that become dominant in families, moreover, laws and state policies governing firms and families themselves are forged through contingent political struggles, only in their case at the national level.

A consideration of the reification of the firm and the family brings us back full circle to my discussion in chapter 1 of Weber's model of modern capitalism. The dominant ideological distinction between the firm and the family among the Como bourgeoisie parallels Weber's distinction between economic action and "other" action. It will be recalled that Weber's definition of "economic action" rests on the distinction between actions oriented toward the satisfaction of a desire for utilities and actions oriented toward the satisfaction of other desires (1978, 68). Although he recognized that actions may be oriented towards multiple ends and shaped by multiple considerations, Weber assumed they could be classified on the basis of their "conscious, primary orientation" (1978, 64). For Weber, this distinction was a heuristic device—an ideal-type that captured a crucial difference between the operation of pre-

modern and modern capitalisms. Modern capitalism, with its calculative spirit and singular goal of profit and accumulation, could be distinguished from premodern capitalism — as found in the large capitalist
households in the medieval cities of northern and central Italy — with its
"primarily non-economic" goal of "solidarity" and "household communism" (359). The latter was structured by a different cultural logic —
one based on "direct feelings of mutual solidarity rather than on a consideration of means for obtaining an optimum of provisions" (156).

In contrast to Weber, I treat the distinction between the family and
the firm not as a heuristic device that differentiates two systems of social action, each with its own distinctive goals and logics of operation,
but as a dominant ideology of capital, kinship, and gender among the
Como bourgeoisie. Rather than providing a useful framework for the
analysis of family capitalism in Italy, the distinction between the family
and the firm is a constitutive element of contemporary family capitalism
in Italy. It does not accurately reflect the practices and operations of
bourgeois families or family firms in Como. Instead, it both shapes their
social actions and misrepresents them. It obscures from view a crucial
part of the complex of activities and social relations through which
family capitalism is produced and reproduced. In other words, the reification of the family and the firm replicates the obfuscation of Weber's
definition of "economic action."

This suggests that the distinction between *family* and *business* and
between *family* and *economy* that is hegemonic in Italy — as well as in
other capitalist societies — may be shaped by struggles within bourgeois
families rather than between the bourgeoisie and the working class. The
exclusion of women's domestic labor from economic models of "the
economy" has been criticized by feminist scholars as a bourgeois justi-
fication of the failure to remunerate the working class for the full extent
of its labor contribution to capitalist production. Abercrombie and his
colleagues (1980) have argued, however, that dominant ideologies function more effectively to secure the coherence of the dominant class
rather than the coherence and integration of capitalist society as a
whole. They reject what they call the "dominant ideology thesis," some
version of which, they argue, "is present in almost all forms of modern
Marxism and . . . is empirically false and theoretically unwarranted"
(1). According to this thesis, the dominant class, through its control of
ideological production, is able to "infect the consciousness of the working class," who come to "experience reality through the conceptual categories of the dominant class" (1). The alternative theory they offer
stresses the "conflictual, unstable quality of modern capitalism," in
which the subordinate classes are controlled by "the dull compulsion of
economic relationships, by the integrative effects of the division of labour, by the coercive nature of law and politics" (6).

My concern here is not whether Abercrombie and his colleagues are correct in asserting that the importance of ideology in explaining the acceptance of capitalism by the working class has been exaggerated. Rather, my concern is with the role of dominant ideologies in securing the coherence of the dominant class itself. My analysis of the reification of the family and the firm among the Como bourgeoisie suggests that securing this coherence entails legitimating the control of purportedly communal family resources by some family members to the exclusion of others. One of the key consequences of the reification of the family and the firm is the exclusion of women from firm management and often from their legal share of the family patrimony, thus facilitating the accumulation and concentration of capital and management and the continuity of the firm. My discussion of patriarchal desire and men's gendered goal of "independence" through entrepreneurship in chapter 3 showed that what Como bourgeois men want has been shaped by their location in a historically contingent process of gender and class formation. Gender is crucial in processes of class-making and self-making among the Como bourgeoisie and, conversely, class-making and self-making are crucial to bourgeois processes of gender-making.

Provincial and Global Capitalism in Como

In 1999 an article about the newly appointed president of the National Association of Italian Fashion appeared in a Milan newspaper, accompanied by his photograph with the caption *Innovazione o morte* (innovation or death). Mario Boselli's remarks on the occasion of his induction into the presidency provided ample evidence of his worthiness of the position. Signor Boselli was quoted as saying,

> Innovation is the only way to survive in a world that is continually getting more difficult, rapid and globalized. . . . One innovates or one dies; and this is true both for family firms such as mine, as well as for the entire Italian fashion industry and the association that represents it. My family has been producing thread for more than 400 years, but in order to continue we had to broaden our production and we had to take risks.

Signor Boselli went on to recount how twenty-five years earlier his family's firm began producing fabric for the first time, how they moved into clothing manufacturing last year, and how only a few months before they transformed themselves from a multiprovincial firm with factories located in three northern provinces of Italy to a multinational firm with factories located in Slovakia. By the end of the article, the Boselli family firm's history of expansion and diversification had been effectively developed as a metonym for the entire industry, endowing Signor Boselli with impeccable credentials to head an association that has broadcast its intention to develop strong international alliances with Paris, London, and the United States.

Mario Boselli's celebration of innovation and expansion echoes the entrepreneurial spirit of the owners of the larger firms in Como. It differs markedly from the one avowed by Piercarlo Venturini, the owner of the small dyeing firm who extolled the virtues of remaining small and specializing in one phase of the production process (see chapt. 4, section on "collaboration and competition"). Expansion, Signor Venturini warned, increased the risk of losing control of the production process as well as of the "human dimension" of work. Citing what he called his "existential philosophy" of *piccolo e bello* (small is beautiful), Signor Venturini declared his intention to maintain the small size of his firm and continue to specialize in the dyeing of only pure silk.

Signor Venturini's commitment to zero growth epitomizes the "provincialism" derided by industry officials and the owners of larger firms in Como. As was seen in chapter 4, the latter blame the "closed" and "provincial" mentality of firms that refuse to share information and collaborate in developing new products, techniques, and markets for keeping Como's silk industry from achieving its potential. Implicit in these complaints is an essentialist theory of difference among capitalist firms, according to which there are two fundamentally distinctive kinds of firms: those that are destined to remain "provincial" and eventually die out and those that have the capacity to thrive and expand in a "global" economy.

This bourgeois theory of capitalist difference is a local version of the essentialist theory of capitalism whose failings I discussed in chapter 1. According to this popular theory, different "cultures of capitalism" have different fates. Some, such as "Hong Kong transnational capitalism," are purportedly endowed with the inherent capacity to transcend location and national boundaries and flow fluidly over the globe. Others, such as "Italian family capitalism," are said to be constrained by their internal limitations and, barring radical transformation, are bound forever to their original site and to eventual extinction in a world of increasing global competition. So compelling is this evolutionary theory of capitalist difference that it has led even some cultural anthropologists to conclude that the kinship foundations of the small family firms of central and northeastern Italy place formidable structural limits on their future prospects. These firms, it is argued, are "essentially conservative—a defensive effort dedicated to assuring the successful reproduction of family and household," which discourages capital reinvestment even as it once acted to sustain rapid accumulation (Blim 1990, 256). In chapter 1 we saw that similar tendencies toward characterizing entire industries, industrial districts, and nations as infused with particular entrepreneurial ethics abound in the scholarly literature on culture and capitalism.

This study has demonstrated that both a "provincial" capitalism and a "global" capitalism are practiced in the same industry by an industrial bourgeoisie that shares common sentiments and meanings of kinship and gender, but differs as regards processes of capital accumulation, diversification, and firm reproduction. The "provincial" capitalism practiced by small firm owners such as Piercarlo Venturini, moreover, is no more a product of a "local" tradition of entrepreneurship than is the "global" orientation of the larger firms. Rather, like the "global capitalism" of Mario Boselli, it is a discursive and material effect of the relations of production between different fractions of the Como bourgeoisie.

As we saw in chapter 4, the dynamic relations of production among firms in Como's decentralized network engenders intense competition among small subcontracting firms that compete with one another to fulfill manufacturing services for the larger firms. All firm owners worry about competition from local firms in their sector of the industry, but the owners of small subcontracting firms are especially anxious about competition from the even smaller firms that are constantly popping up. The survival and success of a small subcontracting firm rests on its ability to increase its number and range of clients, thereby reducing its vulnerability to fluctuating market demands. Yet as we saw in chapter 4, there are formidable constraints on this, not the least of which derive from the hierarchical network of firms that make up this decentralized industry. Expansion into an adjacent sector of production is often impossible because it brings a subcontractor into direct competition with his own clients. Constraints on innovation are also great on subcontracting firms specializing in one phase of production. Dependent as they are on orders from their clients, subcontractors are apprehensive about effecting any changes other than those that decrease production time or increase efficiency and reliability. Instead they are most concerned about maintaining tight control of the labor process in order to control quality. As a consequence, these subcontracting firms jealously guard techniques of production and eschew collaborating and sharing information and knowledge with other firms in their sector. Their outlook and behavior are easily labeled as "closed" and "provincial" by the owners of the larger, more highly capitalized firms whose competitors lie less within the industry than in other industrial districts, including ones overseas.

The competitors of the upper fraction of the Como bourgeoisie are located in the industrial districts and networks of subcontracting firms in the developing nations of Asia. Their concern, consequently, is not that they will lose to local competition, but that the industry as a whole

will be eclipsed by overseas competitors. Hence, they have every reason
to collaborate with other large firms to keep this from happening. The
"cosmopolitan" or "international" outlook of Como's upper bourgeoisie is shaped as well by their transnational distribution and marketing relations. They are, after all, dependent on foreign sales to make a
go of it.

My point is not that the "provincialism" of the small subcontracting
firms is an acultural, utilitarian adaptation to the demands of larger
firms or to the structural constraints of the flexible accumulation of late
capitalism. The entrepreneurial ethos of firms at both ends of the industrial hierarchy in Como is culturally produced by capitalists whose
desires and strategies can be no more satisfactorily explained by a
universal capitalist logic of profit and accumulation than they can be
explained by an essential Italian logic of family and household reproduction. Neither an economic reductionist nor a cultural reductionist
theory of capitalist difference will do. Rather, my point is that the "provincial" and "global" orientations of the different fractions of the
Como bourgeoisie are mutually constituted in an industry that has always been shaped by both regional and international relations of production and distribution.

These findings emphasize the need to move beyond theories of culture and capitalism that tend toward essentialist characterizations of
capitalism as "Western" or "Asian," "early" or "late." Rather than seek
out distinctive "cultures of capitalism" or "capitalist cultures," we need
to employ approaches that enable us to understand the articulation of
heterogeneous capitalist practices that coexist in any particular location.
The diverse entrepreneurial ethics and processes that make up the silk
industry of Como can be loosely categorized as forms of "Italian family
capitalism," but only if we eschew cultural essentialist formulations that
deem it the product of a "traditional Italian" family system or an enduring, stable "Italian culture." Kinship and culture in Italy are themselves
constantly changing in relation to broader cultural, economic, and political transformations. Neither families nor capitalism in Italy are products of Italian culture. Italian culture, after all, is merely a heuristic
device. To claim that it produces Italian families and Italian capitalism—both of which encompass a wide range of forms and practices—is
to succumb to the fallacy of reification. Culture does not produce capitalism; people produce capitalism through culturally meaningful actions that at the same time produce families and selves with particular
desires, sentiments, and identities.

The findings of this study raise questions about the usefulness of the
rhetoric about culture and global capitalism that has become fashion-
able of late in popular and scholarly discussions, despite its lack of support by sustained ethnographic research. In concluding that the spread

of global capitalism portends the end of culture, this rhetoric appears to be caught up in the reification of cultural discourses. Far from heralding the end of culture and the usefulness of cultural analysis, the global spread of capitalism means that a lot more cultural analysis needs to be done.

Notes

❦

Preface

1. In Sahlins's work, for example, the nineteenth-century Hawaiians were able to mediate the effects of the capitalist "world system" by synthesizing the experience "in their own cultural terms" (Sahlins 1992, 215). But the workings of "Western capitalism" itself as a cultural practice shaped by the sentiments and commitments of its agents is unexamined. Sahlins (1992 and 1994) recognizes that "Western capitalism" is a cultural system shaped by its own distinctive cultural terms. In arguing that capitalist forces are realized in many parts of the world in "exotic cultural logics far removed from the native-European commodity fetishism" (1994), he makes it clear that Western capitalism is a cultural system that is always locally mediated in its effects and that these mediating processes shape the "modern global order." His efforts, however, have been focused primarily on demonstrating that "peripheral" peoples have not become the passive objects of a Western capitalist global expansion that replaced their traditional cultural system, but rather that they have employed "Western capitalism" in ways that actually strengthened and developed their own system. His analysis of the early period of European contact in the Sandwich (Hawaiian) Islands, for example, shows how the ruling chiefs appropriated Western commodities to bolster their own hegemonic projects and their sacred divinity. Given his focus on local mediations of "Western capitalism," he has not been concerned with tracing the cultural production of "Western capitalism" itself.

2. See Gibson-Graham 1996 for a critical discussion of recent discourses of globalization.

3. Turning our ethnographic attention to the upper end of hierarchies of wealth and power does not mean, however, ignoring their relations with those at the lower end of them, because interclass relations are crucial in constituting the selves and social relations of people at both ends, as well as those in the middle. In other words, we must steer clear of treating either the bourgeoisie or the working class as if they were autonomous social groups or the primary productive agents of capitalist society. Capitalism, after all, is "intrinsically a class society" (Giddens 1973, 20). It is the product of the dynamic, shifting relations between classes as well as among those within them. We cannot hope to comprehend any moment of capitalism or its historical transformation unless we include in our analysis all the actors participating in these relations.

Chapter One
Producing Culture and Capital

1. These models of global penetration are similar to Sahlins's analytic scheme of how formerly isolated societies such as Hawaii mediated the working of the "world system" of capitalism in the eighteenth and nineteenth centuries (Sahlins 1992, 2). In other words, while capitalism realizes itself through the mediation of local cultural orders, there is but one penetrating capitalist system.

2. For Marx, what distinguishes capitalism from other economic systems is not merely that it is a system of commodity production, but that labor power itself is a commodity bought and sold in the market. As Giddens (1973, 85) notes, this ties the very definition of capitalism to the existence of a class system linking capital and wage-labor. Although I start with this definition of capitalism, like Miller (1997, 10) I am less interested in arriving at a formal definition of capitalism as I am in understanding the sentiments and ideas and the day-to-day practices of people who are engaged in profit-seeking activities loosely classified as capitalist.

3. See Kondo's (1990) ethnography of the production of identities in Japanese family businesses.

4. See, for example, Marx's discussion of the republican opposition to the bourgeois monarchy of Louis Philippe. According to Marx, it "was not a faction of the bourgeoisie held together by great common interests and marked off by specific conditions of production. It was a clique of republican-minded bourgeois, writers, lawyers, officers and officials that owed its influence to the personal antipathies of the country against Louis Philippe, to memories of the old republic, to the republican faith of a number of enthusiasts, above all, however, to *French nationalism*" (1963, 27).

5. Hirschman begins with the question posed by Weber at the beginning of the *Protestant Ethic* of how the acquisitive drive and the moneymaking activities connected with it became honorable at some point in the modern age, "after having stood condemned or despised as greed, love of lucre, and avarice for centuries past" (1977, 9). In attempting to complement Weber's historical explanation of why modern capitalists are motivated to accumulate capital, Hirschman offers a historical explanation of why other people let them do so. Rather than locate its emergence in the development of a new ethic for the

individual, he traces it to a developing theory of the state. Beginning with the Renaissance conviction that harnessing the destructive passions of men is more effective than repressing them through moral philosophy or religious dogma, "society" (i.e., the state) is called on to turn "private vices" into "public benefits." In the seventeenth century, a strategy of pitting passion against passion is devised, leading to a differentiation between the "wild" passions and those that could "tame" them. Indeed, the Hobbesian social contract is, according to Hirschman, an offshoot of this strategy, in which the "interests" of men (their taming passions) can overcome their (wild) "passions."

6. Hirschman is not entirely successful in explaining why this drift from a general concept of interest to the limited meaning of economic interest occurred. Yet his account of how moneymaking became acclaimed once the term "interests" bestowed on it a positive connotation associated with "the idea of a more enlightened way of conducting human affairs" (1997, 41), enables us to appreciate the appeal of the concept.

> Once the idea of interest had appeared, it became a real fad as well as a paradigm. . . . And most of human action was suddenly explained by self-interest, sometimes to the point of tautology. La Rochefoucauld dissolved the passions and almost all virtues into self-interest, and in England Hobbes carried out a similar reductionist enterprise. (42)

7. For Weber, "rational technique is a choice of means which is consciously and systematically oriented to the experience and reflection of the actor, which consists, at the highest level of rationality, in scientific knowledge. What is concretely to be treated as a 'technique' is thus variable. . . . In this sense there are techniques of every conceivable type of action, techniques of prayer, of asceticism . . . of administration, of making love, of making war. . . . All these are capable of the widest variation in degree of rationality" (1978, 65).

8. By now, most cultural anthropologists (Abu-Lughod and Lutz 1990; Leavitt 1996) and some philosophers (James 1997) accept that sentiments entail both ideas and emotions, desires and fears, cognition and feeling.

9. See, for example, Gibson-Graham's (1996) categorization of certain kinds of household work and family production as "noncapitalist."

10. Later refinements of Marx's theory of bourgeois hegemony by Lukacs (1971) and Gramsci (1971) likewise focus on the formation of proletarian consciousness.

11. The miser, according to Marx, seeks to attain this ceaseless augmentation of value by saving his money from circulation, while the capitalist achieves this by "throwing his money again and again into circulation" (1976, 254).

12. Compare this to Marx's analysis of commodity fetishism:

> The mysterious character of the commodity-form consists therefore simply in the fact that the commodity reflects the social characteristics of men's own labor as objective characteristics of the products of labor themselves, as the socio-natural properties of these things. Hence, it also reflects the social relation of the producers to the sum total of labor as a social relation between objects, a relation which exists apart from and outside the producers. Through this substitution, the products of labor become commodities, sensuous things

which are at the same time suprasensible or social. . . . It is nothing but the
definite social relation between men themselves which assumes here, for them,
the fantastic form of a relation between things. (1976, 165)

13. I thank Don Donham for pointing out the ironic intent of Marx's analysis of the fetishism of value.

14. See Chun's (1989, 233) argument regarding the misinterpretation of
Weber and the usefulness of his distinctions among forms of capitalism.

15. This misunderstanding, along with the excesses of the "Occidentalist"
representation of modern capitalism, is in part Weber's fault because his characterization of Asian economy and religion has fueled this dichotomy.

16. Few versions of this tale succumb to the excesses of Huntington's (1996)
prophesy that the "clash of civilizations" — the most crucial of which, for him, is
that of the West against the Rest — will become the major global political conflict in the post–Cold War era. Yet the terms in which the capitalist ethos that
purportedly characterizes East Asia's rising economic nations is commonly represented belies a concept of culture that bears a startling similarity to Huntington's concept of civilizations as broad cultural entities uniting people around
common morals, traditions, and institutions.

17. As Wei Ming Tu notes: "The Confucian values that are thought to have
helped East Asian economic development . . . are very different from those that
never confronted the ruthless questioning of radical otherness. For example, harmony achieved in a highly competitive pluralistic modern society is very different
from harmony assumed in an undifferentiated farming community" (1998, 92).

18. Hertz's study of the Shanghai stock market, for example, concludes that
its "distinctive structure" was forged largely independently from the "capitalist
world system" (1998, 12). The creation of two distinct markets for company
shares, one for domestic investors and another for foreigners, replicated the dual
operation of "tributary" and "petty capitalist" modes of production.

19. According to Ong, "utilitarian familialism" is a term used by Hong
Kong social scientists to describe the everyday norms and practices whereby
Hong Kong families place family interests above all other individual and social
concerns (1999, 118).

20. In the case of transnational Hong Kong corporate elites and Taiwanese
heads of firms, Western liberal-humanist conceptions of self, family, and business are surely among the cultural forces with which people must contend. Ong
and Greenhalgh are tuned into the reflexivity of their Chinese subjects, since
both discuss their informants' manipulation of Orientalist discourses of the family and tradition in constructing family business (Ong 1999, 112; Greenhalgh
1994, 775). Yet in treating these discourses as strategic resources by which their
subjects themselves seem to be unaffected, they place unnecessary restrictions on
the productivity of discourse analysis. Discourse becomes just another resource
appropriated by capitalists whose motives and goals remain unexplicated. Culture — by which I mean the historically situated process of formulating meaningful social action — is obscured behind presumably universal capitalist interests in
profit and accumulation.

21. Yang's (2000) account of the clash between "economic logics and rationalities" in Wenzhou, China, is an example of an analysis that leaves in place a

monolithic concept of "Western capitalism" As Rofel (2000, 500) notes, Yang assumes the existence of an ideal-type of "Western capitalism" informed by a cultural logic that is distinctly different from the "precapitalist logic" of ritual consumption operating in Wenzhou. Sangren adds that the problem with Yang's notion of "hybridity," moreover, is that "*all* social formations are hybrid insofar as individual, familial, communal, and higher-level arenas of social production inevitably exhibit some measure of complexity" (2000, 502).

22. Chakrabarty (2000) and Coronil (1997, 14) both argue that challenging orientalist representations requires not only scrutinizing stereotypical representations of the Orient, but also the implicit conception of the West that underpins them.

23. See Herzfeld 1987.

24. The few exceptions are Carter's (1997) study of Senegalese immigrants and the challenge of immigration to Italian discourses of nation and Kertzer's (1980) study of religion and politics in central Italy. Holmes's (1989) study of worker-peasantries in Friuli contributes to our understanding of the intersections of rural peasant life and proletarian labor. A recent doctoral dissertations has traced the formation of dynastic capitalist families in northern Italy in the eighteenth and nineteenth centuries (Scassellatti 1994), and another traces the development of a northern italian industry specializing in woolen textiles (Leonard 2001).

25. Martinelli and Chiesi (1989, 109) qualify this analysis of Italian capitalist development, which they label the "thesis of the weakness of the Italian bourgeoisie," by pointing out that since the early 1970s "the Italian capitalist class has moved from a position of weak political power and low legitimation to a position of strong political influence and widespread legitimation."

26. Martinelli and Chiesi (1989, 122) comment that it is particularly interesting that family capitalism has persisted in Italy despite the significant presence of state managers.

27. Martinelli and Chiesi (1989, 123) point out that by the end of the 1970s it was still possible for wealthy capitalist families like the Presenti family to control a diversified group with low financial resources, minority control, holdings and subholdings, and the constitution of foreign holdings. They also note that several firms, historically related to well-known entrepreneurial families, are formally controlled by foreign holdings. The family members usually hold the top management positions and officially own only a very small number of shares.

28. Although it is called the *tessitura serica* industry, which literally means "silk weaving," the industry today includes the production of both silk fabrics, including those destined for high-fashion clothing, and the continuous-thread weaving of synthetic fabrics, which are destined for ready-to-wear clothing manufacture.

Chapter Two
The Generation of Firms

1. All names of firms, families, and individuals in the Como silk industry mentioned in this book are pseudonyms, except those that were cited or quoted in newspapers or magazines.

2. When I include an account of what people said, the quotation is indented and set off from the text. Because I did not record interviews and transcribe tapes, I cannot claim that these are verbatim accounts. Rather, they are my unabridged accounts of what informants said, which I reconstructed (almost always on the same day) on the basis of my handwritten fieldnotes. They have not been edited, summarized, or reordered. Wherever there were breaks in informants' statements — as, for example, where I asked another question or asked for clarification — these are noted.

3. Several firms, especially the larger ones, had produced similar "official" firm histories, whether in publicity brochures or glossy hardcover books that were displayed in the reception room of the firm's main office

4. The English phrase "self-made man" was used by this informant as well as by others.

5. In chapter 4, I will explore the issue of the employment of relatives in firms and its significance for the structure and dynamics of the industry.

6. Examples of recent attempts to let ethnographic subjects speak for themselves include Abu-Lughod 1986; Behar 1993; and Visweswaran 1994.

7. There are notable exceptions to this limitation. See, for example, Tsing 1994.

8. For one of the few volumes to focus on the anthropological study of elites, see de Pina-Cabral and de Lima 1999.

9. Marcus studied dynastic families in Galveston, Texas, which had been founded by entrepreneurs in commerce and industry during the later-nineteenth-century era of economic expansion in the United States (Marcus 1985, 1988, 1992).

10. The Chamber of Commerce first appeared in seventeenth-century France, from which it diffused rapidly throughout the world. It was introduced in Italy by Napoleonic legislation and then recognized by the Italian state after unification (*Enciclopedia del Diritto e Dell'Economia Garzanti* 1985, 194).

11. The *capitale sociale* consists of the initial capital that a firm has when it is legally founded. It remains constant unless there is a decision to alter it. It cannot be distributed among the partners unless the firm is dissolved, and its function is to guarantee the survival of the firm and to ensure that debts are paid. There was a rough correlation among the firms in my study between firm size and *capitale sociale*, although there is no legal relationship between the two (Ferrara 1980).

12. In extracting information from the Camera di Commercio files, my research assistants and I recorded all the information in the initial registration form and then kept a running record of any significant changes in ownership (including distribution of shares among partners), type of partnership and corporation, management structure, amount of capital, type of product, and location. Firms with a long history had very thick files that took a considerable amount of time to review and record, but we were aided by a list in the file of all the dates on which reports had been submitted and the reasons for the submission.

13. The Italian term is *rappresentante* and usually refers to a commercial agent rather than a simple salesman.

14. The Italian state requires firms with more than fifty workers to pay a *liquidazione* sum of one month's salary per year of employment to every worker when s/he stops working for the firm, for whatever reason.

15. In a *società a responsibilita limitata* shareholders are not responsible for the firm's debts and can sell their shares to anyone. Upon the death of a shareholder, their shares are passed on to heirs along with the rest of their estate.

16. *Società in accomandita semplice* is a form of incorporation in which there are two types of partners: *soci accomandatari*, who have unlimited personal responsibility for the firm's debts, and *soci accomandanti*, who risk only their initial investment in the firm (Ferrara 1980).

17. *Società per azioni* is a corporation similar to a U.S. joint-stock company, in which shareholders are not responsible for the firm's debts (Ferrara 1980).

18. The mean age of first marriage for both men and women in Italy has remained quite stable over time. For women it was just below 24 years until World War II, rose to a high of 25.1 immediately after the war and was back to just above 24 by the 1960s. For men, the mean age was 27.5 until the 1930s, with the exception of World War I years of 1914–18 when it rose to 28.9. From 1936 to 1965, it remained just above 28 (Livi-Bacci 1977, 100).

19. Leach (1973) discovered a similar pattern among families of the London elite, where despite an ideology of patrifilial transmission — specifically, primogenitural inheritance and succession — it was frequently the case that the wealth that had enabled families to advance their social position came through women.

20. Had Evans-Pritchard (1940, 1951) been a less committed structuralist, he might have been moved by his findings about the "children of daughters" to modify his claim that Nuer society was structured by the principle of agnatic descent. He was, however, unfazed by this seeming contradiction. Instead, he concluded that the Nuer were able to trace agnatic descent through women because of the very strength of the agnatic principle.

21. Italian bourgeois ideas of the generation of firms echo the theme of monogenesis that Carol Delaney (1993) has argued accompanies monotheism. Lest this lead us to the conclusion that Italian capitalism is more pervaded by religious thought than are other forms of European and North American capitalism, I hasten to add that the ideal of being a founding father who creates his own family and his own firm and who comes under no other male authority but God himself is not confined to Italy. For example, when the American film director Steven Spielberg was asked why he had decided to join Jeffrey Katzenberg and David Geffen in founding the first new major studio in Hollywood in more than sixty years despite the high financial risk, Spielberg explained, "Ten years ago this would have been inconceivable because I love having bosses in my life." He that said Steve Ross, the former chairman of Time-Warner, who died in 1992, "was a surrogate father to me" and that Mr. Sheinberg (president of MCA who has been a longtime mentor) "was an older brother figure to me." "I needed them," he added. "But I grew up and began to foster children and have a large family. I have five children. I felt I was ready to be the father of my own business. Or at least the co-father" (*New York Times*, October 16, 1994, 1 and 17).

Chapter Three
Patriarchal Desire

A previous version of this chapter was published as "Patriarchal Desire: Law and Sentiments of Succession in Italian Capitalist Families," In *Succession and Leadership among Elites*, ed. João de Pina-Cabral and Antónia Pedroso de Lima, 53–72 (Oxford: Berg, 1999).

1. The Italian sociologist Pizzorno (1981) has described the entrepreneurial middle stratus as a model and myth representing individualistic alternatives in the minds of Italians. While the Como bourgeoisie share some of these desires, it is important to note that what they pursue is not the same as the individualism that many people in the United States have in mind. The U.S. ideal of individualism emphasizes the freedom of the individual to pursue his or her desires and actualize his or her self independently of others, including family members. Among the Como bourgeoisie, independence means building a family independently from the authority of others.

2. Bottomore (1989) uses this distinction to argue against the "managerial revolution" thesis, that with corporate firms and the diffusion of the ownership of shares, managers and technical experts now control firms.

3. Weberian analysts such as Scase and Goffee (1982) and Mackenzie (1982) also argue for a more fluid view in which the petty bourgeoisie and small-scale capitalists are classified together as "those who own property which, together with their own and other's labour, they use for productive purposes" (Scase and Goffee 1982). Within this sector, four subcategories are distinguished by differences in the relative mix of capital utilized and labor employed. While I concur with this more fluid view of class, I have not used it to demarcate the Como bourgeoisie in this study, as it would include petty bourgeois retail shopkeepers who are not involved in the manufacture of silk.

4. The fact that upward mobility among the thirty-five families is more prevalent than downward mobility is an artifact of my sample, which included only families that had operating firms in 1989, rather than ones that had firms at some previous time. Hence, it would be erroneous to conclude on the basis of my sample that the Como industrial bourgeoisie as a whole has experienced similar success.

5. Information on multiple firm ownership came from two sources: first, from firm owners themselves, who were asked about other firms in which they had invested, and second, from the Camera di Commercio, whose data bank includes a listing of all the firms in which an individual is listed as a partner. Thus, we were able to obtain information on firms that our informants had failed to mention.

6. These real estate holdings were initially discovered in the Camera di Commercio firm files, because families often transferred shares of their firms to family-owned holding companies. My research assistant, Martino Marazzi, then gathered information from records of donations and inheritance in the Conservatoria dei Registri Immobiliari—the state agency in which all notarized acts related to real estate are registered. In addition to wills and acts of donation to family members, sales to nonkin are also included and make up the bulk of the

records attached to any individual's name. It turned out to be too time-consuming to record all the notarized acts for each of my subjects, but Martino's investigation alerted us to the real estate investments of the upper bourgeois fraction. The middle and lower fractions had much more restricted investments. The latter's investments were restricted to the land on which the family home and factory were located.

7. The ownership of multiple firms by families in the upper and middle bourgeois fractions means that the industry is less "decentralized" than it might seem on the basis of the sheer number of firms. Firms that are limited to one or two phases of production are linked by their owners' ownership or investments in firms that specialize in complementary phases of production.

8. According to Martinelli and Chiesi (1989, 117–19), the other three entrepreneurial types that make up the Italian business elite are: the subsidized entrepreneur, who was supported and protected by the state and played a decisive role in the origin and development of heavy industry; the financier, whose main social characteristic was the control of share capital without family ties (what Marx called the "financial aristocracy"); and the manager of state-owned firms, who emerged during the fascist period and continued to develop under the protection of the Christian Democratic party and later the Socialist party after the formation of the first center-left coalition government. None of these three entrepreneurial types is active in the Como silk industry.

9. The landed gentry, on the other hand, did not contribute to the ranks of these entrepreneurs and did not take part in industrial initiatives. The contribution of the proletariat to the formation of entrepreneurship was also very marginal, according to Martinelli and Chiesi (1989), the exception being the few founders of low- and middle-class background who were self-taught.

Chapter Four
Betrayal as a Force of Production

1. At the same time, the growth of the retail clothing industry, which offered inexpensive ready-to-wear clothing to women who had previously sewn their families' garments, shifted Como's sales away from wholesale fabric dealers to clothing manufacturers. Middle- and upper-middle-class women seeking higher quality clothing no longer patronized dressmakers for custom-made clothing, and clothing manufacturers ordered larger quantities and offered more lucrative contracts than did fabric wholesalers.

2. From 1949 to 1986, the population of the province of Como increased by 42 percent (from 551,448 to 782,8710). This was due primarily to a huge influx of immigrants who arrived in the twenty-year period from 1950 to 1970 — mostly from the Veneto, southern Italy, and Sicily.

3. Piore and Sabel (1984, 154) note that the power of organized labor was weakened by the the victory of the Christian Democrats in the 1948 parliamentary election and by the ideological divisions in the trade-union movement. Moreover, rapid industrial expansion brought with it the growing availability of cheap mass-produced consumer goods and farm machinery, which threw in-

creasing numbers of artisans and agricultural laborers out of work and into the labor market. The high wages paid by large, vertically integrated firms such as FIAT helped guarantee labor peace.

4. In the 1980s, printing was the most technologically diverse sector of the industry. *Stampa a quadra* (block printing) was the traditional and still most prevalent technique. It was used for high quality fabrics, because the new technologies — *rotatina* and *transfer* — were just beginning to attain the high-quality production of the traditional machines. *Stampa a quadra* was itself divided into three categories: by hand, by hand machine, and by automatic machine. The fabric was attached to a table and the design plate was passed over the fabric. Even in the mid-1980s printing by hand, which was said to yield the highest quality, was used in 75 percent of the printing firms (Ruggero 1978, 103). The hand machine was found in 30 percent of the firms and the automatic machine in 50 percent (these figures do not add up to 100 percent because different types of printing very frequently coexisted in the same firm). The automatic machine was four times as fast as printing by hand (FULTA 1980, 137).

5. The introduction of mechanical high-speed looms had a profound effect on the organization of production. In particular, it resulted in owners increasing the number of work shifts (commonly to three per day) to amortize the machines more quickly. It also changed the job of the "weavers" from intervening in the weaving process to watching over machinery, and it increased the proportion of employees in weaving firms who did not work directly on the looms.

6. In 1952, the general tax on income was reduced from 3 to 1 percent for artisan firms. In 1954, artisan employers were required to make lower contributions to family allowances for their workers (13 percent in comparison to 22.5 percent for industrial firms) (Weiss 1984, 225).

7. It is important to note, however, as do Piore and Sabel, that large firms benefit as much from special legal provisions as do small firms. For example, the state periodically relieves large corporations of their obligations to contribute to various social-welfare funds, a practice referred to as *fiscalizzazione degli oneri sociali* (1984, 334).

8. See, for example, Sylos Labini 1974 and Weiss 1984.

9. Piore and Sabel point out that the internal division of labor in innovative small firms in Italy tends to be extremely flexible. They describe the contacts between owners, engineers, technicians, the various heads of production, and skilled workers of various grades as "close," with "hierarchical distinctions . . . often treated as formalities" (1984, 224). They do not, however, discuss the kinship character of this flexibility.

10. Blim points to another constraint on attempts to move from being a dependent subcontractor to an autonomous producer.

A parts producer-supplier may respond to these losses — where he can — by more investment, and (perhaps more commonly) by enlarging his network of clientele to include all the possible whole-shoe producers who can use his goods as they are. He may fantasize — as one key informant did — about adding a new line to his inner support products. Here, though, he crosses the very tow line that ties him to the market — his capacity and market strength as a specialist. As his wife — his co-proprietor — consistently reminds him over the kitchen table, it is their collective capacity to produce a low-cost good at high volume with little capital investment in machinery that yields the profits. In her view, a new product means a new machine, another work station, more complicated inventory requirements, and more dispersion of sales efforts. In short—she says—only a leap to higher margin, whole-shoe manufacture would provide a more profitable adaptation. Their game now is volume, and future diversification into another low-margin product would only slow them up. (1990, 126)

11. In the case of small firms in the Marche region, Blim has argued that the so-called new industrialization movement is essentially conservative—"a defensive effort dedicated to assuring the successful reproduction of family and household. The entrepreneurial stratum, through its production and labor systems, engages as much in risk-reduction as it does in risk-taking; it seeks moderate gains at minimum risks" (1990, 10).

12. See Blim 1990, 162–64, for a thorough discussion of the variety of practices falling under the rubric of *lavoro nero* (underground labor). These include *fuori busta*, or outside the envelope, in which employer and employee agree not to report some part of the latter's work for tax, medical insurance, and pension contribution purposes, as well as the generic *lavoro nero* in which a worker is paid a piece rate for work that takes place off the premises of the firm and is not reported to the state, and various forms of fiscal evasion in which mandatory fringe-benefit contributions and taxes to the state are avoided.

13. In a *società in nome collettivo* the firm's assets must be utilized before the owners' assets can be touched. Creditors of the individual owners have no access at all to the firm's assets.

Chapter Five
Capital and Gendered Sentiments

An earlier version of part of this chapter appeared as "Capital and Gendered Interest in Italian Family Firms." In *The Italian Family from Antiquity to the Present*, ed. David I. Kertzer and Richard P. Saller, 321–39 (New Haven: Yale University Press).

1. In identifying the people in the photographs, Renata grouped her nephews and nieces into sibling sets, so that, for example, the wedding pictures of Mario and his four sisters (all of whom are married) were all joined together in one stand-up display.

2. The Italian word for share is *azione*, which also means "action," and a shareholder is an *azionista*. Hence, shareholders are, literally, people with agency.

3. The decline in the birthrate in Italy slowed somewhat in the 1930s, possibly due in part to fascist demographic policy (Istituto di Statistica dell'Università di Firenze, n.d., 40) that included nuptiality allowances for those marrying before the age of twenty-six and tax breaks scaled according to number of children (276). Livi-Bacci (1977, 276), however, emphasizes the difficulty of evaluating the effects of the fascist program given the overall trend to rapid fertility decline.

4. During the 1980s and 1990s, family firms in clothing manufacturing likewise commonly put daughters in charge of marketing and overseas sales. As marketing and retailing, including direct sales, became more important to these firms, daughters who had been assigned to what were considered peripheral sectors of the family business became increasingly central to management, sometimes eclipsing their brothers. Such a shift in the relative importance of marketing had not occurred in Como's silk industry in the same period, although a few of the larger firms were hedging their bets by cautiously building their marketing efforts and setting up retail outlets.

5. Unfortunately, the numbers of daughters in my sample who had begun working in the firm after the 1960s is too small to draw even preliminary conclusions about the comparative rates of attrition among sons and daughters entering the family business.

6. The 1865 Civil Code was revised under Mussolini in April 1942, when the Civil and Commercial Codes were joined, but inheritance provisions were not affected. Although the 1942 code did make some important changes in family law — among them redefining the family as a "social" rather than a "natural" institution — many fascist planners were disappointed that there was not a more sweeping revision (Horn 1994).

7. Davis (1973, 174–86) gives a detailed description of the proportioning of inheritance claims.

8. The Nuovo Diritto di Famiglia, properly speaking termed L. 19 maggio 1975, n. 151, reinforced the position of spouses and "natural" children.

9. Supporters of the 1975 reform of the Civil Code included a broad array of left-wing and progressive political parties, labor unions, and feminists. In advocating the legalization of divorce and the establishment of spousal community property, the left-wing parties appear to have been as interested in breaking up large patrimonial estates as they were in strengthening women's rights.

10. In anticipating the challenge that spousal community property would pose to keeping the family patrimony intact and, thereby, to the concentration of capital, the framers of the 1975 Civil Code created a mechanism entitled *separazione dei beni*. This is a prenuptial agreement that sets apart from community property the property spouses bring individually to the marriage, including inherited property. In the 1980s, *separazione dei beni* became a standard strategy for protecting a firm's assets from in-marrying spouses, especially in the upper bourgeoisie. It could not, however, protect the family patrimony from division among brothers and sisters.

11. Whether the collectivity that women were trying to strengthen after 1975 is construed as a new ideal depends on the unit we define as the carrier of "tradition." If we take actual families and their progeny's families as the carriers of "tradition" it might be construed as an old idea of collectivity. After all, this was an idea of collectivity that the wives of the middle fraction learned growing up in petty bourgeois and peasant families. From the perspective of social class as the carrier of "tradition," however, it is a new idea of collectivity, because in the past the bourgeosie was committed to keeping the patrimony intact and to a less inclusive idea of collectivity. *La famiglia unita* for them did not include married daughters, let alone these daughters' husbands and children. Women raised in older bourgeois families still tend toward this commitment, but women

from nonbourgeois backgrounds have, as it were, imported new ideas into bourgeois family ideology.

12. For information on how the 1975 Civil Code sets forth the division of the patrimony in the case of specific configurations of surviving family members and depending on whether a will is left or the individual dies intestate, see Gallo-Orsi and Bottino 1984.

13. To say that the end of family firms is the beginning of others is not to invoke a timeless model of the developmental cycle of family firms along the lines of Fortes's (1958) model of the developmental cycle of domestic groups. Fortes hypothesized that the varieties of domestic groups found in a community or society at any point in time are merely different phases in the developmental cycle of a "single general form." While such a model can help us to understand the impact of events such as birth, marriage, and death on the composition of families and households, by collapsing variation into a single developmental sequence it blinds us to shifting historical contexts shaping processes of household reproduction and division. In contrast, I have tried to show how the reproduction and demise of family firms in Como's silk industry are shaped by political, legal, economic, and cultural forces that are not constant but constantly changing.

Chapter Six
Conclusion

1. One could argue that even before these shifts, family and firm continuity had been the primary goal and that male filial succession was just a means to that end. That, however, overlooks the strength of people's commitment to an ideology of the masculine self in which independence from the authority of other men was central.

2. Lukacs cites Marx's description of the basic phenomenon of reification as follows:

> A commodity is therefore a mysterious thing, simply because it is the social character of men's labour that appears to them as an objective character stamped upon the product of that labour; because the relation of the producers to the sum total of their own labour is presented to them as a social relation, existing not between themselves, but between the products of their labour. This is the reason why the products of labour become commodities, social things whose qualities are at the same time perceptible and imperceptible by the senses . . . It is only a definite social relation between men that assumes, in their eyes, the fantastic form of a relation between things. (1971, 86)

What is of central importance for Lukacs is that as a result of reification, "man's own labour becomes something objective and independent of him, something that controls him by virtue of an autonomy alien to man" (1971, 87).

3. My point here is not that the idea of "social institutions" is a useless analytic concept. Family and firm, like school, church, and state, can be usefully treated as social institutions so long as they are not reified into things in a

manner that obfuscates the complex ideas, practices and relations that constitute them. In other words, social institutions are useful, analytic concepts as
long as social scientists do not make the mistake of reifying them.

4. There are several types of *società di capitale* that differ according to the
extent of the financial responsibility of officers and shareholders and the administrative structure of the firm (Ferrara 1980).

References

Abercrombie, Nicholas, Stephen Hill, and Bryan S. Turner 1980. *The Dominant Ideology Thesis.* London: Allen and Unwin.

Abu-Lughod, Lila. 1986. *Veiled Sentiments: Honor and Poetry in a Bedouin Society.* Berkeley and Los Angeles: University of California Press.

Abu-Lughod, Lila, and Catherine Lutz. 1990. "Introduction: Emotion, Discourse, and the Politics of Everyday Life." In *Language and the Politics of Emotion,* edited by Lila Abu-Lughod and Catherine, 1–23. Lutz. Cambridge: Cambridge University Press.

Albert, Michel. 1993. *Capitalism versus Capitalism.* New York: Fourth Wall Eight Windows.

Bairati, Piero. 1988. "Le dinastie imprenditoriali." In *La famiglia italiana dall'ottocento ad Oggi,* edited by P. Melograni. Roma-Bari: La Terza.

Bagnasco, Arnaldo, and Rosella Pini. 1981. "Sviluppo economico e trasformazioni sociopolitiche dei sistemi territoriali e economia diffusa." *Quaderni fondazione Giangiacomo Feltrinelli,* no. 14. Milan: Feltrinelli.

Banfield, Edward C. 1958. *The Moral Basis of a Backward Society,* with the assistance of Laura Fasano Banfield. New York: Free Press.

Barberis, Corrado. 1976. *La Società Italiana: Classi e caste nello sviluppo economico.* Milan: Franco Angeli Editore.

Barth, Fredrik. 1966. *Models of Social Organization.* Royal Anthropological Institute Occasional Paper no. 23. London: Royal Anthropological Institute.

Behar, Ruth. 1993. *Translated Woman: Crossing the Border with Esperanza's Story.* Boston : Beacon Press.

Berger, Peter. 1988. "An East Asian Development Model?" In *In Search of an*

East Asian Development Model, edited by Peter L. Berger and Hsin-huang Michael Hsiao, 3–11. New Brunswick, N.J.: Transaction Books.

Berger, Suzanne. 1980. "The Traditional Sector in France and Italy." In *Dualism and Discontinuity in Industrial Societies,* edited by Suzanne Berger and Michael J. Piore, 88–131. Cambridge: Cambridge University Press.

Bessone, Mario, and Enzo Roppo. 1977. *Il diritto di famiglia.* Turin: Giappichelli.

Birnbaum, Lucia Chiavola. 1986. *Liberazione della donna/Feminism in Italy.* Middletown, Conn.: Wesleyan University Press.

Blim, Michael. 1990. *Made in Italy: Small-Scale Industrialization and Its Consequences.* New York: Praeger.

Bohannan, Paul. "The Differing Realms of Law." In *Law and Welfare: Studies in the Anthropology of Conflict.* Ed. P. Bohannan. 1967. New York: Doubleday.

Bono, Paola, and Sandra Kemp, eds. 1991. *Italian Feminist Thought: A Reader.* Oxford: Basil Blackwell.

Bottomore, Tom. 1989. "The Capitalist Class." In *The Capitalist Class: An International Study,* edited by Tom Bottomore and Robert J. Brym, 1–18. London: Harvester Wheatsheaf.

Bourdieu, Pierre. 1977. *Outline of a Theory of Practice.* Translated by Richard Nice. London: Cambridge University Press.

Bouscaren, Lincoln, and Adam Ellis. 1957. *Canon Law: A Text and Commentary.* Milwaukee: Bruce Publishing Co.

Braghi, Paolo, et al. 1978. "Per una analisi della struttura di classe dell'Italia contemporanea." In *La Sociologia delle classi in Italia,* edited by Gerardo Ragone and Cecilia Scrocca, 233–304. Naples: Liguori Editore.

Camera di Commercio Industria Arti e Agricoltura Como. 1987. *Andamento economico in provincia di Como.* Como: Camera di Commercio Industria Arti e Agricoltura.

Carter, Donald Martin. 1997. *States of Grace: Senegalese in Italy and the New European Immigration.* Minneapolis: University of Minnesota Press.

Chakrabarty, Dipesh. 1989. *Rethinking Working-Class History: Bengal, 1890–1940.* Princeton: Princeton University Press.

———. 2000. *Provincializing Europe: Postcolonial Thought and Historical Difference.* Princeton: Princeton University Press.

Chan, Kowk Bun, and Claire Chiang. 1994. *Stepping Out: The Making of Chinese Entrepreneurs.* Singapore: Simon and Schuster.

Chiesi, A. M. 1986. "Fattori di persistenza di capitalismo familiare in Italia." *Stato e Mercato* 18.

Chun, Allen J. 1989. "Pariah Capitalism and the Overseas Chinese of Southeast Asia: Problems in the Definition of the Problem." *Ethnic and Racial Studies* 12 (2): 233–56.

Cipolla, Carlo. 1965. "Four Centuries of Italian Demographic Development." In *Population in History,* edited by D. Glass and D. Eversley, 570–88. Old Woking: Gresham Press.

Coates, Norman. 1987. "The 'Confucian Ethic' and the Spirit of Japanese Capitalism." *Leadership and Organization Development Journal* 8 (3): 17–22.

Cohen, G. A. 1978. *Karl Marx's Theory of History: A Defense.* Oxford: Clarendon Press.

Cole, John. 1971. *Estate Inheritance in the Italian Alps.* Department of Anthropology, Research Report no. 10. Amherst: University of Massachusetts.

Collomp, Alain. 1984. "Tensions, Dissensions, and Ruptures inside the Family in Seventeenth- and Eighteenth-Century Haute Provence." In *Interest and Emotion: Essays on the Study of Family and Kinship,* edited by Hans Medick and David Warren Sabean, 145–70. Cambridge: Cambridge University Press.

Coombe, Rosemary J. 1998. "Contingent Articulations: A Critical Cultural Studies." In *Law in the Domains of Culture,* edited by Austin Sarat and Thomas R. Kearns, 21–64. Ann Arbor: University of Michigan Press.

Coronil, Fernando. 1997. *The Magical State: Nature, Money, and Modernity in Venezuela.* Chicago: University of Chicago Press.

Davis, James. 1975. *A Venetian Family and Its Fortune, 1500–1900.* Philadelphia: American Philosophic Society.

Davis, John. 1973. *Land and Family in Pisticci.* New York: Humanities Press.

De Grazia, Victoria. 1992. *How Fascism Ruled Women: Italy, 1922–1945.* Berkeley and Los Angeles: University of California Press.

Delaney, Carol. 1993. *Seed and Soil: Gender and Cosmology in a Turkish Village.* Berkeley and Los Angeles: University of California Press.

de Pina-Cabral, João, and Antónia Pedroso de Lima. 2000. *Elites: Choice, Leadership and Succession.* London: Berg.

Donham, Donald L. 1990. *History, Power, Ideology: Central Issues in Marxism and Anthropology.* Cambridge: Cambridge University Press.

———. 1999. *Marxist Modern: An Ethnographic History of the Ethiopian Revolution.* Berkeley and Los Angeles: University of California Press.

Enciclopedia Del Diritto e Dell'Economia Garzanti. 1985. Milan: Garzanti Editore, s.p.a.

Evans-Pritchard, E. E. 1940. *The Nuer.* Oxford: Clarendon Press.

———. 1951. *Kinship and Marriage among the Nuer.* Oxford: Clarendon Press.

Ferrara, Francesco, Jr. 1980. *Gli imprenditori e le società.* Milan: Giuffre.

Firth, Raymond, ed. 1960. *Man and Culture: An Evaluation of the Work of Bronislaw Malinowski.* London: Routledge and Kegan Paul.

Fortes, Meyer. 1958. Introduction to *The Developmental Cycle in Domestic Groups,* edited by Jack R. Goody, 1–14. Cambridge: Cambridge University Press.

———. 1960. "Malinowski and the Study of Kinship" In *Man and Culture: An Evaluation of the Work of Bronislaw Malinowski,* edited by Raymond Firth, 157–88. London: Routledge and Kegan Paul.

———. 1969. *Kinship and the Social Order: The Legacy of Lewis Henry Morgan.* Chicago: Aldine Publishing Company.

———. 1970. "The Structure of Unilineal Descent Groups" In *"Time and Social Structure" and Other Essays.* by Meyer Fortes. London: Athlone Press.

Foucault, Michel. 1972. *The Archeology of Knowledge.* Translated by A. M. Sheridan Smith. London: Tavistock.

———. 1978. *The History of Sexuality.* Translated by Robert Hurley. New York: Pantheon Books.

Frey, Luigi, et al. 1976. *Occupazione e Sottooccupazione Femminile in Italia.* Milan: Franco Angeli Editore.

Frigeni, R., and W. Tousijn. 1976. *L'industria delle calzature in Italia.* Bologna: il Mulino.

Gallino, Luciano. 1978. "L'evoluzione della struttura di classe in Italia" In *La sociologia delle classi in Italia,* edited by Gerardo Ragone and Cecilia Scrocca, 98–135. Naples: Liguore.

Gallo-Orsi, Gianfranco, and Federico Bottino. 1984. *Fare Testamento: Principi, consigli, esempi.* 2d ed. Rome: Buffetti Editore.

Geertz, Clifford. 1973. *The Interpretation of Cultures.* New York: Basic Books

Gibson-Graham, J. K. 1996. *The End of Capitalism (As We Knew It).* Malden, Mass.: Blackwell.

Giddens, Anthony. 1973. *The Class Structure of the Advanced Societies.* New York: Harper and Row.

———. 1992. Introduction to Max Weber, *The Protestant Ethic and the Spirit of Capitalism,* vii–xxvii. New York: Routledge.

Golini, Antonio, ed. 1994. *Tendenze Demografiche e Politiche per la Popolazine.* Rome: Mulino.

Goody, Esther N. 1982. *From Craft to Industry: The Ethnography of Proto-Industrial Cloth Production.* Cambridge: Cambridge University Press.

Goody, Jack. 1976. *Production and Reproduction: A Comparative Study of the Domestic Domain.* Cambridge: Cambridge University Press.

Goody, Jack, Joan Thirsk, and E. P. Thompson, eds. 1976. *Family and Inheritance.* Cambridge: Cambridge University Press.

Gough, Kathleen. 1971. "Nuer Kinship: A Reexamination." In *The Translation of Culture: Essays to E. E. Evans-Pritchard,* edited by Thomas O. Beidelman, 79–121. London: Tavistock.

Gramsci, Antonio. 1971. *Prison Notebooks: Selections.* Translated by Quintin Hoare and Geoffrey N. Smith. New York: International Publishers.

Greenhalgh, Susan. 1994. "De-Orientalizing the Chinese Family Firm." *American Ethnologist* 21 (4): 746–75.

Hall, Stuart, 1988. "The Toad in the Garden: Thatcherism among the Theorists." In *Marxism and the Interpretation of Culture,* edited by Cary Nelson and Lawrence Grossberg, 35–57. Chicago: University of Chicago Press.

Hamabata, Matthews Masayuki. 1990. *Crested Kimono: Power and Love in the Japanese Business Family.* Ithaca: Cornell University Press.

Hamilton, Gary G., and Kao Cheng-Shu. 1991. "Max Weber and the Analysis of East Asian Industrialization." In *The Triadic Chord: Confucian Ethics, Industrial East Asia, and Max Weber,* edited by Tu Wei Ming, 107–126. Singapore: Institute of East Asian Studies.

Haraway, Donna. 1991. *Simians, Cyborgs, and Women: The Reinvention of Nature.* New York: Routledge.

Harvey, David. 1989. *The Condition of Postmodernity.* Oxford: Basil Blackwell.

Hegedus, Andras. 1976. *Socialism and Bureacracy.* London: Allison and Busby.

Hertz, Ellen. 1998. *The Trading Crowd: An Ethnography of the Shanghai Stock Market.* Cambridge: Cambridge University Press.

Herzfeld, Michael. 1987. *Anthropology Through the Looking Glass.* Cambridge: Cambridge University Press.

———. 1991. *A Place in History: Social and Monumental Time in a Cretan Town.* Princeton: Princeton University Press.

Hildebrand, George. 1965. *Growth and Structure in the Economy of Modern Italy.* Cambridge: Harvard University Press.

Hirschman, Albert O. 1977. *The Passions and the Interests: Political Arguments for Capitalism before Its Triumph.* Princeton: Princeton University Press.

Holmes, Douglas R. 1989. *Cultural Disenchantments: Worker Peasantries in Northeast Italy.* Princeton: Princeton University Press.

Horn, David. 1994. *Social Bodies: Science, Reproduction, and Italian Modernity.* Princeton: Princeton University Press.

Huntington, Samuel. 1996. *The Clash of Civilizations and the Remaking of World Order.* New York: Simon and Schuster.

Istituto della enciclopedia Italiana. 1980. *Rapporto sulla Popolazione in Italia.* Rome: Istituto Poligrafico. Istituto di Statistica dell'Universita di Firenze. N.d. *Tavole di Fecondità dei Matrimoni per l'Italia, 1930–1965.* Firenze: Scuola di Statistica dell'Università.

James, Susan. 1997. *Passion and Action: The Emotions in Seventeenth-Century Philosophy.* Oxford: Clarendon Press.

Jameson, Fredric. 1984. "Postmodernism, or The Cultural Logic of Late Capitalism." *New Left Review* (146): 53–93.

Janelli, Roger. 1993. *Making Capitalism: The Social and Cultural Construction of a South Korean Conglomerate.* With Dawnhee Yim. Stanford, Calif.: Stanford University Press.

Kao, John. 1993. "The Worldwide Web of Chinese Business." *Harvard Business Review* 71 (March–April): 24–37.

Kemp, Sandra, and Paola Bono, eds. 1993. *The Lonely Mirror: Italian Perspectives on Feminist Theory.* New York: Routledge.

Kertzer, David. 1980. *Comrades and Christians: Religion and Political Struggle in Communist Italy.* Cambridge: Cambridge University Press.

———. 1984. *Family Life in Central Italy, 1880–1910.* New Brunswick, N.J.: Rutgers University Press.

Kim, Choong Soon. 1992. *The Culture of Korean Industry: An Ethnography of Poongsan Corporation.* Tucson: University of Arizona Press.

Kondo, Dorinne. 1990. *Crafting Selves: Power, Gender, and Discourses of Identity in a Japanese Workplace.* Chicago: University of Chicago Press.

Lange, Peter, and Marino Regini, eds. 1989. *State, Market, and Social Regulation: New Perspectives on Italy.* New York: Cambridge University Press.

Lash, Scott, and John Urry. 1984. *The End of Organized Capitalism.* Madison: University of Wisconsin Press.

Leach, Edmund. 1973. "Complementary Filiation and Bilateral Kinship." In *The Character of Kinship*, edited by Jack Goody. New York: Cambridge University Press.

Leavitt, John. 1996. "Meaning and Feelings in the Anthropology of Emotions." In *American Ethnologist* 23 (3): 514–39.

Leonard, David Christopher. 2001. *È di moda la crisi: Crisis and Continuity in the Formation of the Biellese Industrial District.* Vol. 1 (Ph.D. dissertation, City University of New York).

Lessico Universale. 1979. *Successione* 28: 198–99. Rome: Istituto della Enciclopedia Italiana.

Lévi-Strauss, Claude. 1963a. "The Effectiveness of Symbols." In *Structural Anthropology,* edited by Claude Lévi-Strauss, 181–201. New York: Basic Books.

———. 1963b. *Totemism.* Boston: Beacon Press.

———. 1969. *The Elementary Structures of Kinship.* Boston: Beacon Press.

Livi-Bacci, Massimo. 1977. *A History of Italian Fertility during the Last Two Centuries.* Princeton: Princeton University Press.

Livraghi, Renata. 1977. "Le ricerche sul decentramento produttivo," *Quaderni rassegna sindacale* 15 (January–April): 9–22.

Lukacs, Georg. 1971. *History and Class Consciousness: Studies in Marxist Dialectics.* Translated by Rodney Livingstone. Cambridge: MIT Press.

Mackenzie, Gavin. 1982. "Class Boundaries and the Labour Process." In *Social Class and the Division of Labour,* edited by Anthony Giddens and Gavin Mackenzie, 63–86. Cambridge: Cambridge University Press.

Maine, Sir Henry Sumner. [1861] 1931. *Ancient Law: Its Connections with the Early History of Society and Its Relation to Modern Ideas.* London: Oxford University Press.

Malinowski, Bronislaw. 1954. *"Magic, Science, and Religion," and Other Essays.* New York: Doubleday.

Marcus, George E. 1985. "Spending: The Hunts, Silver, and Dynastic Families in America." *Archives of European Sociology:* 224–59.

———. 1988. "The Constructive Uses of Deconstruction in the Ethnographic Study of Notable American Families." *Anthropological Quarterly* 61: 3–16.

———. 1992. *Lives in Trust: The Fortunes of Dynastic Families in Late-Twentieth-Century America,* With Peter Dobkin Hall. Boulder, Colo.: Westview Press.

Martinelli, Alberto. 1980. "Organized Business and Italian Politics." In *Italy in Transition,* edited by Peter Lange and Sidney Tarrow. London: Frank Cass.

Martinelli, Alberto, and Antonio M. Chiesi. 1989. "Italy." In *The Capitalist Class: An International Study,* edited by Tom Bottomore, 140–76. London: Harvester Wheatsheaf.

Martinelli, Alberto, A. M. Chiesi, and N. Dalla Chiesa. 1981. *I Grandi Imprenditori Italiani: Profilo sociale della classe dirigente economica.* Milan: Feltrinelli.

Marx, Karl. [1852] 1963. *The Eighteenth Brumaire of Louis Bonaparte.* New York: International Publishers.

———. 1968. "Preface to the First German Edition of *Capital.*" In *Karl Marx and Frederick Engels: Selected Works.* New York: International Publishers.

———. [1859] 1970. *A Contribution to the Critique of Political Economy.* Translated by S. W. Ryazanskaya. Moscow: Progress Publishers.

————. 1976. *Capital: A Critique of Political Economy.* Vol. 1. Translated by Ben Fowkes. New York: Random House.

Marx, Karl and Frederick Engels. 1976. *The German Ideology.* Moscow: Progress Publishers.

McDonogh, Gary. 1986. *Good Families of Barcelona: A Social History of Power in the Industrial Era.* Princeton: Princeton University Press.

Medick, Hans and David Warren Sabean. 1984a. "Interest and Emotion in Family and Kinship Studies: A Critique of Social History and Anthropology." In *Interest and Emotion: Essays on the Study of Family and Kinship,* edited by Hans Medick and David Warren Sabean, 9–27. Cambridge: Cambridge University Press.

————. 1984b. Introduction to *Interest and Emotion: Essays on the Study of Family and Kinship,* 1–8. Cambridge: Cambridge University Press.

————. Mengoni, Luigi. 1961. *Successioni per causa di morte.* Milano: Giuffre Editore.

Miller, Daniel. 1997. *Capitalism: An Ethnographic Approach.* New York: Berg.

New Encyclopaedia Britannica. 1987. S. V. "Inheritance and Succession."

Ong, Aihwa. 1991. "The Gender and Labor Politics of Postmodernity." *Annual Review of Anthropology* 20:278–309.

————. 1999. *Flexible Citizenship: The Cultural Logics of Transnationality* Durham, N.C.: Duke University Press.

Ong, Aihwa, and Donald Nonini, eds. 1997. *Ungrounded Empires: The Cultural Politics of Modern Chinese Transnationalism.* New York: Routledge.

Ortner, Sherry. 1984. "Theory in Anthropology since the 1960s." *Comparative Studies in Society and History* 26:126–66.

Paci, Massimo. 1982. *La struttura sociale italiana: Costanti storiche e trasformazioni recenti.* Bologna: Il Mulino.

Palomba, Rossella. 1995. "Italy: The Invisible Change." In *Population, Family, and Welfare,* edited by Rossella Palomba and Hein Moors, 158–76. Oxford: Clarendon Press.

Parsons, Talcott. 1943. "The Kinship System of the Contemporary United States." *American Anthropologist* 45:22–38.

Parsons, Talcott, and Robert F. Bales, eds. 1955. *Family, Socialization, and Interaction Process.* Glencoe, Ill.: Free Press.

Patriarca, Silvana. 1996. *Numbers and Nationhood: Writing Statistics in Nineteenth-Century Italy.* Cambridge: Cambridge University Press.

Perez, Margarita Delgado, and Massimo Livi-Bacci. 1992. "Fertility in Italy and Spain: The Lowest in the World." *Family Planning Perspectives* (July–August): 162–168.

Piore, Michael J., and Charles F. Sabel. 1983. "Italian Small Business: Lessons for U.S. Industrial Policy" In *American Industry in International Competition,* edited by John Zysman and Laura Tyson, 391–421. Ithaca: Cornell University Press.

————. 1984 *The Second Industrial Divide: Possibilities for Prosperity.* New York: Basic Books.

Pitkin, Donald. 1985. *The House that Giacomo Built: History of an Italian Family, 1898–1978.* Cambridge: Cambridge University Press.

Pizzorno, Alessandro. 1981. "Middle Strata in the Mechanisms of Consensus."
In *Contemporary Italian Sociology*, edited by Diane Pinto. Cambridge:
Cambridge University Press.

Podbielski, Gisele. 1974. *Italy: Development and Crisis in the Post-War Economy*. Oxford: Clarendon Press.

Poulantzas, Nicos. 1975. *Classes in Contemporary Capitalism*. London: New
Left Books.

Radcliffe-Brown, A. R. 1950. Introduction to *African Systems of Kinship and
Marriage*. Edited by A. R Radcliffe-Brown and Daryll Forde, 1–85.
London: Oxford University Press.

———. 1952. *Structure and Function in Primitive Society*. New York: Free Press.

Reiter, Rayna. 1975. "Men and Women in the South of France: Public and
Private Domains." In *Toward an Anthropology of Women*, edited by
Rayna Reiter, 252–82. New York: Monthly Review Press.

Ricoer, Paul. 1970. *Freud and Philosophy*. New Haven: Yale University Press.

Ricolfi, Luca. 1978. "A proposito del saggio di Sylos Labini." In *La Sociologia
delle classi in Italia*, edited by Gerardo Ragone and Cecilia Scrocca.
Naples: Liguore Editore.

Ricoli, Marco. 1979. "Legislazione economica e piccole imprese." In *L'industria
in Italia: La piccola impresa*, edited by F. Ferreo and S. Scamuzzi, 119–
86. Rome: Editori Ruiniti.

Rofel, Lisa. 1999. *Other Modernities: Gendered Yearnings in China after Socialism*. Berkeley and Los Angeles: University of California Press.

———. 2000. Comment on "Putting Global Capitalism in Its Place," by Mayfair Mei-hui Yang. *Current Anthropology* 41 (4): 500–501.

Ronfani, Paola. 1983. "Sociologia del diritto di famiglia." *Rassegna delle
Ricerche Sulla Famiglia Italiana* 1: 119–32.

Rosaldo, Michelle Z. 1984. "Toward an Anthropology of Self and Feeling." In
Culture Theory, edited by Rick Shweder and Robert Levine, 137–57.
Cambridge: Cambridge University Press.

Roth, Guenther. [1968] 1978. Introduction to *Economy and Society: An Outline of Interpretive Sociology*, by Max Weber, edited by Guenther Roth
and Claus Wittich, translated by Ephraim Fischoff et al., 1: xxxiii–cx.
Berkeley and Los Angeles: University of California Press.

Sabel, Charles. 1982. *Work and Politics: The Division of Labor in Industry*.
New York: Cambridge University Press.

Sacco, Eugenio. 1985. "Come salvare davanti al notaio ditta e patrimonio."
Espansione, no. 185 (October 1985): 88–92.

Sahlins, Marshall. 1992. *Anahulu: The Anthropology of History in the Kingdom of Hawaii*. Vol. 1, *Historical Ethnography*. Chicago: University of
Chicago Press.

———. 1994. "Cosomologies of Capitalism: The Trans-Pacific Sector of 'The
World System.'" In *Culture/Power/History: A Reading in Contemporary Social Theory*, edited by Nicholas B. Dirks, Geoff Eley, and Sherry
B. Ortner. Princeton: Princeton University Press.

Said, Edward. 1978. *Orientalism*. New York: Vintage.

Sangren, Steve. 2000. Comment on "Putting Global Capitalism in Its Place," by
Mayfair Mei-hui Yang. *Current Anthropology* 41 (4): 501–2.

Sassoon, Donald. 1986. *Contemporary Italy: Politics, Economy, and Society since 1945*. London: Longman.

Scase, Richard, and Robert Goffee. 1982. *The Entrepreneurial Middle Class*. London: Croom Helm.

Scassellatti, Alessandro. 1994. "Great Families':" Capital Accumulation and Political Power in Italy. Vols. 1 and 2 (Ph.D. dissertation, City University of New York).

Schneider, David M. 1964. "The Nature of Kinship," *Man* 217:180–81.

———. 1965. "Some Muddles in the Models: or, How the System Really Works." In *The Relevance of Models for Social Anthropology*, edited by Michael F. Banton. Association of Social Anthropologists of the Commonwealth Monograph no. 1. London: Tavistock.

———. 1968. *American Kinship: A Cultural Account*. Englewood Cliffs, N.J.: Prentice-Hall.

———. 1972. "What Is Kinship All About?" In *Kinship Studies in the Morgan Centennial Year*, edited by Priscilla Reining, 32–63. Washington, D.C.: Anthropological Society of Washington.

———. 1984. *A Critique of the Study of Kinship*. Ann Arbor: University of Michigan Press.

Schneider, Jane, and Peter Schneider. 1976. *Culture and Political Economy in Western Sicily*. New York: Academic Press.

Segalen, Martine. 1984. "'Avoir sa part': Sibling Relations in Partible Inheritance Brittany." In *Interest and Emotion: Essays on the Study of Family and Kinship*, edited by Hans Medick and David Warren Sabean, 129–44. Cambridge: Cambridge University Press.

Silverman, Sydel. 1975. *The Three Bells of Civilization*. New York: Columbia University Press.

Smelser, Neil J. 1959. *Social Change in the Industrial Revolution: An Application of Theory to the British Cotton Industry*. Chicago: University of Chicago Press.

Strathern, Marilyn. 1980. "No Nature, No Culture: The Hagen case." In *Nature, Culture, and Gender*, edited by Carol MacCormack and Marilyn Strathern, 174–222. Cambridge: Cambridge University Press.

———. 1988. *The Gender of the Gift: Problems with Women and Problems with Society in Melanesia*. Berkeley and Los Angeles: University of California Press.

———. 1992. *Reproducing the Future: Essays on Anthropology, Kinship, and the New Reproductive Technologies*. New York: Routledge.

Sylos Labini, Paolo. 1974. *Saggio sulle classi sociali*. Rome-Bari: La Terza.

———. 1978. "Sviluppo economico e classi sociali in Italia." In *Capitalismo e classi sociali in Italia*, edited by Massimo Paci, 35–91. Bologna: Il Mulino.

Thomas, Joseph. 1976. *Textbook of Roman Law*. Amsterdam: North-Holland Publishing Company.

Thompson, E. P. 1968. *The Making of the English Working Class*. Harmondsworth, England: Penguin.

Trigilia, Carlo. 1978. "Sviluppo, sottosviluppo, e classi sociali in Italia." In *Capitalismo e classi sociali in Italia*, edited by Massimo Paci. Bologna: Il Mulino. 36–79.

Tsing, Anna. 1994. *In the Realm of the Diamond Queen*. Princeton: Princeton University Press.

Ungari, Paolo. 1974. *Storia del Diritto di Famiglia in Italia*. Bologna: Il Mulino.

Visweswaran, Kamala. 1994. *Fictions of Feminist Ethnography*. Minneapolis: University of Minnesota Press.

Watson, James L. 1997. *Golden Arches East: McDonald's in East Asia*. Stanford, Calif.: Stanford University Press.

Weber, Max. 1978. *Economy and Society: An Outline of Interpretive Sociology*. Vol. 1. Edited by Guenther Roth and Claus Wittich, Translated by Ephraim Fischoff et al. Berkeley and Los Angeles: University of California Press.

———. 1992. *The Protestant Ethic and the Spirit of Capitalism*. New York: Routledge.

Wei Ming, Tu. 1998. "The Rise of Industrial East Asia: The Role of Confucian Values." *Copenhagen Papers in East and Southeast Asian Studies* (April): 81–97.

Weiss, Linda. 1984. "The Italian State and Small Business," *Archives of European Sociology* 25: 214–41.

Wolf, Eric. 1984. *Europe and the People without History*. Berkeley and Los Angeles: University of California Press.

Wolf, Margery. 1972. *Women and the Family in Rural Taiwan*. Stanford, Calif.: Stanford University Press.

Wright, Erik Olin. 1978. *Class, Crisis, and the State*. London: New Left Books.

Yamamoto, Shichihei. 1992. *The Spirit of Japanese Capitalism and Selected Essays*. Translated by Lynne E. Riggs and Takechi Manabu. Lanham, Md.: Madison Books.

Yanagisako, Sylvia. 1979. "Family and Household: The Analysis of Domestic Groups." *Annual Review of Anthropology* 8: 161–205.

———. 1985. *Transforming the Past: Tradition and Kinship among Japanese Americans*. Stanford, Calif.: Stanford University Press.

———. 1991. "Capital and Gendered Interest in Italian Family Firms." In *The Italian Family from Antiquity to the Present*, edited by David I. Kertzer and Richard P. Saller, 321–39. Yale: Yale University Press.

———. 1999. "Patriarchal Desire: Law and Sentiments of Succession in Italian Capitalist Families." In *Succession and Leadership among Elites*, edited by João de Pina-Cabral and Antónia Pedroso de Lima, 53–72. Oxford: Berg.

———. 2002. "Households." In the *International Encyclopedia of the Social and Behavioral Sciences*, edited by Neil J. Smelser and Paul B. Bales. Oxford: Elsevier Science.

Yanagisako, Sylvia, and Jane Collier. 1987. "Toward a Unified Analysis of Gender and Kinship." In *Gender and Kinship: Essays toward a Unified Analysis*, edited by Jane Collier and Sylvia Yanagisako. Stanford, Calif.: Stanford University Press.

Yanagisako, Sylvia, and Carol Delaney, eds. 1994. *Naturalizing Power: Essays in Feminist Cultural Analysis*. New York: Routledge.

Yang, Mayfair Mei-hui. 2000. "Putting Global Capitalism in Its Place: Economic Hybridity, Bataille, and Ritual Expenditure." *Current Anthropology* 41 (4): 477–95.

Yao, Wu The. 1991. "The Confucian Concept and Attributes of Man and the Modernisation of Industrial Asia." In *The Triadic Chord: Confucian Ethics, Industrial East Asia, and Max Weber*, edited by Tu Wei Ming, 397–413. Singapore: Institute of East Asian Studies.

Index